THE BRITISH EMPIRE BEFORE THE AMERICAN REVOLUTION

PROVINCIAL CHARACTERISTICS AND SECTIONAL TENDENCIES IN THE ERA PRECEDING THE AMERICAN CRISIS

VOLUME III

THE NORTHERN PLANTATIONS

LAWRENCE HENRY GIPSON

Author

Jared Ingersoll: A Study of American Loyalism in
Relation to British Colonial Government

Studies in Connecticut Colonial Taxation

Joint Author

The Expansion of the Anglo-Saxon Nations

THE BRITISH EMPIRE BEFORE THE AMERICAN REVOLUTION:

PROVINCIAL CHARACTERISTICS AND SECTIONAL TENDENCIES IN THE ERA PRECEDING THE AMERICAN CRISIS

VOLUME III

THE NORTHERN PLANTATIONS

by

LAWRENCE HENRY GIPSON
B.A. (OXON.), Ph.D., F.R.Hist.S.

*Professor of History and Head of the Department
of History and Government
Lehigh University*

THE CAXTON PRINTERS, LTD.
Caldwell, Idaho, U.S.A.
MDCCCCXXXVI

Printed and bound in the United States of America by
The CAXTON PRINTERS, Ltd.
Caldwell, Idaho
45791

To ALBERT EUGENE GIPSON and LINA MARIA WEST GIPSON who have helped in the building of the West as did their ancestors in the building of colonial New England.

CONTENTS

VOLUME III
The Northern Plantations

CHAPTER I

THE HEART OF NEW ENGLAND

vii

CONTENTS

CONTENTS

CONTENTS

CHAPTER II

IN THE WHITE-PINE BELT

CONTENTS

xi

CONTENTS

CHAPTER III

AN OLD NEW ENGLAND RELIGIOUS FRONTIER

CONTENTS

CHAPTER IV

A PURITAN STRONGHOLD

CONTENTS

CONTENTS

CHAPTER V

THE REGION OF THE OLD PATROONSHIPS

CONTENTS

CONTENTS

CONTENTS

xviii

CONTENTS

CHAPTER VII

THE NEW WORLD PARADISE OF THE SECTS

CONTENTS

CONTENTS

CONTENTS

CONTENTS

CHAPTER VIII

THE IRON MEN

CONTENTS

CONTENTS

CONTENTS

CONTENTS

CHAPTER IX

HUDSON BAY BEAVER

CONTENTS

CONTENTS

CHAPTER X

BANKERS AND SACK-MEN. THE PROVINCE OF AVALON

CONTENTS

CONTENTS

CONTENTS

CHAPTER XI

SUMMARIZATION

CONTENTS

CONTENTS

CONTENTS

MAPS

CONTENTS

THE NORTHERN PLANTATIONS

CHAPTER I

THE HEART OF NEW ENGLAND

UP TO THE present our attention has been chiefly
concentrated upon certain aspects of the civilization of the British Isles and of those portions of the
overseas Empire largely dependent upon slave labor.
It is now necessary to turn to that part of British
North America to the north of the region of the
so-called plantation system of agriculture. From
Pennsylvania to the borders of Maine, farms rather
than plantations were the characteristic unit adopted
by the settlers in the utilization of lands in the raising
of crops.[1] The term farm, as employed in the
eighteenth century, implied at least diversification in
production rather than dependence upon a single
staple; it implied also a unit of land sufficiently small
to be capable of development by means of the personal efforts of the yeoman and his immediate family,
aided by the labor of hired hands or of those bound
by indenture; it implied, further, the existence of no
such social distinctions as were almost universally
manifested in connection with the plantation system.
But farming instead of planting was only one of those
characteristics that set the colonial North apart from
both the tidewater South and the British West Indies.

[1] As we have seen in the preceding volume, farms rather than
plantations were to be found in the South beyond the Tidewater.
In the North something approximating the plantation system
was evolved in such regions as old King's Province in Rhode
Island as will subsequently be made clear.

3

Already great strides had been taken in the development of handicrafts, in the production of flour, in the manufacture of rum and iron, in shipbuilding, and in the exploitation of the North Atlantic fisheries. In so far as such activities were carried on in the South these were rudimentary or sporadic, with the exception of the production of flour and crude iron in Maryland and Virginia. But in the North development along some of these lines, at least, had proceeded so far as to arouse the apprehension of Englishmen who found themselves faced with a destructive type of competition and who consequently could not feel that this region was properly adjusted to the mercantilistic theory regarding the part that colonies should play in supplementing the efforts of the Mother Country. The oldest of the northern colonies, Massachusetts Bay, was in some respects the most dangerous rival in America of England's vital economic interests, owing to its strategic position, its considerable population, and its success in the fisheries, in shipbuilding, and in the manufacture of iron and rum. It may therefore be well to describe first of all the activities of this Colony that not only historically but, as the result of the dynamic power of leadership, was in 1750, as in 1650, the heart of old New England.

The Province of Massachusetts Bay possessed in the town of Boston, "the Metropolis of North-America,"[1] undoubtedly the greatest commercial and shipping center within the British Empire outside of the British Isles. Situated on a peninsula in the security of the Bay, protected by the frowning batteries of Castle William, the buildings of the town

[1] See *infra* p. 186, note.

4

rose gradually from Long Wharf and extended southward for about two miles. The traveller, Daniel West,
who visited the town in 1720, was so impressed not
only with the polite quality of the conversation of
the merchants but with the evidence of their prosperity as to declare, "that a gentleman from London
would almost think himself at home at Boston, when
he observes the number of people, their houses, their
furniture, their tables, their dress and conversation,
which perhaps is as splendid and showy as that of the
most considerable tradesmen in London."[1] Another
English traveller in 1740 stated that the houses and
streets were little inferior to some of the best in
London.[2] In 1750 Captain Goelet of New York
recorded in his diary, on the occasion of a visit to
this seaport, that of its three thousand houses two
thirds were of wood, the remainder of brick, "much
better and Stronger Built, more after the Modern
Taste all Shashd and Prety well Ornamented haveing
Yards and Gardens adjoyning Also." The better
buildings, he stated, were very spacious, two and
three stories in height, and, together with the gardens
that surrounded them, covered a good deal of ground.[3]
In fact, in the course of a century the town had become a real center of wealth and aristocracy. The
Tramount,[4] the exclusive residential section of that
period, indeed possessed some of the finest houses of
any part of North America, such as the Bromfield

[1] *The Memorial History of Boston*, II, 440-441.
[2] *Ibid.*
[3] "Extracts from Capt. Francis Goelet's Journal," *The New-
England Historical and Genealogical Register* (Boston, 1870),
XXIV, 62.
[4] First called Trimountaine, the word is now Tremont.

Mansion, the Ewing Mansion, and that of Peter Faneuil. Over the paved streets of the town rolled the coaches of the leading families. Many of these equipages were drawn by four spirited horses and accompanied by blacks in livery. Indeed, taking all things together, one traveller was so impressed that he was led to assert that "considering the bulk of the place they outdo London!"[1] It is only necessary to add as a further proof of the aristocratic spirit of the town that in the early '50s of the century, Boston could boast almost a thousand slaves.[2]

From this seaport at least a thousand vessels sailed each year.[3] It appears that most of the ships were not only owned by the local mercantile interests but had been built in the various shipyards of the Province, for, even early in the eighteenth century, these were launching annually from one hundred and forty to one hundred and fifty vessels, large and small, among the leading types of which were the three-masted ships, sloops, snows, and brigs. Later appeared the schooners.[4] Many of the vessels, after picking up a cargo for the maiden voyage across the Atlantic,

[1] The Memorial History of Boston, II, 441.

[2] The number of slaves in Boston in 1754 was 989 and in Suffolk County, 1266. Mass. Hist. Soc. Coll. (second series), II, 95-97.

[3] William Douglass, A Summary, Historical and Political . . . of the Present State of the British Settlements in North America (1755), I, 538. In the second decade of the eighteenth century almost twice the number of vessels sailed from Boston as from New York, and the total tonnage was almost three times as great. Boston averaged 415 vessels and 20,929 tons; New York 215 vessels and 7,464 tons. Shelburne Papers, 45: 270-271.

[4] Boston, it appears, declined as a shipbuilding center in the eighteenth century. In 1738 some forty-one vessels of 6,324 tonnage were constructed there; in 1749 but fifteen vessels of

THE HEART OF NEW ENGLAND

were thereupon sold by their owners to London, Liverpool, or Bristol merchants and thus lost their identity with Massachusetts Bay, as did also many others built upon order of British firms.[1] For it was found that the cost of ship construction was less in New England than in any other part of the Empire.[2] The importance of Boston as a commercial center is also indicated by the fact that in the early '40s over one hundred and sixty warehouses were needed, not only to contain the great supplies of commodities brought to Massachusetts from foreign parts for distribution, but also to house the produce of this and other American plantations that had been gathered for exportation.[3] In these warehouses were stored bales of broadcloth, flannel, and baize; haberdashery, ironware, canvas, twine, and cordage, with East India goods and numberless other articles from England and certified goods from Europe. There were

2,450 tonnage. See A. P. Usher in the *Commonwealth History of Massachusetts*, II, 399-400 for a discussion of shipbuilding in Massachusetts.

[1] The sale of New England vessels to England had, ever since the days of the navigation legislation beginning with the law of 1660, been a factor of great significance in the economic relations of the two portions of the Empire. In 1715 it was estimated that from forty to fifty were purchased by the mercantile interests of the Mother Country and that the total value of all the ships sold was over ninety thousand pounds. V. S. Clark, *History of Manufacturing in the United States*, I, 95; C. P. Nettels, *The Money Supply of the American Colonies before 1720*, pp. 92-93.

[2] According to figures presented by Usher *(op. cit.)*, a vessel could be built in Massachusetts for £8 per ton; in the middle colonies it cost £8.10; in the Carolinas £10.10; in England from £15.5 to £16.5.

[3] Wm. Douglass, *A Summary, Historical and Political . . . of the Present State of the British Settlements in North America* (1755), I, 531.

also hogsheads of rum, molasses, and sugar, with log-wood from the West Indies and Honduras Bay, wines from the Madeiras and the Canary Islands, countless barrels of cod, mackerel, alewives, and other pickled fish—the latter the product of the Bay and also of the Straits of Canso and of Newfoundland—together with oil and bone brought by the whalers, and, lastly, the products of the New England forest, such as timber, deals, tar, and turpentine.[1]

The multifarious activities of the Boston merchants are well illustrated in the person of Thomas Hancock who, starting his career as a bookbinder, turned to foreign trade in which he engaged extensively in partnership with other local men. He shipped rum, fish, oil, flour, and other goods to Newfoundland, the West Indies, and Europe, loading his ships for the return voyage with the products of these places. Business correspondents in London and at many other seaports enabled him to buy and sell successfully in light of information received through these channels. Not only did he thus carry on an extensive wholesale and retail business but he acted as a banker, selling and purchasing bills of exchange. It must, however, be added that in the building up of the family fortunes he was, it seems, none too scrupulous with respect to the observance of the customs laws, but apparently rather consistently engaged in illegal traffic in foreign wares.[2] The career of Hancock is, it would

[1] "The Answer of the Governor of Massachusetts to several Queries" March 2, 1736-37. Shelburne Papers, 45: 345. Salem, however, was perhaps the greatest fish-exporting town of New England.
[2] Edward, Edelman, "Thomas Hancock, Colonial Merchant," *Journal of Economic and Business History*, I, 77-104.

seem, typical of that of many of the most successful colonial merchants not only of Boston but of Newport, New York, and Philadelphia.

The busy and energetic people of the Colony, taken as a group, seem to have maintained a high standard of living during this period. It was asserted that to discharge the heavy annual trade balances against them in their relations with the merchants of the Mother Country as the result of large importations "all the produce of their cod fish at the markets in Spain and Portugal—all the oil they catch—all the ships they build—all the freights they make—all the money they get by specie or bills of exchange—and all the profits from every branch of their trade, center in Great Britain annually"[1]—which evidences, moreover, the prevailing triangular nature of their commercial activities. But this is not the whole story by any means.

According to Robert Dinwiddie, acting at the time as a surveyor-general of customs, the total value of the commodities shipped from Great Britain directly or through the Guinea trade to the plantations in 1743 was estimated to be £3,635,000; almost one sixth of this amount or a total of £600,000 worth of goods came to Massachusetts Bay. These imports carried a higher value than all the goods shipped directly to the combined colonies of North Carolina, Pennsylvania, New Jersey, New York, Connecticut, Rhode Island, New Hampshire, and Nova Scotia.[2] Impres-

[1] See G. R. Minot's *Continuation of the History of the Province of Massachusetts Bay*, I, 155-161 for a discussion of this.

[2] This amount included British manufactures, East India goods, German linens, and the Madeira trade. Dinwiddie's report is embodied in James Abercrombie's "Examination," the Shel-

THE NORTHERN PLANTATIONS

sive as this is, the total value of exports of the Province, including ships for sale, oil, fish, deer skins, ironware, naval stores, bricks, horses, cattle, earthenware, and furs, amounted in the same year to not less than £800,000, out of a total export of commodities valued, according to these estimates, at £5,036,000 sent out from the plantations. In other words, the value of its exports almost equalled the combined exports of Pennsylvania, New York, Connecticut, Rhode Island, New Hampshire, and Nova Scotia.[1]

It is clear, if the above estimates have the slightest validity, that Massachusetts Bay imported from the

burne Papers, 47: p. 30. Dinwiddie gives the following estimates for the other colonies: Pennsylvania, £250,000; the Jersies, £40,000; New York, £150,000; Rhode Island, £30,000; Connecticut, £30,000; New Hampshire, £30,000, and Nova Scotia (before 1748), £10,000.

These figures differ remarkably from those returned by the Governor of Massachusetts Bay. For example, in an account sent by Belcher in 1736-37 to the Board of Trade the total value of British manufactures and India goods imported into the Province was placed at the modest sum of £120,000. The natural produce was rated at £100,000. For his report see the Shelburne Papers, 45: 344-345. The official figures for colonial imports and exports are of course notoriously defective.

The predominance of New England in trade relations with England in the early part of the century is indicated by the fact that between 1716 and 1719 there sailed from London to that region 101 vessels, while to New York the number was but 19, to Pennsylvania, but 25, to South Carolina, but 26; during the same period 123 sailed from New England to London, while from New York there were 44, from Pennsylvania, 8, from South Carolina, 91. This is taken from a "List of ships trading with the colonies from the port of London," C.O. 390: 5, No. 45; quoted by C. P. Nettels in his *The Money Supply of the American Colonies before 1720*, p. 101, note.

[1] Dinwiddie's estimates for the above colonies are as follows: Pennsylvania, £300,000; New York, £250,000; Connecticut, £90,000; Rhode Island, £90,000; New Hampshire, £96,000; Nova Scotia, £10,000. *Ibid.*, pp. 28-29.

Mother Country far beyond its requirements. Indeed, the great mercantile houses of Boston had made that town the entrepôt for a vast territory that embraced much more than New England; in fact, it dominated Nova Scotia and Newfoundland to the north and even North Carolina to the far south. Building its own ships, using these as the carriers of its own commerce and much of that of its neighbors, it levied financial tribute in the form of freights, commission services, insurance policies, and credit and other facilities from all those communities which it habitually served. For over a century, indeed, it had been the undisputed commercial metropolis of the English possessions in North America.

In spite of what has just been said relative to the importance of the commercial activities of the Province, it may be well to point out that in the middle of the eighteenth century the trade of Boston was much disturbed, because of the fact that the Colony had just reorganized its financial system as the result of the receipt of funds from Great Britain, amounting to one hundred and seventy-five thousand pounds sterling, as reimbursement for the expense involved in the Louisbourg expedition in King George's War. This step was of such importance that it deserves further brief consideration.

When the General Court came to the determination to apply the reimbursement funds so as to place the provincial finances upon a hard money basis, it passed in January, 1749 an act for drawing in the bills of credit which had at any time been issued by the Province and for ascertaining the value of coined silver within its borders. This law, providing among other things for the exchange of silver for the depreciated old tenor bills of credit upon the basis of ten pounds in these to one pound sterling, was thereupon, in conformity with the charter requirements, submitted to His Majesty in Council, which accepted in June of that year a Board of Trade representation favoring its confirmation. The language employed by the Board on this occasion should be of interest to students of today, in light of the important decision of the United States Supreme Court in 1935 respecting the fulfillment of promises to pay in gold. The Lords Commissioners referred to the fact that the plan of redemption "may appear at the first View to be in some Degree a Breach of the public Faith of the Province and an Injustice to the possessors of the said Bills" but then went on in referring to the bills of credit to emphasize the fact "that by far the greatest part thereof have passed from hand to hand and been received by the present possessors at even a lower Rate than is set upon them by this Act." As to redemption at face value, they declared that since "the first possessors never did or could receive near that Nominal Value so it would be unreasonable that the present possessors should avail themselves of a Benefit which they have never purchased and cannot in Equity be entituled to."[1]

Massachusetts Bay now returned in everyday business practice to its old proclamation money basis, for the law provided that all Spanish-milled pieces of eight of full weight should be valued at the rate of six shillings for the discharge of every contract en-

[1] *Acts of the Privy Council, Col., 1745-1766*, pp. 85-89.

12

tered into after a specified day in 1750, with a penalty of fifty pounds to be levied upon any person taking or paying a higher rate. Further, to prevent the depreciated bills of credit of the other New England colonies circulating within the Province it also provided severe penalties for anyone attempting to circulate these bills during a period of four years, beginning with March, 1750.[1]

The old, badly depreciated bills of credit were thereupon called in; yet it appears not at the rate signified in the law but at the higher rate of seven and one half to one, and Spanish pieces of eight were paid to the holders.[2] This ultimately was advantageous, for the people were at last furnished with a stable hard money which had not been the case since the gradual disappearance of their old Pine Tree shillings that had first been struck in the middle of the preceding century, the minting of which had been prohibited in 1686.[3] But conditions in 1750, due to

[1] *Ibid.* It may also be pointed out that after the passage of the act under consideration a petition signed by merchants and other inhabitants of Boston was submitted to His Majesty praying that he would take effectual measures to compel the governments of New Hampshire, Connecticut, and Rhode Island to redeem their bills at the same rate at which Massachusetts Bay had covenanted to do and to refrain from issuing any additional paper money. *Ibid.*, pp. 81-82.

[2] Boston Correspondence. *Pennsylvania Journal*, June 14, 1750. For a discussion of this see C. H. J. Douglas, *Financial History of Massachusetts Bay from the Organization of the Colony to the American Revolution* (Columbia University Studies I, No. 4); J. B. Felt, *An Historical Account of Massachusetts Currency*; A. M. Davis, *Currency and Banking in Massachusetts*, I, 203, ff.

[3] For the fate of the Pine Tree shilling see C. P. Nettels, *The Money Supply of the American Colonies before 1720*, pp. 171-175.

the dislocation of business resulting from a rather sudden resumption of specie payments, were, temporarily, deplorable. One gentleman, writing from Boston in June, declared that "Trade is quite dead" and that "the Town is as dull and still as on Sunday." Although it was full of goods, there was no money with which to buy, by reason of the fact that not only was there less Massachusetts Bay current money "by five hundred thousand pounds" but that of the other colonial governments which previously had circulated there freely was no longer a tender. "All countenances are dull; we curse one another; especially those are cursed that were for the Act.[1] As soon as the dollars come out they are shipped to London, New York, Philadelphia, or Hispaniola or are laid up to worship ... *What a deplorable picture is here.*"[2]

In spite of the extent of the territory of Massachusetts Bay, the inhabitants, who, according to an estimate made in 1755, numbered two hundred and twenty thousand,[3] were largely employed in the

[1] "An Act in addition to an Act pass'd in 22ᵈ Geo: 2ᵈ 1., Entitled, An Act for drawing in the bills of credit of the several denominations," etc. "List of Acts of Massachusetts Bay, 1753." Shelburne Papers, 49: 53. See letter in *Pennsylvania Journal*, June 7, 1750.

[2] *Ibid.*, June 7, 1750. See also a letter from Boston printed in the August 2 issue of the *Pennsylvania Journal*: "You can't possibly imagine what an alteration there is in our affairs for want of a medium there being scarce any money of any sort to be seen except a few coppers, and they seem to diminish; all trade seems to be stagnated, and little else goes on but drinking." "The effect was frightful. Ruin stalked in every home; the people could not pay their taxes; and were obliged to see their property seized by the sheriff," assserted with some exaggeration Alexander Del Mar in his *History of Money in America* (p. 83), referring to Boston of this period.

[3] New Hampshire Hist. Soc., *Coll.*, V, 230; Green and Harrington, *Population before ...* 1790, pp. 5-6.

THE HEART OF NEW ENGLAND

fisheries, in navigation, and in the building of ships as well as in providing materials for their construction.[1] So busy, in fact, were the people in the pursuit of these particular interests and so unsatisfactory was the cultivation of wheat, owing to the barberry rust, that it was necessary to import annually from North Carolina, Virginia, Maryland, and other southward points, large quantities of flour and bread, together with corn and pork, in order to subsist the great seafaring, as well as the town-dwelling, population. Of the manufactures carried on by the latter, rum was the chief, the exportation of which had reached to upwards of fifteen thousand hogsheads by 1750, or not far from two million gallons a year.[2] According to the opinion of the men of the period, this article was the foundation of all the happy prosperity and material welfare evidenced by the inhabitants of the Province. It was called "the great support of all their trade and fishery; without which they can no longer subsist,"[3] for it was the common beverage of practically all their laborers: their loggers, timber men, sailors, and fishermen. Men asserted that they could

[1] G. R. Minot, *Continuation of the History . . . of Massachusetts Bay*, I, 155-161.
The comparative value of the exports of farm produce and of wealth derived from the sea by Massachusetts Bay in 1715 was, according to Captain Thomas Banister, £113,000 and £491,000 respectively. "Essay on the Trade of New England" (1715), C.O. 5: 866, No. 67; quoted by C. P. Nettels in his *The Money Supply of the American Colonies before 1720*, p. 100.

[2] G. R. Minot, *op. cit.*, I, 155-161. In 1750 there were sixty-three distilleries in Massachusetts Bay. Charles W. Taussig, *Rum, Romance and Rebellion*, p. 16.

[3] G. R. Minot, *op. cit.* Out of a total of some fifteen thousand hogsheads of rum exported by the Province, nine thousand went to the Newfoundland fisheries, three thousand to the south-

not endure the hardships of their employment or the rigors of the seasons without it. The precious article was the basis of the trade with the southern continental colonies, with the Indians for furs, with Newfoundland for prize fish, and with the Guinea Coast for gold and slaves. To obtain the molasses from which it was distilled, to the West Indies was carried an immense quantity of "refuse" or "Jamaica" fish. The profitable disposal of this inferior article was indeed a vital matter, for it constituted between one fourth and one half of the total catch of the cod fishermen and made up a very large proportion of the cargoes brought from Newfoundland. Happily, the British sugar planters were eager to receive it for their slaves and usually agreed to pay for it in specie. As the planters on the French sugar islands were usually faced with a surplus of molasses which they were naturally anxious to sell, it was highly advantageous for the Massachusetts Bay skippers to carry to them this specie by means of which they drove excellent bargains with the Frenchmen. It is, however, to be feared that much of the abundant supply of molasses thus purchased for the Boston distillers found its way into Massachusetts Bay without the payment of the duties provided for by the Molasses Act of 1733.

The inhabitants of the Colony from the very beginning had shown an interest in the development of

ern colonies, thirteen hundred to the Straits of Canso and other adjacent places, seventeen hundred to Africa. See *Publications of the Col. Soc. of Mass.*, XIX, 386-387. It is asserted that a gallon of molasses would make almost a gallon of rum. Witt Bowden, *The Industrial History of the United States*, p. 86.

the fisheries. In the course of the seventeenth century they succeeded in appropriating the great cod and mackerel beds of the waters now known as the Gulf of Maine,[1] and in the eighteenth century those that were equally valuable to the south of the Straits of Canso which lie between Nova Scotia and Cape Breton Island. By 1750 four hundred vessels were employed in the cod fisheries—principally in the Gulf of Maine and about Nova Scotia and Newfoundland —while two hundred sought the mackerel and other small fish about the inshore grounds of the coast.[2] Some 280,000 quintals represented the annual harvest. These activities laid the fortunes of such men as Peter Faneuil of Boston, who showed his munificence to his own town by the erection of the famous market building that bears his name. Moreover, as will be stressed in a later chapter, the interest of the men of Massachusetts Bay in Newfoundland had become so pronounced that this had become a matter of public consideration in England. For it was frankly viewed with some apprehension by those who looked to the annual sailing of the fleets from the fishing towns of the Mother Country as one of the principal guarantees of the maintenance of English naval supremacy.

[1] It seems that no codfish of finer quality was cured within the Empire than in New England where, according to the testimony of Governor Bellomont in 1700, it was caught and cured during the period of cold weather and was therefore considered so superior that it brought in the markets of Portugal a piece of eight per quintal more than the Newfoundland fish. His letter to the Board of Trade of Nov. 28 is quoted by C. P. Nettels, *The Money Supply of the American Colonies before 1720*, p. 78.

[2] W. B. Weeden, *Economic and Social History of New England*, II, 641; Raymond McFarland, *A History of the New England Fisheries*, Chapter I.

They feared that, just as the fisheries previously mentioned had been monopolized by New Englanders, so might even those of the Banks—resulting in the decay of English shipping and the western seaports.

In addition to the fishing interests just mentioned, one must not fail to point out that from the towns of the Bay, such as Gloucester—with New Bedford and Nantucket soon to assume first importance—a hundred whalers, carrying hardy, adventurous crews, sailed into the subarctic regions and especially into the Gulf of St. Lawrence in pursuit of sperm oil, head material, and whalebone.[1] These seldom failed to return with an annual supply.

All that has been said indicates the extreme aggressiveness of the Massachusetts Bay seamen. The same can be said of her agriculturists. They had dotted with townships the whole region from the Merrimac on the north to the neighborhood of Narragansett Bay on the south, from Cape Cod on the east to the Connecticut and beyond to the west.[2] In the course of the seventeenth century they had swallowed up the Province of Maine and the Colony of Plymouth and had threatened with extinction, by reason of their extravagant boundary claims, New Hampshire to the northward, and Rhode Island to

[1] W. B. Weeden, *New England*, II, 644. By 1771 there were 665 Massachusetts Bay ships engaged in the cod fisheries, 304 in whaling, and 90 in catching mackerel and other fish. See *The Commonwealth History of Massachusetts*, II, 404, for these and other figures. For whaling see G. F. Dow, *Whale Ships and Whaling* (Marine Research Society), pp. 3-40.

[2] According to *A Short Description of the American Colonies* (p. 167), published in 1749, there were "above 80 good towns and more to be." The figures are manifestly for an earlier period since the census made in 1765 gives a total of one hun-

the southward. By 1750 they were, with an insatiable land hunger, crowding along the western border and were about to challenge the rights of those great land magnates of the Province of New York established to the east of the Hudson. For Massachusetts still held to the ancient limits from sea to sea laid down by royal patent in the Charter of 1629.[1]

In the seventeenth and the early part of the eighteenth century vacant lands had been granted by the government to church congregations or other groups desiring a change of location, but this method of land settlement, with the growing influence not only of the secular in government as against the clerical, but of individualism as against the old Puritan conception of social solidarity, had been sufficiently modified so that it was possible for an individual interested in land speculation to secure a very considerable grant, frequently in payment of military services. This in turn he disposed of in small allotments to actual settlers,[2] which resulted in an accele-

dred and eighty-four towns with Suffolk County credited with eighteen; Essex, with twenty-one; Middlesex, with thirty-seven; Hampshire, with twenty-nine; Worcester, with thirty-five; Plymouth, with fifteen; Barnstable, with ten; Bristol, with eleven; Dukes, with three; Nantucket, with one; and Berkshire, with six. Besides this, in Maine, York County had seven, Cumberland, seven, and Lincoln, six. For a discussion of this see *The Commonwealth History of Massachusetts*, II, 112-113.

[1] The Governor of Massachusetts Bay to the Board of Trade, March 2, 1736-37, Shelburne Papers, 45: 343.

[2] See the *Publications* of the Colonial Society of Mass., 18: 69; also the petition of Samuel Waldo and Windham Beawes, attorneys for Robt. Mackey and John Corner of London, Merchants, praying for a grant of land. Board of Trade Journal, Apr. 4, 1753, 51: 91, 96-97. For a discussion of land speculation in New England see Roy Hidemichi Akagi, *The Town Proprietors of the New England Colonies, 1620-1770.*

ration of the tendency to seek isolated farms on the part of individuals rather than the establishment in the wilderness of a community center.

Nevertheless, the conditions under which Penacook[1] to the west of the upper Merrimac River was settled may be accepted as characteristic of the processes of Massachusetts Bay colonization down to 1750. In the beginning of the year 1725, upon petition of a group of intended settlers, mostly of Haverhill it appears, the government created a township of seven square miles in the region of the intended settlement. This was granted to the petitioners under certain specified conditions among which were these: that the tract should be divided into one hundred and three equal shares or lots; that one hundred families should settle thereon within the space of three years; that each settler should build a good dwelling house and break up and fence six acres of land within the time aforesaid; that the houses should be erected within twenty rods of each other on the home lots and "in a regular and defensible manner"; that a convenient house for the public worship of God should be completely finished within the time first mentioned; and finally, that each settler should pay the Province five pounds for his right. As soon as one hundred were admitted settlers they were empowered to hold proprietary meetings to care for their interests. As to the three remaining rights, out of the one hundred and three, one was reserved for the first settled minister, one for a parsonage, and one for

[1] This later became the parish of Concord after it had been awarded to New Hampshire.

"the use of the church forever."[1] In 1726 a committee of the grantees proceeded to lay out the lots, and the following year the settlers were admitted under the terms laid down, and thereupon proceeded to the place. By 1730 a church was built and a minister ordained, and three years later the community was incorporated as a township by act of the Massachusetts Bay General Court under name of Rumford.[2]

The century of pioneering on the part of the descendants of those who crowded into Massachusetts Bay during the days of the Great Migration had had the result, taken together with other influences exerted from across the Atlantic, of profoundly modifying the character and general outlook on life of the majority of the people. The Congregational Church, in spite of its powerfully entrenched position in 1750, was no such force within the commonwealth as it had been in 1650. At the earlier period the local church had possessed an extraordinary authority over the lives of individuals, whether members or nonmembers, regulating the most minute, most private interests of all.[3] The members were those in fellowship who not only had received baptism but had qualified by open confession to participate in the church com-

[1] New Hampshire Hist. Soc. *Coll.* I, 154-156. For a study of the early land system of Massachusetts Bay see Melville Egleston, "Land System of the New England Colonies," Johns Hopkins University *Studies*, 18: 69, IV, Nos. 11 and 12; R. G. Akagi, *Town Proprietors of the New England Colonies*; H. E. Osgood, *American Colonies in the Seventeenth Century*, I, Chap. XI.

[2] *Acts of the Privy Council, Col.*, 1745-1766, pp. 239-243.

[3] See Perry Miller, *Orthodoxy in Massachusetts, 1630-1750, A Genetic Study*; H. M. Dexter, *Congregationalism of the Last Three Hundred Years*; Williston Walker, *The Creeds and Plat-*

munion and were consequently designated as being of the communion. It was this group which had looked after the ecclesiastical functions of the town and in addition had controlled its civil interests. The pastor of the congregation, alone of the group, had been considered competent to unlock the mysteries of the word of God, and he had ruled without a serious rival. However, the expanding frontier, with the exigencies that grew out of it, together with other forces almost equally as potent, had in the course of a century brought about certain changes that had profoundly affected the Congregational Establishment. In 1657 and 1662 synods of the church made concessions by establishing the halfway covenant. This required baptism alone as the condition for the enjoyment of the civil privileges of church membership, although not for participation in the sacrament of the Lord's Supper, which presupposed testimony of conversion. Subsequently, however, individual pastors, such as Solomon Stoddard of Northampton, went beyond this, holding that the Lord's Supper was a converting ordinance in itself, and that baptism was therefore a sufficient title to all the privileges of the church. Such changes had the effect of introducing gradually certain elements into the local ecclesiastical societies that proved hostile in the end to the maintenance of the prestige of seventeenth-century Congregationalism. Moreover, the new charter granted to the Colony in 1691 struck squarely at the church

forms of Congregationalism; Champlin Burrage, *Early English Dissenters in Light of Recent Research*; S. E. Morison, *Builders of the Bay Colony*; and J. T. Adams, *The Founding of New England*.

Establishment, although it is true that the provincial government continued to pass measures that had as an objective the maintenance of the old and still cherished ecclesiastical system.[1] In 1692 came the witchcraft terror, the rationalistic aftermath of which was not conducive to the continued great prestige of the church. Further, the Anglicans and especially the Quakers, always in opposition, gradually became most formidable enemies of the Establishment,[2] and these groups, together with the Baptists, in the course of the first half of the eighteenth century succeeded in gaining special exemptions[3] which freed them from the necessity not only of attending the religious services of the Congregational Church but also of contributing financial support to the same. All others of course remained under the same compulsions, legally at least, as had existed in the seventeenth century.[4]

Moreover, in the eighteenth century the Establish-

[1] For an excellent statement regarding this point see the "Opinion of Messrs. York & Talbot respecting certain grievances complained of by the Church of England Clergy in the Massachusetts Bay" submitted in 1732 to the Board of Trade. W. S. Perry, *Historical Collections Relating to the American Colonial Church*, III, 274-288.

[2] This topic has been carefully treated by Susan M. Reed in her *Church and State in Massachusetts, 1691-1740* (University of Illinois *Studies* in Social Science, III, No. 4). See also J. C. Meyer, *Church and State in Massachusetts Bay, 1740-1833*.

[3] Shelburne Papers, 49: 46.

[4] William Stevens Perry, *Historical Collections Relating to the American Colonial Church*, III, 440-441. Here is a brief description of Boston in 1751: "The three Episcopal Congregations of this Town are large, and tho' mine is not so well situated for services, yet is increasing. The independent congregations are 10 large ones, and two small ones, owing to and leaven'd with Methodism. We have two small Anabaptist Congregations, one

ment was weakened by other forces[1] than those just described. First, there had taken place a dispersion of the sons of its earlier supporters; many of them, leaving their ancestral abodes, went to live on the outskirts of new townships and consequently far from the Church's ministrations and discipline. Again, in the region of the old seated towns and especially in Boston the press undoubtedly introduced factors that struck at ecclesiastical authority. Further, the prevailing latitudinarianism in England of this period was undoubtedly exerting its influence even in Massachusetts Bay, and there was an acknowledged weakening of the old religious ardor, with the growth of the doctrines of Arminius in New England which struck at the Calvinistic foundations of the Church.

In 1731 Jonathan Edwards, New England's leading eighteenth-century theologian and preacher, who had succeeded his grandfather, the Rev. Mr. Stoddard, at Northampton, started a powerful drive against this religious drift, in his Boston public lecture on "God Glorified in Man's Dependence." His preaching, together with that of George Whitefield and others, resulted in gradually stirring up the most astonishing religious revival in all American history, known as the Great Awakening. It may better be described as the coming of the Great Fear. To Edwards, God was the embodiment not only of supreme love but of supreme and stern justice who, to quote

springing from Methodism. Papists are among us not a few, but how many or whether increasing I cannot find." Mr. Cutler to the Secretary, Boston, N. Eng. Dec[r] 26, 1751, *ibid.*

[1] See H. B. Parks, "New England in the Seventeen-thirties," *New England Quarterly,* III, 397-419.

from one of his sermons, "though he will know that you cannot bear the weight of omnipotence treading upon you, yet will he not regard that, but he will crush you under his feet without mercy; he will crush out your blood, and make it fly, and it will be sprinkled on his garments so as to stain all his raiment. He will not only hate you, but he will have you in the utmost contempt."[1] The sinner once condemned was beyond all hope of salvation and redemption in face of the inflexible will of God, and only a few out of each generation would escape this terrible fate.

The titles of Edwards' sermons are sufficiently indicative of the development of his theological conceptions. Examples of these are: "The Eternity of Hell Torments," "Sinners in the Hands of an Angry God," and "The Justice of God in the Damnation of Sinners." The immediate effect of this sort of preaching upon the simple-hearted, receptive people who gathered to hear the great Northampton theologian and his followers is really beyond description. They wailed, they wrung their hands, they fell to the floor in emotional fits.[2] While many of the pastors of Congregational churches gave themselves over enthusiastically to the promotion of the revival, welcoming the itinerant evangelists who now appeared in every town and village to further the work, others saw in this tremendous excitement an enemy of true religion and of an orderly church.

Started as a movement to restore the prestige of Congregationalism and its ministry in New England,

[1] *Life and Works of Jonathan Edwards* (ed. by S. E. Dwight), IV, 320.

[2] See A. V. G. Allen, *Jonathan Edwards* (1889); J. T. Adams, *Revolutionary New England*, Chapter IX.

by the middle of the century sober men had become convinced that the revival had left the Establishment in a shattered condition. For in practically every town of importance the more ardent supporters of the new movement had led secessions from the community congregation to set up a rival organization generally known as the New Light Church. The reaction from this, known as the Old Light movement, was equally pronounced. Even Edwards became a victim of it. By a vote of the Northampton town meeting in 1749 he was forbidden the use of the pulpit from which for over twenty years he had preached with almost unprecedented power. Indeed, never again after the revival had died down was theology the all-absorbing interest in New England.[1] There was something really prophetic in the decision made by young Samuel Adams in 1743 to base his master's thesis at Harvard upon politics in discussing the query, "Whether it be Lawful to resist the Supreme Magistrate, if the Commonwealth cannot otherwise be preserved."

The gradual change in the attitude of many people toward the ecclesiastical system is well illustrated in the appearance in 1721 of the *New England Courant* under the editorship of James Franklin, the elder brother of the later distinguished Benjamin, with its fiery and coarse attacks upon the clergy and the prevailing social order of things. That the paper was able to survive until 1727 indicates that it supported the point of view of a respectable number of people, even granting that they may not have been considered

[1] Thomas H. Billings, "The Great Awakening," Essex Inst. Hist. *Coll.*, 65: 89-104.

by their contemporaries a number of respectable people.

The press, in fact, was destined to usurp in a great measure the place of the pulpit in Massachusetts. The first news sheet printed in America had made its appearance in the Colony in 1690 under the title of *Public Occurrences, Both Foreign and Domestic.*[1] But the printer, Richard Pierce, had not the temerity to put forth more than one issue in view of the denunciations of the authorities. However, in 1704 John Campbel gave to the world *The Boston News-Letter,* which under different editors exerted considerable influence and continued to appear until in the midst of the Revolutionary War it ceased publication. In 1719 *The Boston Gazette* was founded by William Booker and soon after passed into other hands, surviving until its absorption by the publishers of *The New England Weekly Journal,* which came into existence shortly after the disappearance in 1727 of *The New England Courant* to which reference has been made; then came *The Rehearsal* in 1733, which after about four years was changed to *The Boston Weekly Post* and was owned by Thomas Fleet. Finally, in 1748 appeared *The Independent Advertiser.* While the earlier newspapers had perhaps wisely avoided politics, the change in the attitude of the public was evidenced by the fact that the last-named paper, although going out of existence in 1750, was mainly interested in things governmental and had as contributors such men as Samuel Adams.

[1] For a treatment of the press in Boston see D. A. Goddard, "The Press and Literature of the Provincial Period," *Memorial History of Boston,* II, Chap. XV.

27

However, all of them printed more or less extensive news items relating to the affairs of the outside world, which irresistibly had a broadening effect upon the people. This was supplemented by the growing influence of Harvard and Yale where, it is asserted, there were five times as many students in attendance in 1740 as were in college in all New England in 1680,[1] in spite of the decline in the number of grammar schools with their stress upon classical, college-preparatory studies.[2] For these institutions of higher education, by the middle of the eighteenth century, had indeed become real cultural centers where were trained such men as Thomas Hutchinson, Jared Ingersoll, and William Samuel Johnson, with their broad-minded approach to issues of public importance. It would also seem that many of those who secured their preparation for the ministry, especially at Harvard, entered upon their pastoral duties at this period carrying with them the growing spirit of catholicity and comprehensiveness evidenced by their *Alma Mater* which, for example, led them into sharp opposition to the fanaticism involved in the Great Awakening. Indeed, one may question whether in any portion of the Empire was a greater proportion of the population influenced by what may be called the new humanism than in Massachusetts Bay. And

[1] Yale was, of course, not founded until 1701.

[2] C. K. Shipton, "Secondary Education in the Puritan Colonies," *New England Quarterly*, VII, 646-661. For the decline of the secondary schools in Massachusetts Bay see M. W. Jernegan's important study in the *School Review*, Vol. XXVII and also E. D. Grizgell, *Origin and Development of the High School in New England*, Chap. I; J. T. Adams, *Provincial Society, 1690-1763*, pp. 132-134; Charles Angoff, *A Literary History of the American People*, I, 64.

in the spreading of enlightenment the clergy apparently were among the most effective of the agencies.[1]

Massachusetts Bay was one of the three corporate colonies surviving within the old British Empire. Due to its extraordinary aggressiveness and self-sufficiency in the course of the seventeenth century, its original charter had been voided in the Court of Chancery in 1684. Two years later the government of this plantation was embodied in the so-called Dominion of New England, which was ruled by Edmund Andros as governor with the assistance of a council from 1686 until 1689 when his power collapsed as the result of the Revolution in England. In 1691 a new charter was granted by William and Mary.[2] This has been well described as "the nearest approach to the creation of a constitution for a royal province by means of a single document that we have before the passage of the Quebec Act in 1774."[3]

Under the terms of the charter all of the lands comprehended within the Colony under the first patent, together with Plymouth Colony, the Territory of Maine, and Acadia or Nova Scotia, as well as all intervening lands, were erected into the Province of Massachusetts Bay.[4] By this instrument the freedom of action of the Colony was greatly restricted

[1] For the development of this theme see C. K. Shipton, "A Plea for Puritanism," *Amer. Hist. Rev.*, XL, 460-467.

[2] For the text of the charter see *Acts and Resolves of the Province of Massachusetts Bay*, I, 1-20; F. N. Thorpe, *The Federal and State Constitutions, Colonial Charters and Other Organic Laws*, III, 1870-1886.

[3] L. W. Labaree, *Royal Government in America*, pp. 7-8.

[4] *Acts and Resolves of the Province of Massachusetts Bay*, I, 1-2; William MacDonald, *Select Charters, 1606-1775*, p. 206. After the Treaty of Utrecht, Acadia was placed under a separate administration.

in the provision that the governor, the lieutenant or deputy governor, and the secretary should be royal appointees. The Great and General Court of Assembly, consisting of the governor, a council of twenty-eight assistants,[1] and the deputies of the freeholders of the various towns,[2] was empowered to make laws, create courts of judicature, grant lands except to the east of the Sagadahoe River [the Kennebec], erect towns, and appoint and settle all civil officers not holding patents from the Crown. But the power of law-making did not extend to the denial of religious freedom, except to Roman Catholics, or to erection of any vice-admiralty jurisdiction, or to the restriction of freedom of fishing granted to all subjects of England.

This charter gave to the governor the power of controlling the course of legislation, possessing as he did an absolute veto on all bills and elections.[3] As a

[1] For lists of active assistants in 1754, see "Council Records, 1747-1755" (Mass. Archives), pp. 330, 333, 334.

[2] To vote one had to possess either a forty shilling freehold or other estate to the value of forty pounds sterling. A town with one hundred families was allowed to send two deputies, with forty families, one. Boston was given four. The Governor of Massachusetts Bay to the Board of Trade, March 2, 1736-37, Shelburne Papers, 49: 20-40. That the responsibilities involved in the sending of deputies were not infrequently considered irksome, especially when no crisis confronted the Commonwealth, and public affairs were running smoothly, is indicated by the fact that in the year 1753 fifteen towns were fined, in amounts ranging from £5 against both Sunderland and Dudley to £26 against Plymouth, for failure to send any representative for that year. *Journal of the House of Representatives of Massachusetts Bay* (1753), p. 13.

[3] An issue arose as to the power of the governor to negative the choice of a speaker of the House of Representatives. In 1725 an explanatory charter issued by the Crown upheld the

further check upon the Colony it was provided that all laws were to be transmitted home by the first opportunity after engrossment, and, upon being presented to His Majesty in Council, could be rejected within a period of three years.

That the provisions of the new charter just described had the effect of making the legislature of a province, distinguished in the seventeenth century for its recalcitrancy, much more solicitous in the course of the eighteenth to frame measures in harmony with the spirit of the imperial conceptions of government would seem to be abundantly evidenced.[1] Out of three hundred and four acts passed between the years 1703 and 1753 that were referred to England for approval only six were reported for disallowance and two for repeal.[2] As a further safeguard

authority of the chief magistrate. *Acts of the Privy Council, Col., 1720-1745,* pp. 94-95, 103.

[1] However, between 1695 and 1701 some thirty-three acts were disallowed. *Acts of the Privy Council, Col., 1680-1720,* pp. 841-844.

[2] Two of these acts disallowed were passed in 1718; one related to imposts and tonnage and the other regulated the culling of fish; another, passed in 1723, was for apportioning and assessing a tax; a fourth, of the year 1731, was for ascertaining the number of representatives; the fifth, for granting imposts and tonnage, was passed in each of the years 1731, 1732, and 1733 and led to the issuing of an additional instruction to Governor Belcher forbidding any future import duty on negroes and felons; and the sixth, passed in 1750, granted His Majesty an excise upon sundry articles. Of the acts reported for repeal, one was passed in 1733 to prevent the currency issued by a New Hampshire society from circulating in Massachusetts; the other, of the year 1742, sought to take off the entail from certain lands in Ipswich belonging to the estate of John Wainwright. See "A List of Acts passed in Massachusetts Bay reported between the year 1703 and the present time, 1753," Shelburne Papers, 49: 34-54. *Acts of the Privy Council, Col., 1720-1745,* pp. 329-334, 845, 848.

against the spirit of independence on the part of the Assembly, the governor was given the power to adjourn, prorogue, and dissolve that body. In the respects above noted—with the exception of the existence of a charter which preserved the power of the Assembly over the lands as well as over certain provincial appointments—the government of Massachusetts Bay differed little from that of a normal royal colony, with the governor in each case receiving his commission under the great seal and acting under royal instructions.[1] However, with respect to the selection of the councillors of the Province there was a fundamental difference. Under the Massachusetts Bay charter this was not to be by Crown appointment but by action of the General Assembly. These men not only served in the capacity of an upper chamber of the Assembly but seven of them with the governor could constitute a council for directing the affairs of the province, which was authorized, among its other duties, to appoint judges and other officers for the courts of justice.

Finally, the charter, anticipating subsequent parliamentary regulation of the King's Woods in North America, placed the people of the Province under special restrictions by providing a penalty of one hundred pounds sterling for the destruction of any white-pine tree growing within the Province reserved by the Crown for the royal navy.[2]

In 1750 Massachusetts Bay possessed perhaps the most energetic and capable governor of any of the

[1] L. W. Labaree, *Royal Government in America*, pp. 195-196.
[2] For an interesting analysis of the Massachusetts Bay charter in the year 1752 see the Shelburne Papers, 47: 20-24.

British plantations, in the person of William Shirley.[1] He was the son of a London merchant and had made something of a reputation in the law in England, but finally came to America in 1731, accepting thereupon the office of Surveyor of the King's Woods; in 1734 he was appointed Advocate-General. Later he was selected by the Massachusetts Assembly to serve on the boundary commission to settle the disputed line separating the Province from Rhode Island and in general was favorably regarded, especially in light of the fact that he was known not to be in sympathy with Belcher, who was governor jointly of Massachusetts Bay and New Hampshire and was by no means popular in either. Upon the recall of the latter, who was later transferred to New Jersey, the way was opened up for Shirley, who in 1741 was given a commission limited to Massachusetts Bay, over which he acted as governor for a period of some fifteen years. A man of tremendous energy and enthusiasm, he set himself to promote the interests of the Commonwealth. He was especially concerned with the situation in Nova Scotia when in 1744 news arrived of the British declaration of war against the French King.[2] The great Canso fisheries, which had been under the control of the fishermen of his own province, had already fallen to the French with the cap-

[1] For an excellent account of the administration of Shirley see G. A. Wood, *William Shirley, Governor of Massachusetts, 1741-1756. A History*, Vol. I. (Columbia University *Studies*, Vol. XCII, No. 209). Shirley's abilities are put in a much less favorable light by S. M. Pargellis in his *Lord Loudoun in North America, 1756-1758*.

[2] See J. B. Brebner, *New England's Outpost*, for an extended treatment of this.

ture of Canso; Annapolis Royal, the only English stronghold in the northern province, was also menaced. Moreover, the Indians along the border of Maine, an integral part of Massachusetts Bay, were now assuming a threatening attitude, as they were much under the influence of French missionaries. Not only did he succeed in entering into treaties with these Indians, but he raised a force for the relief of Annapolis. Early the following year he recommended to the Assembly the reduction of the great fortress of Louisbourg that not only guarded the mouth of the St. Lawrence but threatened Nova Scotia. His advice was acted upon and, with the assistance of the other New England colonies, an expedition under the leadership of William Pepperrell and Admiral Sir Peter Warren succeeded in its capture. He thereupon formulated plans for the overthrow of the French power in Canada. These were approved in England and some eight thousand troops were assembled for that purpose, although nothing was done as the result of a change in the conduct of the war by those in general charge at home. Indeed, in the subsequent peace of Aix-la-Chapelle, much to his despair, even Louisbourg was returned to the French under an agreement of the *status quo ante bellum*. However, the ministry could not let pass unrewarded his notable achievement. He and Pepperrell were knighted by the King, and the colonies that had participated in the Cape Breton adventure were voted compensation by Parliament for the expenses entailed in it.

Shirley was now at the height of his power and influence in public life. His distinguished achievements in North America and also his knowledge of the respective rights and claims of the English and French in the regions south of the St. Lawrence and including the Peninsula of Acadia at this juncture led to his appointment as one of the two English commissioners to meet in Paris with those designated by the French government to settle all outstanding issues between the two nations—especially those arising out of conflicting claims in North America and the West Indies. Leaving for England the latter part of the year 1749, he carried with him striking proofs of the confidence of the people of Massachusetts Bay, as embodied in the answer of the two houses of the General Assembly to his address notifying them of his intended departure for a year's absence. "And when we reflect," they declared, "on your knowledge of the present Circumstances of the Province and the great ability to set the same in a true light, our expectations are justly raised, that you will in every Respect consult and by all proper Methods in your Power promote the real Interest of his Majesty's good Subjects... under your charge."[1] Well, therefore, might Shirley declare to the Duke of Newcastle upon arriving in London, "that throughout my whole Administration a perfect Harmony has ever subsisted between me and the Assembly... and that I left 'em in perfect tranquility and well affected to his Majesty's Government; whilst some of the Neighbouring Colonies are involved in Factions and the utmost Confusion."[2] In view of this pleasant relationship established between the Governor and the people of the Province

[1] A copy of this answer is printed in the *Pennsylvania Journal and Weekly Advertiser*, Aug. 31, 1749.
[2] *Correspondence of William Shirley*, I, 494.

it may be considered surprising to find the former during his leave of absence, which was extended to 1753, seeking a change of post. For not only did he solicit Newcastle in 1750 for an appointment to the governorship of New York, should it fall vacant, but in 1752 he sought the same office for the Leeward Islands.[1]

During the absence of the Governor from the Province the control of administration was intrusted to Lieutenant Governor Spencer Phips. The latter, however, was so remiss in communicating with the Board of Trade and in keeping it in touch generally with the state of affairs in Massachusetts Bay by answering the heads of inquiry that in May of the year 1751 it determined to rebuke him, pointing out in this connection that "Their Lordships consider this neglect as a great mark of disrespect and disregard to His Majesty's Service and a Breach of the Trust." Phips, in reply to this, sought to excuse himself by stating that he was unable to find among the public papers addressed to Shirley the document in question. Thereupon the Board, forwarding a copy of this, admonished him not to fail to send a full answer to the heads every six months.[2] Massachusetts Bay, however, was at that juncture quite free from dangerous agitation and designs against the imperial unity. The Colony was proud of its able and popular royal governor and gave such appearance of growing sympathy with the Mother Country in things religious that a proposal was actually made in the year 1750 for the erection in Cambridge in the vicinity of Harvard

[1] Op. cit., I, 508-509; II, 1-3.
[2] C.O. 5: 918, pp. 257-262.

College of "a College for University Learning according to the Church of England."[1] In fact, its devotion to the Crown was expressed in almost extravagant terms early in the same year when the General Court in an address to His Majesty denounced the disloyal tendencies of the French-speaking inhabitants of Nova Scotia and at the same time petitioned the King either to compel "such uncertain and precarious subjects" to leave his dominion or to reduce them to a more perfect obedience. It ends with these words:

"It is the high sense we have of the Happiness we enjoy as we are the subjects of the Crown of Great Britain, and the Dread which proceeds even from the most distant prospect of being ever subjected to the Yoke, and Tyranny of the French, that induces us to this our humble Address to your Majesty and it is our Constant and devout Prayer to almighty God, that your Majesty may long continue to Reign over us, and that our Posterity may remain the faithful subjects of your Royal House to the end of time."[2] Further, in the year 1754, an address was voted on the part of the two chambers that returned "their humble thanks to His Majesty for His Paternal Goodness to His Subjects in that Province."[3] Here, surely, one might have thought, was a colony committed irrevocably to sentiments of devotion to His Majesty, the King of England! Yet not many years were to pass before the faintest expression of loyalty to the Crown

[1] Thomas Coram to George Onslow, May 12, 1750. "Morrison Papers," Hist. Mss. Com. *9th Rep.*, p. 478.

[2] This was signed January 31, 1750 by Lieutenant Governor Phips, as well as by Josiah Williams for the Council and by Speaker Thomas Hubbard, "in the name and by Order of the House of Representatives." P.R.O. A. 40, Nova Scotia, 1751, 63: 189.

[3] *Acts of the Privy Council, Col., 1745-1766*, p. 203.

on the part of any inhabitant led to furious denunciations on the part of the deputies of the towns and to threats and even acts of terrorism on the part of the people.

In fact, it may be affirmed that by the middle of the eighteenth century the Province, in common with the rest of New England which it dominated in many respects, had come to the point in its development as a center of population and wealth, and of experience in things political, that signs were not lacking that it possessed, in spite of all formal testimony of loyalty to the King and to the imperial ideal, a sense of almost complete self-sufficiency. The successful capture by New England volunteers of the great French fortress of Louisbourg, the most conspicuous stroke on the part of the British in King George's War, did not fail to reënforce that sense. It was also doubtless based upon the conviction that New England had become the seat of a peculiar and superior civilization. John Adams later gave very forcible expression to this idea and at the same time set forth why, in his opinion, this portion of the Empire had an advantage over "every other colony in America and, indeed, of every other part of the world that I know anything of." The statement is so illuminating, as setting forth a point of view that doubtless was widespread among the inhabitants of the commonwealth at the period under consideration, that it would be well to close this chapter with his exact words. He finds this superiority due to five causes which he enumerates as follows:

"1. The people are purer English blood; less mixed with Scotch, Irish, Dutch, French, Danish, Swedish, etc., than any other; and descended from Englishmen, too, who left Europe in purer times than the present, and less tainted with corruption than those they left behind them.

"2. The institutions in New England for the support of religion, morals, and decency exceed any other; obliging every parish to have a minister, and every person to go to meeting, etc.

"3. The public institutions in New England for the education of youth, supporting colleges at the public expense, and obliging towns to maintain grammar schools, are not equaled, and never were, in any part of the world.

"4. The division of our territory, that is, our counties, into townships; empowering towns to assemble, choose officers, make laws, mend roads, and twenty other things, gives every man an opportunity of showing and improving that education which he received at college or at school, and makes knowledge and dexterity at public business common.

"5. Our law for the distribution of intestate estates occasions a frequent division of landed property, and prevents monopolies of land."[1]

[1] *Familiar Letters of John Adams and His Wife* (ed. Chas. Francis Adams, 1876), pp. 120-121.

CHAPTER II

WEDGED between the geographical divisions of Massachusetts Bay, which after the year 1677 included the former Province of Maine, lay the Province of New Hampshire. The chief source of wealth of the Colony lay in its forests, for in the eighteenth century there extended from Nova Scotia southward into New Jersey a broad belt of white pine. With reason was this tree called "the prince of the American forest," owing to "its size, age and majesty of appearance." One may well picture the slopes of the mountains and hills with the valleys of this region covered here and there with these splendid trees, many of which towered above the sky line with their lower branches at least a hundred feet from the ground and with a trunk measuring over seven feet in diameter at the base. These giant conifers when sound were especially prized. They were not only valued for the lumber they yielded but especially for their availability as ship timber; for from them the great masts as well as bowsprits and yards were procured. There was, however, considerable waste in the harvesting of these; in the words of a contemporary, "trees of the largest size, fit to make 34 to 38-inch masts, 48 out of 50 may happen to be defective, although while standing they appear to be perfectly sound. . . ." He further added, "Some very good trees are broke in falling, nor is it possible to prevent it. Trees of 45 or 50 yards long, and from 4 to 6 feet in diameter, are of such immense weight it is almost beyond the power of man to use any secure management in lowering them. Much is done by bedding with bushes and small trees to help secure them, but notwithstanding there still remains a very great risque."[1] Burnaby declared that the largest of these pine trees were never cut but in times of deep snow. "When the trees are fallen," he wrote, "they yoke seventy or eighty pair of oxen, and drag them along the snow. It is exceedingly difficult to put them first into motion, which they call raising them; and when they have once effected this, they never stop upon any account whatever till they arrive at the water's side."[2] The "sticks," as the trunks cropped of all limbs were called, were then floated down the river to Portsmouth where they were dressed by expert ship timber workers. Only then were they ready for export.

In spite of these difficulties many of the ships of the royal navy required masts which could be provided only from trees of the largest size, and these had to be secured from some source, whatever the expense or hazard.

The existence of this growth of virgin white-pine forest in America had been known to the people of England for over a century and was held to be a

[1] John Wentworth to the Earl of Hillsborough, Dec. 4, 1771, "Wentworth Letter Books," quoted in Mayo's "The King's Woods," Massachusetts Hist. Soc. *Proceedings*, October-November, 1920, p. 53.

[2] Andrew Burnaby, *Travels through the Middle Settlements of North America, 1759-1760*, I, 115-116.

matter of first importance. While their oak trees provided superb material for the hulls of the ships, they had for centuries been dependent upon the forests of Scandinavia for masting materials. This was considered highly undesirable. As early as 1692 the first steps were taken by the government in the direction of the proper preservation and utilization of this imperial asset by the appointment of a Surveyor-General of His Majesty's Woods in North America in the person of the famous Edward Randolph,[1] who was succeeded by Jahleel Brenton. Brenton was in turn followed by John Bridger, then came in turn Charles Burniston, Charles Armstrong, and David Dunbar, the latter serving until 1744.[2]

The task assigned to the Surveyor-General was by no means trifling. Not only was he to protect the best of the white pine standing in the unappropriated forest regions for the King's use, but he was expected to encourage the production of various naval stores on the part of the settlers. Under Queen Anne and her immediate successors appropriate legislation was passed which strictly forbade, without special license, the cutting of any white pine of a diameter of two feet and over twelve inches from the base, within the entire region of the growth of these trees, except on land that then was private.[3] All lands subsequently granted were under limitation which provided for the reserve of these trees; there was also the require-

[1] *Calendar of State Papers, 1689-1692*, Par. 1830.
[2] C.O. 391: 51, p. 52. For this topic see E. L. Lord, *Industrial Experiments in the British Colonies of North America* (Johns Hopkins Univ. *Studies*, XVI).
[3] 3 and 4 Anne, c. 9, Sec. 2; 9 Anne, c. 22; 8 George I, c. 72; 2 George II, c. 35.

ment that no white pine of any description should be felled without express license from the Surveyor-General.[1] And not only was the King's broad arrow ordered to be placed upon these reserved trees by the Surveyor-General or his deputies, but violators of the regulations were subject to trial in a vice-admiralty court—an extraordinary extension of the authority of this tribunal and an indication of the degree of importance attached to this imperial resource by the British government.[2]

On the other hand, to bring about the legitimate production of ship timber made from these trees, and its exportation to the Mother Country, Parliament provided that those who transported masts, bowsprits, and yards from the plantations to the latter should be entitled to a premium of one pound sterling per ton.[3] That this bounty was a decided encouragement may be appreciated especially in light of the fact that a good mast of twenty-four inches in diameter at its base would bring, on contract with the royal navy, something over thirteen pounds sterling, and one of thirty-four inches as high as ninety pounds. Bowsprits ran in value from two pounds ten shillings to over fifty-two pounds, and yards from six pounds and a half to some thirty-two pounds, according to the accounts of the contractor of the royal navy.[4]

[1] Mayo, "The King's Woods," Mass. Hist. Soc. *Proceedings,* Oct. and November, 1920, pp. 53-54.
[2] 8 Geo. I, c. 12.
[3] 2 Geo. II, c. 35, Par. 3; 25 Geo. II, c. 35; 32 Geo. II, c. 23.
[4] These figures were secured by Belknap from the books of Mark Hunking Wentworth, contractor for the royal navy. Jeremy Belknap, *History of New Hampshire,* III, 80. In 1769

So greatly were these contracts for ship timber prized that those interested, it appears, brought about the passage of a provincial law laying a fine of one hundred pounds sterling upon any one cutting down one of these masting trees without license.[1] There came, however, signs of the gradual lessening of the importance of New Hampshire as a lumbering center. As early as 1727 Colonel Westbrook, contractor for the royal navy, transferred many important contracts for timber to the lumbering interests of Maine; in 1737 Governor Belcher, in his report on the state of the Province of New Hampshire, declared that within the past decade the trade in pine lumber had decreased by three quarters and that the trees growing on private property located near the seashore had all but disappeared.[2] In fact, it was necessary to go some distance from the water, even well up the Piscataqua, for suitable ship timber, especially for masts, which entailed additional labor, expense, and time.

It is therefore probably true that by 1750 there existed in Maine and on the upper Connecticut River bodies of white pine suitable for the needs of the

the value of the masts sent to England was placed at £7819 before exportation. G. L. Beer, *Commercial Policy of England Toward the American Colonies*, pp. 98-99.

[1] 5 Anne, c. 17, Par. 1; *New Hampshire Provincial Papers*, V, 19-20. In tracing the history of the supply of New England masts to the Mother Country upon contract one finds that during the years 1689-1696 Samuel Allen agreed to furnish a shipload annually; he was followed by Isaac Taylor who supplied as many as four annually; then a Francis Collins, between 1708 and 1713, furnished three annually. See C. P. Nettels, *The Money Supply of the American Colonies before 1720*, p. 74, note.

[2] Jonathan Belcher to the Board of Trade, April 4, 1737. Shelburne Papers, 45: 311-318.

royal navy that could be tapped more economically than the timber growing in New Hampshire. However, the contractor for the royal navy, Mark Hunking Wentworth, was one of a powerful group of New Hampshire capitalists and a brother of the Governor. He seems for various reasons to have looked to the exploitation of the resources of that Colony, with the result that he favored his provincial associates with lucrative contracts.[1] Indeed, the deep personal interest of the Wentworth group in the masting trade could hardly be questioned, even if there existed no other evidence, in light of the fact that Governor Wentworth was furnished £2,000 by interested New Hampshire parties to buy the relinquishment of the post of Surveyor-General of His Majesty's Woods in 1744 from the incumbent, David Dunbar, although the stipend attached to it was only £200 a year.[2] One may further venture to assert that there is abundance of proof that this great power of the Wentworth family was fully used to protect the Portsmouth lumbering interests.[3]

In spite of the success of the New Hampshire lum-

[1] E. L. Lord, *Industrial Experiments in the British Colonies of North America*, p. 99.

[2] At the time of Wentworth's appointment as governor, his friend, John Thomlinson, London agent of New Hampshire, wrote regarding him, "I have good hopes of having something more done for him that will put him into a capacity soon to discharge all obligations of this sort." John Thomlinson to Theodore Atkinson, May 9, 1741. *New Hampshire Provincial Papers*, II, 930. This "something" was the office of Surveyor-General of the King's Woods.

[3] For a discussion of this see the author's *Jared Ingersoll: A Study of American Loyalism in Relation to British Colonial Government*, Chap. IV.

bering group in maintaining temporary control of the ship timber contracts, evidence is not lacking that the leaders looked to the future of the Province with concern. Since its most conveniently located timber had been largely cut away, as was stated, the time was not far distant when the cost of lumbering within its borders would become prohibitive, especially that carried on for obtaining ship timber. However, it seemed that without a continuation of this industry the Colony would hardly fail to sink to insignificance. To insure, therefore, the continued prosperity of New Hampshire through the maintenance of the mast trade became indubitably the mainspring of much of the activity of Benning Wentworth during the period of his governorship, which lasted from 1741 to 1767. Most intimately related to this problem was that involving the exact nature of the geographical limits of the Province.

When Governor Belcher, Wentworth's predecessor, reported on the New Hampshire boundaries to the Board of Trade in 1737 he stated that although the reputed southern boundary was a line "three miles to the northward of the Merrimac River and every part thereof," dividing New Hampshire from Massachusetts Bay proper and that to the east was the county of York in Maine, these limits were in dispute. Yet, even the most moderate claims of her powerful neighbor, he judged, would leave the Province narrowly restricted and almost surrounded by the lands of the other. In his commission as governor, no boundaries were given, and in none of the earlier commissions, he declared, was any mention made of any, "at the head or at the sea." In fact, as he saw it the Province of New Hampshire was "but a small strip of Land, no more than fifteen Miles wide by the Sea, and not so big by the half as some counties of Massachusetts."[1] It is, however, well known that he was prejudiced and was actively seeking the union of the two colonies of New Hampshire and Massachusetts Bay over both of which he was serving as governor.[2]

In the very year, indeed, that Belcher's report was made, an order in Council was issued referring the disputed boundaries to a commission drawn from the governors' councils of New York, Rhode Island, and Nova Scotia. Ultimately the commission made a report on the eastern limits which vindicated the New Hampshire contentions, but it experienced difficulty in coming to a satisfactory conclusion regarding the southern limits, owing to the peculiar reading of the charter of Massachusetts Bay. Nevertheless, in 1741, largely by reason of the powerful influence of the Wentworths and those intimately associated with them, especially the London provincial agent, John

[1] J. Belcher to the Board of Trade, April 4, 1737. Shelburne Papers, 45: 312. According to a memorandum drawn up by the Board of Trade in 1721 New Hampshire included "all that part of the main land in New England lying upon the Sea Coast, beginning from the middle part of Merrimack River and from thence to proceed Northwards along the Sea Coast to Pescattaway River & so forewards up within the said River and to the furthest head thereof, and from thence north westward untill 60 Miles be finished, and from thence to cross overland to the 60 Miles accounted from Piscattaway River, together with all Islands, & Isletts within 5 Leagues distance of the Premises, and abutting upon any part of parcell thereof." "Memorandum relating to State of the . . . Colonies . . . ," Sept. 8, 1721, *ibid.*, 45: 210.

[2] W. H. Fry, *New Hampshire as a Royal Province*, pp. 256-257.

Thomlinson, an order in Council was secured establishing this boundary along "a line corresponding to the course of the Merrimac from three miles north of its mouth to three miles of Pawtucket Falls at its most southerly bend and then due west to the next English Province"—a decision that quadrupled the hitherto supposedly restricted limits of New Hampshire and actually went far beyond the most sanguine expectations of the inhabitants of the Colony. Indeed, so liberal was this decision, at the expense of Massachusetts Bay, that the former government was temporarily embarrassed when it was found that these new limits included Fort Dummer on the upper Connecticut, far removed from the most western of the settled townships.

The fort had been built by Massachusetts Bay, as a result of a vote of the House of Representatives in 1723, to protect her own outlying western settlements. As it was located at the most but a three or four days' march distant from the powerful French stronghold at Crown Point, its strategic importance was not to be questioned. From the time of its construction until the decision against her, she had supported it, keeping it garrisoned and in a fair state of repair. Thereupon the question arose, Which province should pay the cost of its maintenance, the one that requires its protection or the one within the territory of which it now stands? The people of New Hampshire, as a group, felt that it was unjust to expect them to defend the frontiers of Massachusetts Bay, especially in light of the fact that along the line of their own settlements there were nine posts that had to be maintained in time of hostilities as a barrier to the French and their Indian allies.[1] Not only did the deputies of the people in 1745 take this position strongly in the General Assembly but the dispute continued for years, with Massachusetts during the interim reluctantly garrisoning the fort.[2]

As to Governor Wentworth, his far-seeing plans comprehended the newly acquired region, and he brought pressure at all times to persuade the representatives of the people to undertake the responsibility of western frontier defense. In this connection he summoned to the Assembly representatives from the unprivileged towns of Chester, Haverhill, South Hampton, Rumford,[3] Methuen, and Dracut to gather needed support in that body. These, however, were denied the right to seats by the older towns,[4] with the result that Wentworth carried the issue to His Majesty in Council, who in 1748 ordered an instruction to be prepared empowering certain New Hampshire towns and districts to send deputies to the As-

[1] These were Rochester, Barrington, Nottingham, Chester, Londonderry, Juncook, Penacook, Contacook and Canterbury. See the statement of John Thomlinson, Agent of New Hampshire, before the Board of Trade, March 2, 1748-49. Board of Trade Journal, Vol. 57. For an excellent account of the progress of this dispute see the testimony of the agents of the two provinces before the Board at the session of Feb. 17, 1748-49. Ibid., 57. For fuller details see the "Thomlinson Papers," New Hampshire Provincial Papers, V, 921-931.

[2] Ibid., VI, 2-3.

[3] In the case of Rumford, as was brought out in the preceding chapter, it had been established by Massachusetts people to the west of the Merrimac and, much against the desire of the inhabitants, had been included in those lands that New Hampshire received in the settlement of the boundary.

[4] New Hampshire Provincial Papers, V, 261, VI, 70, 74-79. W. H. Fry, New Hampshire as a Royal Province, pp. 156-161.

sembly.[1] Even in the face of this royal authorization the latter body, up until the year 1752, stoutly stood by what it considered to be an inherent right of determining, without interference from the executive, all questions involving the right of the towns to be therein represented.[2] A change, nevertheless, gradually took place in the attitude of the public over the larger question, involving as it did the support of the Governor's policy in western New Hampshire. This seems to have been true especially after the return of Major Goffe and Matthew Patten who had gone into the region of the upper Connecticut to view Fort Dummer in 1749.[3] The information gradually spread that the new acquisition lying adjacent to the river was not only "the Garden of New England,"[4] but also afforded an abundant supply of white-pine trees and was therefore an asset of vast importance, the benefit of which might be generally shared by the people. This seems to have had the desired effect. At least, late in the year 1752 Wentworth was able to write to the Board of Trade that harmony within the provincial government had been restored and that the new members had been seated.[5] Soon after this, detachments of New Hampshire troops were posted on the upper Connecticut both at Fort Dummer and at Keene. The Governor now found himself possessed of the necessary support for

[1] Board of Trade *Journal, 1741-1749*, p. 292.
[2] L. W. Labaree, *Royal Government in America*, pp. 180-183.
[3] *New Hampshire Provincial Papers*, VI, 581.
[4] See Grant Powers, *The Coos Country, 1754-1785*, for valuable source material covering the period under consideration.
[5] Board of Trade *Journal, 1749-1753*, pp. 379-380.

the ambitious project which for years he had been evolving.

This project involved the immediate exploitation of the lands of the upper Connecticut Valley. As the first step in this direction, he had secured in 1748 a special commission from the Crown to make grants within the Province upon a quit-rent basis of one shilling sterling for each one hundred acres.[1] Early in 1750, in communicating with Governor Clinton of New York, he announced in the name of his own colony, a claim to lands a considerable distance to the westward of the Connecticut.[2] Two years later came the first of a series of grants of townships each six miles square which ultimately extended sixty miles along the Connecticut and westward to a point not many miles removed from Albany. This was done in face of the continued protests of the government of New York, which also claimed that the lands were under its jurisdiction. It also alleged that settlers were especially attracted by Wentworth's invitation to take out New Hampshire patents rather than those of New York, for the quit-rent asked was but one shilling per hundred acres instead of two shillings and six pence charged by the latter under terms of the royal instructions.[3]

In all, some one hundred and forty townships were allotted to favored parties; in connection with this Wentworth reserved for himself, in lieu of a fee for affixing the seal, five hundred acres for each grant or

[1] See "The New Hampshire Grants (so called) 1749-1791," *Documents and Records Relating to New Hampshire*, X, No. 3.
[2] *New York Colonial Documents*, VII, 598.
[3] *Ibid.*, VII, 595-598.

a total of some seventy thousand acres of land, undoubtedly selected for its potential white-pine harvest.[1]

New Hampshire, therefore, during the period under special consideration, instead of struggling for existence, as had been the case from the very beginning of her history until the year 1741, in the face of the intense pressure of Massachusetts Bay, was now not only relieved of this pressure but, in fact, had become so extraordinarily aggressive under the leadership of her powerful governor as thoroughly to alarm the Province of New York.

In 1750 the population of the Province may be estimated roughly at between twenty and twenty-four thousand people.[2] Outside of the lumbering and commercial activities the next most important interest was doubtless general farming, which seems to have engaged the attention of the majority of the inhabitants. However, ships were built at Portsmouth, and various articles of wood were manufactured, such as house frames, desks, chests of drawers, and other furniture, which were carried southward, especially to Virginia and to the Carolinas.[3] In religion the people were inclined strongly toward Con-

[1] W. H. Fry, New Hampshire as a Royal Province, pp. 265-274.

[2] In 1737 the population, according to Gov. Belcher, was eleven thousand whites and about two hundred blacks; it was given in 1755 as thirty thousand. "Account of the Several Provinces in North-America," from Ames' Almanack for 1756. New Hampshire Historical Society, Coll., V, 228-230. For other figures see Greene and Harrington, American Population before ...1790, p. 72.

[3] Shelburne Papers, 45: 313-318.

gregationalism[1] and came so much under the influence of the preaching of Whitefield that upon the
banners of the New Hampshire forces furnished for
the reduction of Fort Louisbourg was placed his
motto, *"nil desperandum Christo duce."*

At this point it may be affirmed that the rise to
importance of the Province was in many ways bound
up with the rise of the Wentworth family to a dominating position in its affairs. This family of Lincoln-
shire origin was represented among the early settlers
of Exeter where a William Wentworth was not only
a selectman of the town and an elder in the church,
but an extensive landowner. The father of Benning
and Mark Hunking was John Wentworth, who was
Lieutenant Governor of the Province between the
years 1717 and 1730 and who made the family the
first in importance in New Hampshire both in political life and in the field of commercial undertaking.
His sons inherited his instinct for money-making and
power, and each of them, in spite of financial reverses
in the case of Benning previous to his attaining the
governorship, became exceedingly wealthy. The degree to which the government of New Hampshire,
under the latter, was a family arrangement could
probably not be duplicated in any other part of the
old British Empire. In the course of his governorship,
George Jaffrey, who had earlier married his sister,
was not only the President of the Council but also the
Provincial Treasurer; the Chief Justice of the Su-

[1] New Hampshire Historical Society *Coll.*, I, 150-152. Burnaby declared that there were only two missionaries of the Church
of England within the Province and that one of them had applied
to be removed to Rhode Island. *Travels through the Middle
Settlements* (1759-1760), p. 115.

preme Court, Theodore Atkinson, another brother-in-law, was likewise in the Council; Jotham Odiorne, also a councillor and second judge, was related in marriage to Mark Hunking Wentworth, his brother; Henry Sherburne, a cousin, was a councillor; while Samuel Solley, another councillor, was married to Jaffrey's daughter; and finally Thomas Packer, his brother-in-law, was High Sheriff.[1] In keeping with this was his method of caring for public affairs. Out at Little Harbour, not far from Portsmouth, still stands the Wentworth mansion, where the owner once lived in semiregal fashion. This spacious residence, at one time containing some fifty-two rooms, could be approached by land or water. It was prepared for defense with an armory off the hallway and with underground quarters for the horses in times of danger. Within was the great chamber set apart for the meetings of the Provincial Council and also the amusement room with its billiard tables and inviting buffet.

Wentworth, as may be appreciated, was so powerfully entrenched in the government as to be for years quite safe from the attacks of his enemies. It is true that in the '40s Richard Waldron, whom he had dismissed from the Council, headed a movement to displace him, and became speaker in the Assembly. But the Wentworth influence was too great in England to be successfully overcome, and the contest rather added to the latter's strength than weakened it.[2]

[1] See John Wentworth, *The Wentworth Genealogy*, I, 287; New Hampshire Hist. Soc. *Coll.*, V, 232-233.

[2] *New Hampshire Provincial Papers*, VI, 39-61. Waldron was a brother-in-law of former Governor Belcher.

CHAPTER III

AN OLD NEW ENGLAND RELIGIOUS FRONTIER

SOUTH of Massachusetts Bay and even more narrowly confined than was New Hampshire before 1740 was the corporate colony of Rhode Island and Providence Plantations, lying mostly to the westward of Narragansett Bay, although fringing its northern and eastern shores. "Rhode-Island with a portion of the adjacent Continent under the same Government," declared Bishop Berkeley in a sermon before the Society for the Propagation of the Gospel in 1731,[1] "is inhabited by an English Colony consisting chiefly of sectaries of many different Denominations who seem to have worn off that part of Prejudice which they inherited from their Ancesters against the National Church of this land, though it must be acknowledged at the same time that too many of them have worn off a serious sense of all Religion." The Colony, in fact, came into existence in the fourth decade of the seventeenth century as the result of the efforts of religious refugees fleeing from Massachusetts Bay's iron rod of church discipline. By the middle of the eighteenth century most of the inhabitants were comprehended by four religious denominations, the strongest and most articulate of which was the Baptist, followed by the Quaker, Presbyterian, and Episcopalian in order of numerical strength and influ-

[1] See Berkeley's *Miscellany*, pp. 213-235.

ence.[1] However, as the result of the Great Awakening which came upon the Colony with dramatic force, other sects than those just mentioned made their appearance, largely on account of secessions from the older groups, and it may be said that there still survived in 1750, especially outside the towns, much of the spirit of the seventeenth century religious zealots.

Since the days of Roger Williams and Samuel Gorton the Colony had stood for soul liberty as against religious restraints and for the separation of the affairs of church and state. In spite of this, a much-disputed religious clause had crept into the Rhode Island code of laws by a process not entirely clear, but apparently as one result of the sharp reaction throughout the Empire to the attempts of the Old Pretender, a devout Catholic, to gain the throne of England in 1715. This clause, which denied all political rights of citizenship, including the franchise, not only to non-Christians but to Roman Catholics, first appeared in the digest of the laws of the year 1719 and was reprinted in those of 1730 and 1745 and reads as follows:

"And that all rights and privileges granted to this Colony by his Majesty's Charter be entirely Kept and preserved to all his Majesty's subjects residing or belonging to the same: and that all men professing Christianity and of competent estates and of civil conversation, who acknowledge and are obedient to the civil Magistrates, though of different judgements in religious affairs (Roman Catholics only excepted)

[1] In 1739 the little Colony possessed thirty-three church edifices of which number twelve were Baptist, ten were Quaker, six were Presbyterian, and five were Anglican. Frederic Denison, *Westerly and its Witnesses*, p. 88.

shall be admitted Freemen and shall have liberty to choose and be chosen officers in the colony both Military and Civil."[1]

Granting the presence of this restriction in her laws, Rhode Island in practice set a worthy example of religious tolerance to her neighbors. While her Baptist preachers in going into Connecticut were visited with sharp persecution and were not exempt from bodily violence,[2] it appears that at home no one was molested in the pursuit of his religious principles. In the face of political issues, the Baptists willingly maintained their Quaker friends in office. Even the Sabbatarian center at Westerly showed a remarkable spirit of generosity toward other sects.[3] One is therefore not surprised to find Jewish merchants in Newport playing a leading rôle in the life of the Colony.[4] It may be asserted that by 1750 the Colony had attained an attitude toward religious matters that might be characterized as broad and secular.

Rhode Island does not abound in natural resources. The soil in most places is just tolerably good, composed as it is of boulder clay or hard pan; however, it possesses the quality of endurance, and after being cleared of the glacial surface rocks and smaller stones, frequently a very arduous task, is capable of yielding

[1] *Acts and Laws of the Colony of Rhode Island, 1719*, p. 3. For an extensive treatment of this see Sidney S. Rider, *An Inquiry Concerning the Origin of the Clause in the Laws of Rhode Island (1719-1783) Disfranchising Roman Catholics (Rhode Island Historical Tracts*, second series, No. 1).

[2] See A. G. Palmer, *Early Baptists of Connecticut.*

[3] Frederic Denison, *Westerly and its Witnesses.*

[4] For the importance of the Jews in the commercial life of Rhode Island see M. J. Kohler, "The Jews of Newport," *American Jewish Historical Publications*, No. 6.

under careful management fairly abundant crops of cereals as well as other produce. Indeed, from this stony soil apparently came a surplus of food beyond local needs in the middle of the eighteenth century. At least there were considerable quantities of beef, pork, butter, cheese, Indian corn, horses, and sheep available, whether obtained locally or from neighboring colonies, for export each year from the Colony. If one were to assume that this surplus was produced locally, it must have been obtained only by the sustained and intelligent efforts of the agricultural population made up largely of small farmers whose holdings probably did not average beyond one hundred acres. In general, the conditions confronting the dwellers in rural Rhode Island opposed aristocratic tendencies and the operation of large land units. However, it is true that the leading people in the neighborhood of Kingston, within the region of old South County, possessed large bodies of land and rather numerous slaves, and had developed a modified plantation system, all of which had survived from the days when this region, known as King's Province, was the object of dispute between Rhode Island and Connecticut.[1] Elsewhere, as a rule, the entire labor on the land was supplied by the farmers and their sons. These men, strongly independent and individualistic, bore the reputation of doing their own thinking to a surprising extent.

During the period under discussion the population of the Plantations was increasing perhaps more rapidly than at any other similar period in the eighteenth

[1] Edward Channing, *The Narragansett Planters*, pp. 12-16, 19-23.

century. In 1730 there were but 17,935 people; by 1755 the number had mounted to 40,636. The increase after this was slow; by 1783 there were only 51,869 people and by 1790 but 68,825.[1] This would imply that conditions during the middle of the century were particularly favorable, not only for a natural increase in the number of inhabitants, but for those from other regions who were attracted to the Colony. As a matter of fact, Rhode Island not only had sustained her agricultural population in a state of self-respect and comfort but she had acquired by 1750 real importance and very considerable wealth in the field of foreign trade. This latter had come since the beginning of the eighteenth century. According to a report sent to the Board of Trade in 1708, but twenty-nine vessels were accredited to the people of the Plantations,[2] which, however, represented a sixfold increase in the amount of shipping owned locally twenty years previous to that date; by 1721 there were sixty vessels; by 1740 the number had amounted to one hundred and twenty,[3] and by 1750 there must have been three hundred, made up largely of sloops, brigantines, and small ships engaged in foreign as well as in the coasting trade.[4] The explanation of this increase lies not only in the en-

[1] E. B. Greene and V. D. Harrington, *American Population before . . . 1790*, 63-64.
[2] *Rhode Island Col. Rec.*, IV, 55-56.
[3] *Rhode Island Col. Rec.*, V, 8-14; see also the letter of Gov. Richard Ward to the Board of Trade of Jan. 9, 1740, printed in E. R. Potter and P. S. Rider's *Some Account of the Bills of Credit on Paper Money of Rhode Island.*
[4] W. F. Crawford, "The Commerce of Rhode Island with the Southern Continental Colonies in the Eighteenth Century," Rhode Island Hist. Soc. *Coll.*, XIV, 99-110; 124-130.

terprise of the men of Newport and later of Providence[1] but in the favorable location of the Colony with respect to the interior of the Province of Massachusetts Bay, which seems to have become in the course of the eighteenth century increasingly dependent commercially upon the ports of Narragansett Bay.[2]

The leaders in the expanding commercial life of Rhode Island in the middle of the eighteenth century were such men as Stephen Wanton, Abraham Redwood, Joseph Whipple, Godfrey Malbone, Aaron Lopez, Stephen Ayrault, Daniel Ayrault, Nathan Angel, William Vernon, Philip Wilkinson, and Stephen Hopkins. The ships of these and other merchants haunted all the ports of the West Indies, carrying on a vast traffic, especially in rum, molasses, and sugar secured in the French islands. The general course of this West India trade may well be illustrated by articles of agreement that Philip Wilkinson and Company, owners of the *Charming Polly,* entered into with the captain, one Richard Penmure. According to this, after the latter had loaded his ship at Newport with suitable goods he was to sail to the Windward Islands and, if possible, dispose of these articles at St. Vincent; otherwise he was to sail to Dominica and, should there still be any portion of the cargo left, he was to proceed to the Dutch island of St. Eustatius, where the

[1] Arnold in his *History of the State of Rhode Island* quotes Bulls' *Memoirs* of Rhode Island to the effect that by 1769 the Plantations had some two hundred vessels employed in foreign commerce and between three and four hundred in the domestic trade.

[2] H. C. Dorr, *Planting and Growth of Providence (Rhode Island Historical Tracts,* No. 15), pp. 172 and 207.

residue should be sold. With all of his goods thus converted into money he was thereupon to sail with the greatest despatch to the French island of Hispaniola for the purchase of molasses, muscovado sugar, and indigo with which he was to return to Rhode Island.[1]

It was this type of activity, in which scores of Rhode Island vessels were engaged, that assumed such importance as to lead the British West India planter interests in 1750 to protest to the Board of Trade that the commerce between the Colony in question and Hispaniola was no casual traffic but part of a well-formed plan on the part of the Court of France for the destruction of the British interests in the Caribbeans. These planter interests, as has been noticed in an earlier chapter, called upon the officials of the Mother Country for protection from such competition, and in this connection they asked for an investigation of the extent of the enforcement of the Sugar Act of 1733, which had placed upon foreign-produced sugar, molasses, and rum brought into the English plantations, a series of high duties.[2] Well they might. For there is no evidence that at this period the local collector of the customs at Newport made any effort to secure the duties on these articles.[3] There were many circumstances favoring the activities of the smuggler. He would customarily appear at his port of entry with his ship in ballast. Should a com-

[1] This agreement is printed in *The Commerce of Rhode Island 1726-1774* (Mass. Hist. Soc. *Coll.*, seventh series, IX), I, 60-61.
[2] C.O. 137: 25, 112. See Chapter IX, "The Struggle for the Muscovado Markets" in Volume II.
[3] F. W. Pitman, *Development of the British West Indies, 1700-1763*, p. 275 for "An Account of all Duties Collected." No duties are placed to the credit of Rhode Island between the years 1733-1750.

plaint be lodged against him he could boldly produce a certificate of having sailed from some British West India island also in ballast and would thereby be acquitted. For in approaching the Colony with his dutiable cargo, he would slip into some secluded cove and there discharge his sugar and molasses, perhaps under cover of darkness. Admiral Knowles asserted in 1752 that "nothing could be a stronger proof of this Practice than their Sailing . . . in Ballast all the winter Season, when it was Certain no Vessels in the world in a set of Ballast only could Encounter the Weather on their Coasts."[1]

A vice-admiralty court case of the year 1751 will illustrate how deeply the Jamaican authorities felt regarding the commerce of the Colony with the foreign sugar islands, and on the other hand, the even-handed justice that all colonials might expect of His Majesty's Privy Council. This involved the sloop *Jupiter* owned by Gideon Cornell of Newport. The vessel was loaded with lumber and horses furnished by a number of Rhode Island merchants for sale at Hispaniola with orders to return with a lading of articles from that island. The master, a Frenchman by the name of Bontin, naturalized in Ireland, after disposing of his cargo took on board French sugar and molasses, partly on credit for one de Pond and other residents of Hispaniola, and, by reason of desertions among his crew, a sufficient number of French mariners to man the sloop for the return voyage. Unfortunately, the vessel ran into a hard gale and broke her boom, with the result that she

[1] Governor Knowles to the Board of Trade, November 10, 1752. Library of Congress Accessions, No. 2413.

sought the nearest anchorage for repairs, which was at Port Royal, Jamaica. While there the vessel, together with the cargo, was seized by the Receiver-General of Customs, Benjamin Hume, as not operated according to navigation laws, and was libelled and condemned in the local vice-admiralty court upon charges of bringing into the Island foreign sugar and molasses, of failure to have the proper complement of British seaman, and of irregular registration.

Bontin thereupon appealed to His Majesty in Council. However, upon petition of the advocate of the Vice-Admiralty Court of Jamaica, James Innes, and Hume, his appeal was dismissed in 1753 for non-prosecution, with the assessment of £80 additional costs. The owner of the vessel the following year petitioned that the order dismissing the appeal be discharged, alleging the death of Bontin, who preceding this had become bankrupt. This was finally done, after the payment of costs by Cornell and the furnishing of proper security by himself and the Rhode Island London Agent, Richard Partridge. Finally, in the summer of 1758 the Lords of the Committee on Appeals reversed the sentence after the case was heard *ex parte*, restoring the ship and cargo with interest and levying upon the respondent £100 costs.[1]

In conclusion, one may venture the hope that when the *Jupiter* finally returned to Newport there was no effort to smuggle her cargo of French sugar and molasses into the Colony, little as may have been the inclination or previous expectation of the owners to pay the high duties levied thereon. However, if this

[1] *Acts of the Privy Council, Col., 1749-1766*, pp. 191-194.

were done, it must have been in the nature of an exceptional gesture in the direction of good citizenship and loyalty, for the whole spirit of the people of the trading towns was in direct opposition to compliance with the law. This may be illustrated by an incident of the year 1764, after the passage of the Sugar Act of that year lowering the duties on foreign-produced sugar and molasses.

The government had at last determined to make an effort to put an end to smuggling into the continental colonies. In this connection His Majesty's cutter the *St. John* was dispatched to Narragansett Bay and its commander, Lieutenant Hill, was also placed in charge of the custom-house. The Lieutenant, in attempting to perform his duty, found himself confronted by an overpowering opposition in June of that year when a mob forced the governor at Fort George on Goat Island to fire upon the cutter, with the result that several of the men in the custom service were wounded. They also threatened to burn the vessel should the keeper of the customs not desist in his activities.[1]

The West India commerce was but one angle of a great triangular trade developed by the Colony. The molasses thus brought from the West Indies was distilled into rum.[2] The quantity produced at this period can perhaps be judged by an assertion made in 1764 by the merchants of Rhode Island that fourteen thousand hogsheads of molasses were annually imported and that all the British West India islands together

[1] *Op. cit.*, pp. 690-692.
[2] According to Bull's *Memoirs* of Rhode Island quoted by Arnold, there were in Newport in 1769 twenty-one distilleries.

could not supply the demands of their distilleries.[1] The rum not consumed domestically and sold in neighboring colonies was largely transported to the Guinea Coast, for at this period the Rhode Islanders were the great American slavers.

While large profits were undoubtedly made from these voyages, serious difficulties sometimes arose. David Lindsay of Newport, riding in his rum ship off the great slave mart of Anamaboe on the Gold Coast,[2] gives a vivid description of the problems presented to those who came to trade with the expectation of quick profits in the middle of the eighteenth century. His letter to the Newport owners of the ship, dated Feb. 20, 1752, reads as follows:

"Gentlemen,
"This third of mine to you, and now I am to let you Know my proceed'gs Since my Last Daited 3th Jan.[y]; . . . I have Gott on bord 61 Slaves and upards of thirty ounces of Goold, and have Gott 13 or 14 hhd.[s] of Rum yet Left on bord, and God noes when I shall Gett Cleare of it ye trade is so very Dull it is actuly a noof to make a man Creasey [;] my Cheef mate after making foor or five Trips in the boat was taken Sick and Remaned very bade yett [;] then I sent Mr. Taylor and he got not well and three more of my men has sick. James Dixson is not well now, and wors [;] then I have wore out my Small Cable, also ockam, and have ben oblige to buy one heare; for I thought the Conciquance of yr Intrust on bord this vessel was Two Great to Rusk with bot a cable to trust to. Therefore I begg you not Blam me in so doeing [.] I should be Glad I cood Com Rite home with My slaves, for my vesial will not Last to proceed

[1] See Edward Channing, *History of the United States,* III, 41.
[2] For the importance of Anamaboe see Volume II, Chapter X of this treatise.

farr [;] we can See Day Lite al Roond her bow under Deck [;] however I hope She will carry me Safe home once more. I need not inlarge. Heare Lyes Captains hamlet, James, Jepson, Carpenter, Butler, Lindsay; Gardner is Due; Ferguson has Gone to Leward all these is Rum ships. Buttler is in a brig with 150 hhds from Barbados belong to Cape Coast Castle. Ivve sent a small boye to my Wife. I conclude with my best Endevors for intrust, Gentlemen, your faithful Servant at Command.

DAVID LINDSAY.

N.B. on the whole I never had so much trouble in all my voiges I shall Write to barbadoes in a few days."[1]

The above indicates the degree of importance to which slaving had attained in the commerce of the Colony. Indeed it was asserted before the Board of Trade in 1750, in its investigation into the African trade, that almost one half of all the vessels engaged in slaving that came from the American plantations were owned by the people of Rhode Island.[2]

Once the cargo of the Rhode Island slaver was completed, the ship was dispatched, as a rule, to the English sugar islands, stopping at either Barbados or St. Christopher, and then if the cargo had not been

[1] This is printed in *Commerce of Rhode Island*, 1726-1800, I, 59-60. In 1736 Captain John Cahoone in a letter to the owner of his ship, which also stood in the roadway of Anamaboe, writes in a similar vein. On October 27 he wrote that there never was so much rum on the coast at one time before "Nor the like of French skipers—never seen before for no. for the hole Coast is full of them." He declared that he had purchased but twenty-seven slaves and there had been as many as nineteen ships at one time in the road; that with his own vessel at the time of writing there were seven rum ships and that they were "Ready to Devour one another; for our Case is Despart ... Cap. Hammond hath ben hear six months and has but 60 Slaves on Bord." *Ibid.*, I, 46-47.
[2] Board of Trade *Journal*, 1749-1753, p. 23.

disposed of it was carried to Jamaica where, owing
to the contraband sale of negroes to the Spaniards of
the Main, as well as to the legal sale under the *cedules,*
and to the steady demand from the local sugar
planters, a sale was sure to be consummated, at least
for all healthy blacks.[1] With this ready money the
ship was then again stored with French sugar island
products before returning home, and the owners were
thereupon ready to continue the process.

In the middle of the eighteenth century, Newport,
it must be kept in mind, was a commercial and business center at least equal if not superior to New York
in importance.[2] Besides her extensive distilleries she
possessed sugar refineries and a number of establishments for producing spermaceti candles, in addition
to being deeply interested in shipbuilding and the
production of iron nails,[3] while in the warehouses of
her merchant princes were large assortments of European and East India commodities. Burnaby thus suc-
cinctly described the commercial activities of the
enterprising men of Rhode Island:

"Their mode of commerce is this; they trade to
Great Britain, Holland, Africa, the West Indies, and
the neighboring colonies; from each of which they
import the following articles: from Great Britain,
dry goods; from Holland, money; from Africa,

[1] See the instructions to Captain David Lindsay of the schooner
Siraleone by its owners, Philip Wilkinson and David Ayrault,
Commerce of Rhode Island, 1726-1800, I, 64.
[2] For a view of Newport in 1740 see Rhode Island Hist. Soc.
Coll. XVIII, 91-93.
[3] There were, however, at least according to the governor's
report to the Board of Trade, no forges or furnaces within the
Colony in 1750. *Records of Rhode Island,* V, 313-315. For iron
works in 1766, see A. C. Bining, *The Colonial Iron Industry,*
p. 14.

slaves; from the West Indies, sugar, coffee and molasses; and from the neighboring colonies, lumber and provisions: and with what they purchase in one place they make their returns in another. Thus with the money they get in Holland, they pay their merchants in London; the sugar they procure in the West Indies, they carry to Holland, the slaves they fetch from Africa they send to the West Indies, together with lumber and provisions, which they get from the neighboring colonies; the rum that they distil they export to Africa; and with the dry goods, which they purchase in London, they traffick in the neighboring colonies. By this Kind of circular commerce they subsist and grow rich."[1]

Newport, moreover, was the cultural center of that region economically dependent upon her and from which she drew much of her wealth. Such families as the Callendars, Ellerys, Wards, Honeymans, Cheekleys, Updikes, and Johnstons strove to maintain those traditions which were established as the result of the sojourn of the great Bishop Berkeley in the town.[2] It was here also that the accomplished Dr. Ezra Stiles resided for many years preceding his acceptance of the presidency of Yale College. This flourishing community, however, was involved at this period in a sharp political struggle over issues that were destined to destroy her prosperity and which had the effect of dividing Rhode Island into two sectional zones with the southern zone, roughly speaking, including the aristocratic Narragansett planters, supporting the principles of the Newport commercial interests as against the financial program of the main body of the agricultural population.

[1]Andrew Burnaby, *Travels through the Middle Settlements,* pp. 93-94. [2] *Newport Historical Magazine,* II, 174-175.

The government of Rhode Island was based upon the charter of the year 1663, giving title to the "Governor and Company of the English Collonie of Rhode Island and Providence Plantations in New England, in America."[1] This instrument placed the actual control of the government in the hands of the freemen of the company. It was these who each May and October, meeting in Newport in person or by proxy, voted for the deputies of the towns to the General Assembly and who, together with the representatives of the towns, formed at the May meeting a court of election for the purpose of selecting a governor, a deputy governor, the ten assistants, a secretary, and a treasurer for the ensuing year.[2] Upon the General Assembly there had further devolved the task of choosing, in addition to the above, some three hundred local officials, such as the colony judges, the judges of the county courts, the sheriffs, the justices of the peace, the field officers and those of the regimental companies and the grand committees on the bills of credit—a task that consumed most of the month of May. With the growth in the importance of these offices and of the work of the Assembly there took place a gradual increase in the qualifications for freemanship. In 1724 the right to vote was limited to white men owning land valued at one hundred pounds; in 1730 this was increased to two hundred pounds; and in 1746 to four hundred pounds.[3]

[1] *Rhode Island Col. Rec.*, II, 3-21.
[2] This system originating with the beginning of the charter government survived until 1760. *Rhode Island Col. Rec.*, VI, 256-7; W. E. Foster, *Town Government in Rhode Island*, p. 26.
[3] For other aspects of these laws see A. E. McKinley, *Suffrage Franchise in the ... Colonies*, pp. 453-459.

As a result, Providence with a population of 3,452 people in 1748 could count but ninety-six voters.[1]

This growth in aristocratic tendencies with reference to the franchise seems to have gone hand in hand with the growth of a new attitude toward government on the part of the people. Previously they had sought through political organization to regulate and guard certain common interests, but from 1715 onward the Colony became the dispenser of valuable favors in the creation of a series of so-called "banks" or government loans to private individuals. The first of these banks was provided for by act of the Assembly in 1715 when £30,000 in bills of credit were distributed to those who offered security in land double the value of the loan, which was to run for ten years. To provide an equitable distribution among the inhabitants, £6,500 was assigned to Providence, £11,511 to Newport, £5,993 to Portsmouth, and £2,363 to Warwick; and the remainder was in like manner allotted to the five other towns of Kingston, Westerly, Greenwich, Jamestown, and New Shoreham.[2] Here one doubtless finds an important cause for the progressive raising of the barriers to acquiring freemanship within the Colony. For who but freemen would, under ordinary circumstances, stand the slightest prospect of securing a loan? Moreover, the fewer the freemen the better would be the opportunity for each one with more land than ready money for extending his enterprises, to obtain financial assistance.

[1] W. A. Green, *The Providence Plantations*, p. 53.
[2] See Elisha R. Potter and Sidney S. Rider, *Some Account of the Bills of Credit or Paper Money of Rhode Island. (Rhode Island Historical Tracts* No. 8).

It will be of interest to observe the working out of this program of government financing of private industry.

When the ten years had passed in the life of the first bank, the final period of repayment was extended to 1728, at which time it was arranged that this should be liquidated by a series of partial payments to be completed by 1738.[1] In 1721 the second bank was meanwhile established, with the same relative allotments to the towns, when £40,000 was loaned for five years and the time of repayment of this was lengthened in 1728, at the same time of extending the period for the repayment of the first bank. In that year the third bank was provided for, with £40,000; in 1731, a fourth bank, with £60,000; and in 1733, a fifth bank, with £100,000; in 1738, a sixth, with £100,000; in 1740, a seventh, with £20,-000 now of new tenor;[2] in 1743-44 an eighth bank, with £40,000, also of new tenor, loaned at ten years at four per cent, and finally, in 1750 a ninth bank, with £25,000. It is needless to suggest that in the intoxication of this easy method of acquiring wealth the money began to depreciate in value. Between the years 1710 and 1747 there was issued, in addition to these banks, £312,300 in bills of credit for the supply of the Treasury, of which sum £134,335 was unredeemed in 1749, making a total of five hundred and fifty thousand pounds outstanding.[3] By 1752 the

[1] See Governor Richard Ward to the Board of Trade, January 9, 1740. This letter is printed in *ibid.*, pp. 145-163.

[2] One pound of the new tenor was worth four of the old bills of credit issues at this juncture.

[3] Report of the Committee on Bills of Credit Feb. 27, 1749, *ibid.*, pp. 182-192; see also *ibid.*, p. 66.

bills of credit of the older issues that had first circulated at a value not far removed from the proclamation or lawful value, as established by Queen Anne, that is, of six shillings to the Spanish-milled dollar, had sunk to the point that it required fifty-six shillings to purchase one of the latter.[1]

The dangers in this situation, however, were for a long time ignored. Governor Richard Ward in a letter to the Board of Trade, sent early in 1740 replying to their request for an account of the issue of bills of credit, defended the soundness of the policy. "In short," he declared, "if this colony be in any respect happy and flourishing, it is paper money, and a right application of it, that hath rendered us so." His argument was "that navigation is one main pillar on which this government is supported at present; and we never should have enjoyed this advantage had not the government emitted bills of credit to supply the merchants with a medium of exchange, always proportioned to the increase of this commerce."[2] Nevertheless, in the course of the decade following this defense the paper money advocates found their colony involved in deep difficulty. Although Massachusetts Bay had also been guilty of issuing great quantities of paper money, she emerged in 1750 with a hard-money program, having previously forbidden the circulation of the paper money of Rhode Island issued after 1742.[3] Connecticut, her neighbor to the

[1] Henry Phillips, *Historical Sketches of the Paper Currency of the American Colonies*, p. 111.

[2] Richard Ward to the Board of Trade, Jan. 9, 1740. *Rhode Island Historical Tracts*, No. 8.

[3] *Acts and Laws of the Colony of Massachusetts Bay* (Boston 1743), p. 99.

west, also in the early '50s forbade the circulation of all of her bills of credit. Her trading interests indeed saw the danger when too late and petitioned the British Government against the orgy of money bills.

In this petition, sent in the fall of 1750, they declared that during the past seven years the currency had depreciated by one half of its value, "whereby all the creditors of the colony, have been greatly defrauded." They asserted that the landholders of the Colony "having generally mortgaged their farms or plantations, as a security for the bills of credit they have taken upon loan, have found it to their interest to multiply such bills, that they may depreciate and lessen in value, and which they have recourse to, as a legal expedient of wiping away their debts without labor."[1] This situation not only struck a deadly blow at the business interests of the Colony but manifestly had the most adverse effect upon the British merchants with Rhode Island connections. To check this financial irresponsibility the Board of Trade two years before had intimated to the agent of the Colony, Richard Partridge, that Rhode Island need not look to reimbursement of her expenses connected with the war just closed unless it would call in its bills of credit.[2]

The Rhode Island Assembly, however, dominated by inflationists, was in nowise deterred by the threat. This body not only went ahead with its plans for the establishment of an additional bank, but in 1750

[1] Petition to the King. Newport, September 4, 1750. *Rhode Island Col. Rec.*, V, 311-313.
[2] E. R. Potter and S. S. Rider, *Some Account of the Bills of Credit or Paper Money of Rhode Island*, p. 24, note.

voted to instruct Partridge to oppose strenuously any bill that might be brought into Parliament for regulating colonial paper money. In the face of this determination on the part of the debtor agricultural elements of the Colony to continue the process of repudiation, Parliament the following year passed its famous act narrowly restricting further issues of bills of credit by the New England commonwealths.[1] But the damage had already been done, and the enormous mass of old tenor bills continued to depreciate until by 1762 these had a value in relation to the Spanish-milled dollar of but one hundred and forty shillings to one, as against six to one the proclamation, lawful money, rate. The ultimate effect on Rhode Island business was paralyzing. It is therefore not surprising that Newport, in the following decades, largely as a result of this situation, together with other concomitant causes, gradually lost all importance as a commercial center. In other words, the repeated issue of bills of credit "devised and designed as a protection to the trade and commerce of the Colony were the very means by which it was utterly lost and driven from the Colony forever."[2]

[1] 24 George II, c. 53.

[2] E. R. Potter and S. S. Rider, *Some Account of the Bills of Credit or Paper Money of Rhode Island*, p. 24, note.

The depreciation of the Rhode Island currency is well illustrated by a case of trover that came before the superior court of that colony in 1753 in which 3,840 gallons of molasses was given a value of £3,840. When the issue came before the committee of the Privy Council, the Rhode Island agent, Richard Partridge, tactfully referred to this sum as "New England" currency. *Acts of the Privy Council, Col., 1745-1766*, p. 275.

CHAPTER IV

A PURITAN STRONGHOLD

AMONG all the British plantations in North America and the West Indies, Connecticut in 1750 was organized on perhaps the most democratic constitutional basis. This plantation and Rhode Island were the only colonies that were fully corporate and that had retained unaltered seventeenth-century charters; but in the former alone the freemen voted directly and locally for their governors; its provisions for the exercise of the franchise were also more liberal than those of its eastern neighbor; with the exception of Rhode Island it was the only colony with an assembly in which the governor did not possess an absolute veto upon the measures of that body;[1] and also excepting Rhode Island and Maryland, it was the only colony not required to send its laws to England for acceptance or rejection by the King's Council. In common with New Jersey it had no fixed governmental center, the Assembly meeting alternately at Hartford and New Haven; in common with this province and also North Carolina, it had neither a chief city[2] nor any important direct com-

[1] Georgia was, of course, a trusteeship at this period and was about to pass under royal control. William Stephens was the President of the Georgia Board under the Trustees. See Volume II, Chapter VI.

[2] In the year 1756 Middletown had 5,446 white inhabitants; Norwich, 5,317; New Haven, 5,085; Wallingford, 3,713; New London, 3,171; and Hartford, 2,926; in 1774 New Haven stood first, with 8,022 whites; then came Norwich, with 7,032; New

mercial intercourse with the Mother Country.[1]
Wealth, moreover, was neither in the hands of a few
as against the many nor was it concentrated
geographically.[2]

Possessed of no first-class port nor of a town with
as many as six thousand inhabitants before the last of
the intercolonial wars, the Colony, with a population
of over one hundred and twenty-five thousand in
1756,[3] was primarily interested in farming and stock
raising. Its export staples were beef and pork which,
together with ship timber, wheat and other cereals,
flax, potashes, and horses, brought in a return of some
£130,000 sterling that in turn was largely spent in
the purchase of European commodities.[4] While most
of the produce of its farms went to Boston and New

London, with 5,366; Hartford, with 4,881; Wallingford, with
4,777; and Middletown, with 4,680. See *Connecticut Colonial
Records*, XIV, 483-492.

[1] Between the years 1755 and 1764 the firm of Williams,
Trumbull, and Pitkin with establishments at Lebanon, Norwich,
Wethersfield, and East Haddam developed very active relations
with England and the continent of Europe. Likewise, the Mc-
Aulays of New Haven in the early '60s sent their little schooners
to Lisbon for salt and wine. See Stuart's *Life of Trumbull*, pp.
67-70; T. F. Trowbridge, "Commerce, Foreign and Domestic"
in the *History of the City of New Haven*, p. 484.

[2] The following was the rating for taxation in 1750 of the
six towns standing highest on the list: New Haven, rated at
£54,448; Norwich, at £51,881; Middletown, at £48,456; Fairfield,
at £47,561; Windsor, at £38,597; Farmington, at £38,396. In
the year 1770 the six towns standing highest on the list were
Norwich, rated at £63,870; New Haven, at £63,335; Farmington, at £60,727; Woodbury, at £54,099; Stratford, at £49,-
210; and Fairfield, at £49,008. It will be noticed that neither
Hartford nor New London appear in these lists, which indicates
that the wealth of the colony was largely agricultural in character. *Conn. Col. Rec.*, IX, 563; XIII, 368.

[3] *Ibid.*, X, 618. See Greene and Harrington, *American Population before . . . 1790*, pp. 49-50 for other figures.

[4] *Conn. Col. Rec.*, X, 622-623.

York, there was a ready demand for Connecticut beef, pork, flour, horses, and lumber in the West Indies in return for which rum, sugar, molasses, and salt, together with bills of exchange were received. The shipping of the Colony at this period was composed of some seventy-five sloops, brigantines, schooners, and snows, the largest of which possessed a capacity of but ninety tons and carried a crew of but ten men.[1] However, it appears that these diminutive ships built in Connecticut yards were adequate to meet the modest commercial needs of the people, unimpressive as they were.

In spite of its major emphasis upon agriculture and its commercial backwardness, at least with respect to European trade, industrially Connecticut was far ahead of its western neighbor, New York, as evidenced by the production and manufacture of iron. While the latter had in operation but one pig-iron furnace and no forge in the year 1750, the former could boast not only of a steel furnace, built at Killingsworth in 1744, but also of some eight forges with tilt hammers, three of which had been erected in 1732, the remainder during the period from 1742 to 1748. It is to be noticed that all of these ironworks were in eastern Connecticut within the counties of New London and Windham.[2] In fact, the great Connecticut River, winding its way southward through the heart of the Commonwealth, divided it into two rather distinct regions or sections which had somewhat different interests and on occasions

[1] *Ibid.*, X, 625.
[2] C.O. 5: 1273, p. 88. East Haven in western Connecticut, it is true, also produced pig iron at its ironworks, although it is not listed.

manifested opposing points of view, particularly during the decade preceding the outbreak of the American Revolution. Eastern Connecticut tended to look in the direction of Boston, western Connecticut in the direction of New York. This was true not only with respect to commercial contacts but to those that were cultural as well.[1]

For example, in the '50s most of the commerce that New Haven had with any other part of North America was with New York. As a result of influences flowing from the latter place, an Anglican church was erected on her town commons during the same period. Stratford, in Fairfield County, lying to the west of New Haven and even closer to New York, by 1750 had become something of an Episcopalian center, and furnished, in the person of Dr. Samuel Johnson, the first president for the newly created King's College in New York. On the other hand, to the east of the Connecticut the trade contacts were largely with Boston; moreover, the towns of this region were deeply interested in whatever issues agitated the citizens of that seaport and were generally among the first to espouse at least their radical ideas.[2]

Accepting the existence of this regionalism within the Colony, it may nevertheless be suggested that even western Connecticut had more in common with Massachusetts Bay than with New York and that in many fundamental ways the greatest solidarity existed between this section and that of eastern Con-

[1] See the author's *Jared Ingersoll: A Study of American Loyalism in Relation to British Colonial Government,* p. 198, note.
[2] *Ibid.,* pp. 176 and 268.

necticut. For the Colony embodied in its organized life a political and social system evolved in its fullness in New England alone, and which, in the middle of the eighteenth century, was preserved more faithfully here perhaps than in any of the other New England plantations. Connecticut may truthfully be called the last of the Puritan commonwealths. For this reason, therefore, it may be well to present in some detail certain aspects of government, both local and central.

New England Puritanism took the form of a community or small-town movement based upon adherence to certain common religious principles and practices. It, therefore, had its foundation in the conception of social solidarity in all matters that touched the common life, demanding as it did uniformity of thought and action. This social solidarity expressed itself through certain distinct avenues regulated by law, such as the church communion, the ecclesiastical society, the proprietors' meetings, the freemen's meetings, and the town meetings.

The church communion was limited to those in full Christian fellowship who before admittance had publicly testified to their conversion and had subscribed to the church covenant. Among these were the so-called "seven pillars" of the local church or its founders, provided that it had been erected according to the old New Haven Colony rule. The communion seems to have embraced all the consecrated Christians of the community, unless these were dissenters from the established Congregational Church. It gave a vitality and, in a sense, a spiritual validity, to the work of the ecclesiastical society of which it was an inner circle. From its membership also were chosen almost without exception those to whom had been delegated important powers within the community. When they acted on issues of first importance having to do with the religious life of the community they doubtless were guided, as a rule, by the sense of this body, the heart and conscience of the town.

The Great Awakening of the '40s brought with it a breaking-down of the old solidarity of the communion in many Connecticut towns, with the division of the church fellowship into the Old Lights and the New Lights. As a result there was generally a secession of the latter from the parent body for the purpose of establishing a separate communion. In most places this was apparently accomplished only after considerable agitation in which bitterness and intolerance were much in evidence. Especially was this true in eastern Connecticut where, for example, in 1744 at Saybrook, fourteen Separatists were arrested and fined for "holding a meeting contrary to law on God's holy Sabbath day" and, upon refusal to make payment, were driven through the mud to New London, twenty-five miles distant, and there thrown into prison without fire, food, or beds.[1] This deplorable and unneighborly treatment of men and women whose only crime was loyalty to religious conviction can be explained only in the light of the long history of religious persecution. In almost every

[1] See M. L. Greene, *Development of Religious Liberty in Connecticut* (pp. 276-277), who also gives an account of the branding of Deacon Nathaniel Drake of Windsor and the imprisonment of Rev. Ebenezer Frothingham "for nothing but exhorting and warning the people."

case there is felt to be at stake the precious causes of conformity and solidarity with all the blessings these have in store for mankind in an ordered existence. And so the hostility of the Connecticut ecclesiastical authorities was particularly directed against these secessionists from the Establishment. Even as late as 1777 a writer bitterly complained of the plight of the Separatists. "They have been persecuted, oppressed, and most cruelly treated, their property has most unjustly been taken from them to support ministers that in conscience they would not hear preach; and at the same time, they have had ministers of their own to support; they have been imprisoned for not paying the rates to the clergy and fined for not attending public worship with the standing churches."[1]

The ecclesiastical society previous to 1746 legally comprehended all those living within the bounds of the town. This seems to have been the case, in spite of the act of the General Assembly in 1727 exempting from church attendance and the payment of local church rates, under certain conditions, those who were communicants of the Church of England and the acts of the year 1729 extending these immunities, under similar terms, to Quakers and Baptists.[2] After

[1] *The Connecticut Journal*, March 26, 1777. A penalty of ten shillings was to be levied against any person assisting in forming a "separate company for worship in a private House." *Acts and Laws of Connecticut* (1750), p. 139. Unitarians and Deists were struck at by a statute which declared that anyone convicted of denying "any one of the Persons of the Holy Trinity to be God," or denying that the Scriptures were of divine authority should be incapable of enjoying any office, ecclesiastical, court, or military. *Ibid.*, p. 69. See M. L. Greene, *The Development of Religious Liberty in Connecticut*, pp. 234 and 239.

[2] *Conn. Col. Rec.*, VII, 106, 237, 257.

the year mentioned, the law provided that those groups which had been expressly exempt by law from the payment of the ecclesiastical society dues should be debarred from further participation in the activities of the society.[1] This marks the disappearance of the all-inclusiveness of the local societies. Within them still remained not only the membership of the communion but those who had never taken the covenant nor made any profession of faith, as well as those who belonged to religious bodies other than the Anglican, Quaker, and Baptist organizations. Unless prevented by bodily infirmity, all under the jurisdiction of the local society were expected, on pain of fine, to attend its church services and while there to conduct themselves in a seemly fashion. They were also permitted, if they were adult males possessed of a freehold within the society limits rated at fifty shillings or were rated at forty pounds or more in the common list, to be present at the business meetings of the society and to participate not only in the choice of a pastor but also in the selection of society officers, in decisions regarding church rates, and in the regulation of the parish school.[2]

While every effort was made to include all living within the limits of the ecclesiastical society in its activities, there was no corresponding solicitude to see that all men should share in the privileges and responsibilities of freemanship. For it was only the freemen who could vote for the filling of the offices of the Colony and were entitled to occupy the same.

[1] *Ibid.*, IX, 218-219.
[2] *Acts and Laws of Connecticut* (1750), pp. 165-168; *Conn. Col. Rec.*, VII, 211.

To become a freeman one had to be a male twenty-one years of age in possession either of a freehold estate to the value of forty shillings per annum or of forty pounds personal estate in the general assessment list for that year and to be "of a quiet and peaceable Behaviour and Civil Conversation"; in addition, one was required to secure a certificate of endorsement from a majority of the selectmen of the town and in a freemen's meeting to take the prescribed oath.[1] Once having attained this privilege, one apparently remained in the enjoyment of it irrespective of the vicissitudes of fortune, except when, upon judgment of the superior court that he had been guilty of "walking scandalously," he was, as a penalty, disfranchised.[2]

Exactly what proportion of the adult male population was in the exercise of freemen's privileges in colonial Connecticut in the middle of the eighteenth century is difficult to estimate with accuracy. However, it is likely that not one fourth of the adult males were qualified voters. This at least seems to have been the case of New Haven.[3]

[1] This oath is given in *Acts and Laws of Connecticut* (1750), p. 175. By this the applicant was obliged to swear that he would be true and faithful to the King and his successors and to the government of the Colony and act according to conscience "without Respect of Persons, or Favor of any Man."

[2] *Ibid.* This law struck Francis Fane, legal adviser of the Board of Trade, as deserving of disallowance, since "walking scandalously" was too vague a phrase for disfranchisement. See Charles M. Andrews, *Fane's Reports on the Laws of Connecticut* (Acorn Club *Publications*, 1915), pp. 44-45.

[3] For the discussion of this question see the Introduction to the *Wolcott Papers* (edited by A. C. Bates); *The American Historical Review*, XXIII, 403; *Jared Ingersoll*, p. 19.

The semiannual freemen's meetings were held
regularly on the Monday following the first Tuesday
in April[1] and the second or third Tuesday in September in all the towns of the Colony.[2] At the last-
named meeting not only were deputies elected to
represent the towns in the October session of the
Assembly but each freeman gave his vote by written
ballot for twenty persons whom he judged qualified
"to stand in nomination for election in the month of
May following." These ballots were forwarded to
the General Assembly by the town clerk, and counted.
The twenty freemen receiving the greatest number
of votes were thereupon declared to be nominated to
stand as the candidates at the spring election when
all the elective offices of the Colony were filled. At
the April meeting of the freemen, after the deputies
to the May meeting of the Assembly had been chosen,
they then proceeded to ballot for the governor, the
deputy governor, the treasurer and secretary of the
Colony as well as for the twelve assistants who acted
both as a governor's council and as an upper house
of the General Assembly.[3] Once again the ballots
were sent to the General Assembly where the final
results were declared.

[1] Down to 1740 the freemen met the last Tuesday in April.
Conn. Col. Rec., VIII, 297.
[2] The freemen in New Haven, Hartford, and Fairfield counties
were to meet the third Tuesday while those of New London and
Windham counties met the second Tuesday in September. *Acts
and Laws of Connecticut* (1750), pp. 45-47.
[3] Although it was necessary to select the assistants and the
treasurer and secretary from the list of twenty nominees, the
Connecticut code of 1750 stated that "the Free-men shall have
Liberty to choose the Governor and Deputy-Governor, where
they see cause, of all, or any of the Free-men within this Colony."

The freemen, representing the propertied element in each community, were inclined toward conservatism in action. They, rather than the nonpropertied element, naturally determined the political tone of the Commonwealth. Only on the approach of the Revolution would it seem that the nonfreeman elements, who constituted an overwhelming majority of the people of the Colony, through violent and terroristic means wrenched, for the moment at least, political control from the hands of the more cautious and legal-minded freemen.[1]

In eighteenth-century colonial Connecticut one might be not only an inhabitant of a town but also a freeman without being a town proprietor. Prior to 1685 there seems to have been no clear-cut differentiation between the proprietors of the unoccupied lands within the limits of the towns and the rest of the settled population. The general town meetings from time to time granted lands to individuals on petition.[2] In that year the General Court authorized a confirmation to the so-called proprietors and settled inhabitants of the titles to the common and un-

---

Ibid., pp. 45-46. From 1670 to 1750 a freeman might go to Hartford to cast his vote for colonial officers or do so at his local freemen's meetings. The code of 1750 did away with personal attendance. *Ibid.*, p. 46. See A. E. McKinley, *The Suffrage Franchise in the Thirteen English Colonies*, pp. 416-417.

[1] For example, Thomas Darling and Joshua Chandler, ultra-conservatives, were sent by the New Haven freemen to the General Assembly as late as 1774. In opposition within that town were members of the train band, sailors, and those who made up the mobs in times of excitement. See *Jared Ingersoll*, pp. 20, 31.

[2] See, for example, the action of the New Haven town meeting of April 29, 1684. New Haven Town Records (Ms.), IV, 2-3.

divided lands in twenty-eight of the towns.[1] This legislation was brought about as the result of disputes between the old established families and newcomers as to who were entitled to share in the periodic land divisions. The law was so ambiguous in its meaning that it only added to the keenness of the struggle between the two groups. As a result, in 1704 the Assembly specifically confined the proprietorial rights within the towns to those who had been considered proprietors in 1685, and their children.[2] From this time on a sharp distinction was drawn between the proprietors and other inhabitants, and all matters having to do with the township lands were cared for in distinct meetings attended only by the former. At any regularly called meeting, taxes might be levied upon those with proprietorial rights for the purpose of making fences, gates, and bridges. According to the law, on the first Monday in March a special meeting was to be held for the purpose of choosing a committee to care for the common lands during the year to follow. This committee was empowered to select fence viewers and haywards and to make other necessary arrangements regarding the lands.[3]

Proprietors' meetings, those of the freemen and those of the members of the ecclesiastical societies, were but offshoots of the parent gathering,[4] the meeting of the inhabitants of the town, which was by all odds the most comprehensive of all the local assemblages both in scope of action and in respect to the

[1] *Conn. Col. Rec.*, III, 177; IV, 432-433.
[2] *Ibid.*
[3] *Acts and Laws of Conn.* (1750), pp. 61-68.
[4] This is made clear by the action of the General Assembly in 1746. *Conn. Col. Rec.*, IX, 218-219.

number of dwellers within the town admitted to its privileges. Nevertheless, it should be understood that a man might be a dweller in a New England colonial town and yet technically not be an inhabitant. Three classes of individuals: transients or "single persons newly come," indentured servants, and slaves were not entitled to such recognition.[1] The code of 1750 declared that, whereas "several Persons of Ungoverned Conversation thrust themselves into the Towns in the Colony and by some Underhand way, as upon pretence of being Hired Servants, or of Hiring Lands or Houses or by Purchasing the same endeavor to become Inhabitants in such Towns," it should be understood that no newcomers would thereafter be admitted as such but those of honest conversation. The law further stated that strangers might not even abide in any town without consent of the selectmen or the major part of the town and that those who had been warned out of town by the former were liable to a penalty of ten shillings a week or be whipped ten stripes if they did not leave.[2]

But not even all adult male inhabitants were qualified to participate in the proceedings of the town meetings. One not only had to be a lawful inhabitant twenty-one years of age but in addition a householder in possession either of a freehold estate rated at fifty shillings on the tax lists, or of personal estate valued

[1] At a New Haven town meeting held January 18, 1702, it was laid down that the above classes "never were or are inhabitants in the Town." New Haven Town Records, IV, 133.

[2] *Acts and Laws of Conn.* (1750), pp. 99-100. "The settled and approved Inhabitants qualified and having estate shall have power, provided they are of a Prudential Nature and that their penalties for one offense do not exceed 20s." *Ibid.*, p. 240.

at forty pounds. There was, however, one exception: no one could be debarred from voting in the town meeting who had established himself as a freeman.[1] It will be noticed that there was no provision of the law, as it stood in the middle of the eighteenth century, disqualifying anyone, by reason of religious nonconformity, from taking part in the activities of the town meeting,[2] although deists and Unitarians were debarred from holding any civil, ecclesiastical, or military office within the Colony.

One of the most important functions performed by the town meeting was the annual selection of the host of local officials required to carry out the manifold activities of the community, where few matters, even in the middle of the eighteenth century, were considered to be so personal in nature as not to be subjected to the inquisitorial scrutiny of those delegated for that purpose. Selectmen, some seven in number, were elected to have general oversight of local affairs when the town meeting was not in ses-

[1] *Op. cit.*, p. 241.

[2] This is denied by Channing *(History of the United States,* II, 439), who gives as his authority the act of 1728 which he asserts was in force in 1760. The act is entitled, "An Act directing how Persons shall be qualified to vote in Society Meetings." It does not refer to the town meetings, although it is true that at that period these occasionally dealt with church matters, but is carefully worded so as to limit its application to the periodic meetings of the ecclesiastical society. Further, it did not debar nonconformists from voting even in these meetings, provided that they had established a residence within the bounds of the society and were rated at fifty shillings or forty pounds in the common list. Not until 1746 were Episcopalians, Baptists, and Quakers, who had previously been exempt from financially supporting the ecclesiastical society, finally debarred from the privilege of voting in this. *Conn. Col. Rec.,* VII, 439; IV, 218-219; *Acts and Laws of Conn.* (1750), pp. 231-233.

sion: a clerk, to keep the town records; a treasurer, to guard and disburse the funds of the town; a varying number of constables, to watch over the peace and quiet of the community, and tithingmen, to maintain the ecclesiastical regulations by watching over the moral welfare of the inhabitants on week days, and on the Sabbath by preserving order in the meeting house during the sermons, with authority, in the words of the old formula, "to smite such as are unruly or of uncomely behaviour in the meeting." Many other officials were chosen whose work was scarcely of less importance: key keepers, to impound stray animals; branders, to place the town brand on all the horses;[1] highway surveyors, to care for the miserable township roads and in this connection to see that each man not exempt did his required two days' work; fence viewers, to supervise the maintenance of fences and other boundaries of the community; haywards, to carry out the work of fence repairs and to secure animals that were straying;[2] gaugers and packers, to supervise the packing of beef, pork, and fish in casks for export; sealers of leather,

[1] Each town in the Colony had its own brand. The town branders were required to keep a record and description of every animal branded and also of all sales of the same. All branding was to be done at one of the town pounds, under heavy penalties. This applied only to horses. The brands of cattle, sheep, and swine were to be placed by the owners, but the marks were to be registered.

[2] The term hayward is used also to designate one who keeps the cows. (See G. E. Howard, *Local Constitutional History*, p. 221.) Toward the middle of the century the hayward is no longer found in many communities. For example, in 1727 twelve haywards were chosen in New Haven, but after 1740 the office disappears. This seems to have come about as the result of the erection of more permanent fences.

89

of measures, and of weights; excise masters, to collect locally the colonial excise on rum, brandy, and other distilled liquors; listers, to prepare the assessment rolls; and, finally, tax collectors.

In other words, it was necessary in many Connecticut towns to find those qualified to fill over one hundred public posts. That public service was not infrequently considered a burden is indicated by the code of 1750 which provides for a fine of twenty-five shillings from any person who refused to exercise the office to which he was elected unless he could show that he was "Oppressed by such Choice; and that Others were unjustly exempted."[1]

The town meetings, beyond those given over to holding courts of election, were concerned with an infinite variety of local interests. The killing of crows, the straying of geese, the yoking and ringing of pigs allowed to run at large, the hiring of bulls and boars for the town commons, and the eradication of the barberry bushes were among those things during the first half of the century that greatly concerned the people and were the objects of deliberation and action. Fairly trivial as many of these matters that occupied the attention of the inhabitants in these town meetings may now appear to be, they were, nevertheless, among the things that bulked largest in the eyes of the average man and really conditioned his immediate welfare far more than most of the weightiest imperial legislation. Indeed, these meetings dealing with matters of vital personal importance were excellent schools in which to gather political experience, and no colony produced shrewder politicians

[1] *Acts and Laws of Conn.* (1750), p. 241.

than those that had their training at the local gather-
ings. Controlled largely by the same elements that
directed the freemen's meetings and those of the proprietors, the town meetings, while considered to be
centers of radicalism by the home authorities, were
generally the strongholds of conservative influence
during the decades preceding the Revolution, especially so in western Connecticut, standing for the
maintenance of the old order of things and discoun-
tenancing change and the extreme policies of the
radical group dwelling within the town.

Over against these influences which could be
counted on to oppose hasty and radical political
action within the community stood the train bands.
Under the law all males between sixteen and fifty
years of age, except those holding posts under the
colonial government, those connected with Yale
College, Masters of Arts, justices of the peace, physi-
cians, surgeons, schoolmasters, attorneys at law, one
miller to a gristmill, constant herdsmen, mariners
and ferrymen, as well as lame and otherwise disabled
persons, negroes, and Indians, were required to attend
musters and to engage in military exercises.[1] Although
the train bands under the terms of the law were not
required to meet more frequently than four days
annually for training, yet this conveys little idea of

[1] *Ibid.*, pp. 155-164. Each band had the following complement: a captain, a lieutenant, an ensign, four sergeants, and
sixty-four privates. While the smaller towns would support but
one train band, larger towns would have six or seven. Every
listed soldier, and indeed all householders, were required by law
to possess a well-regulated firelock, the barrel of which was not
less than three and one half feet long, a good sword or cutlass,
a trimming-wire fit for his gun, a cartridge box, a pound of
powder, four pounds of bullets, and twelve flints. *Ibid.*, 155-157.

the degree of solidarity that existed within the ranks of these military units and the extent of the influence exercised by them in times of crises. It should in this connection be kept in mind that, while the regimental officers were appointed by the colonial authorities, the officers of the train bands from captain downward were selected by the enrolled men. As a result of the exemption from military service of the more responsible men of the communities, the election of officers was quite under the control of the radical and more irresponsible elements, who naturally supported those who sympathized with their point of view. These popular officers, many of them adventurous characters, such as Benedict Arnold of New Haven and John Durkee of Bean Hill in eastern Connecticut, at times exercised a degree of authority in the affairs of the Colony that resulted in the brushing aside of any and all opposition to their program.[1]

The next units of local government larger than the Connecticut towns were the probate districts within which a court of probate was erected to care for matters relating to wills, letters of administration, and guardianship;[2] and above these were the counties, the officials of which were not elected by the people but appointed by the General Assembly or by the Governor and Council or in some cases by the county courts. In 1698 a law was passed providing that in each county at least four of the most able freemen should be appointed justices of the peace;

[1] This influence was manifested during the periods of crises connected with the Stamp Act and the preliminaries of the Revolution.

[2] *Ibid.*, p. 34.

three of whom, a quorum, with a judge to preside, were empowered to hold court.[1] At first these appointments were during pleasure but subsequently they were made annually.[2] The county courts were authorized by the code of 1750 not only to try all civil cases and those criminal cases not extending to life, limb, banishment or to divorce, but also to levy taxes for paying the debts of the county.[3] They were empowered to appoint a king's attorney to prosecute all criminal offenders "and to doe all other things necessary or convenient to suppress vice and immorality."[4] Twice a year a superior court of judicature met at the county seats with power to try by jury or otherwise all pleas of the Crown.[5] Before these lower and higher courts the county sheriffs, appointed by the governor and council of the Colony, brought offenders and subsequently carried out the judicial mandates.[6]

It would now be appropriate to consider the laws that bound the people and were applied in the courts of the Colony in the middle of the eighteenth cen-

[1] *Conn. Col. Rec.*, III, 95.

[2] *Acts and Laws of Conn.* (1750), pp. 105-106.

[3] Taxes were raised for the payment of county officials, for the upkeep and building of jails, and for the other limited county activities.

[4] This office came into existence in 1704. *Conn. Col. Rec.*, IV, 468. Virginia alone of the other American colonies seems to have made use of this county official. For a discussion of this office see the author's *Jared Ingersoll*, pp. 42-54.

[5] *Acts and Laws of Conn.* (1750), pp. 30-32.

[6] *Ibid.*, pp. 221-224. The sheriff in Connecticut was expected to serve and execute all lawful writs, to have the power of a water bailiff to search vessels, to command assistance when necessary and, with the advice of an assistant or a justice of the peace, to raise the militia.

tury. How far were these, on the one hand, still influenced by the religious conceptions of the preceding century and, on the other hand, how far modified by the newer forces assaulting even this, the chief stronghold of Puritanism within the old British Empire?

For purposes of comparison, the Connecticut codes of 1650 and 1750 will indicate the nature of the changes that had taken place during the period of a century. The first named was based upon the "Body of Libertys" adopted in Massachusetts Bay in 1641 and supplemented by the twelve capital laws of the following year.[1] These capital offenses were: worshipping a strange god, witchcraft, blasphemy, wilful murder, slaying another through guile, bestiality, sodomy, adultery, rape, kidnapping, false testifying, and rebellion against the Colony, and were supplemented by two other capital offenses: the cursing of parents by a child over sixteen years of age and "stubbornness" on the part of a child over sixteen years. The penalty for the third offense of burglary or of robbery was also capital.

Besides the death penalty, branding, mutilation, whipping, the pillory, the stocks, imprisonment, and fining were employed. For example, the punishment of burglary or robbery for the first offense was branding on the forehead with the letter "B," for the second, another branding and a whipping, for the third, death as an incorrigible;[2] for drinking more than one-

---

[1] These appear in the Massachusetts Bay Code of 1648.

[2] For the code of 1650, see *Conn. Col. Rec.*, I, 509. See also the author's study entitled, "The Criminal Codes of Colonial Connecticut," *American Journal of Criminal Law and Criminology*, June, 1915.

half pint of wine at one time or for tippling for more than one-half hour or after nine o'clock at night, a fine of five shillings; with whippings and the stocks for excessive drinking; for the use of tobacco, on the part of those under twenty years of age or not already addicted, and for using it publicly, a fine of six pence; for keeping bachelor house alone, a fine of twenty shillings for every week; for staying away from church services, five shillings; and for behaving contemptuously toward the Word of God or messengers thereof, for the first offense, open reproval by the magistrate, for the second offense, either a fine of five pounds or the humiliation of standing two hours upon a four-foot block on lecture day, bearing a placard reading, "An open and obstinate Contemner of God's Holy Ordinances."

In the code of 1750, under the heading of "Capital and other Felonies," seven offenses are enumerated. Among the old fourteen capital laws of 1650 blasphemy in the name of God the Father, Son, and Holy Ghost, bestiality, sodomy, and false testifying still find a place.[1] On the other hand, the old laws against worshipping a strange god, witchcraft, wilful murder,[2] slaying another through guile, adultery, rape, kidnapping, rebellion against the Colony, the cursing of parents by a child, and stubbornness on the part of a child, have either disappeared from the category of capital crimes in favor of other laws or, if still capital, are not classified with the capital felonies. On the other hand, among capital laws not found in the code of 1650 that were embodied in the later code

[1] *Acts and Laws of Conn.* (1750), pp. 68-69.
[2] Still punishable by death.

is that relating to conspiracy against the Colony, given the place of first importance, taking the place of the old law against worshipping a strange god;[1] then there is the law against the crime of arson and that against mayhem when the victim thereby is deprived of his tongue, an eye, or a private organ.[2] Other crimes in the code of 1750 not found in the earlier code that were punished capitally were counterfeiting the King's seal, levying war against him, or compassing his death. Counterfeiting of money, another crime not mentioned in 1650, while not capital, was very severely punished by the eighteenth-century code under discussion; the offender was not only branded, but lost his right ear, was debarred from all trade, was deprived of his estate, and committed to the workhouse for life. The crime of adultery, a capital offense in 1650, in the later code was punished by means of whipping, branding, and the wearing of a halter about the neck outside the garments of the guilty party.

While the above changes have been noted in the laws of the Colony, the keeping of the Sabbath as a holy day was as vigorously enjoined in the middle of the eighteenth century as earlier. The law declared that on the Sabbath all persons were to apply themselves to private and public duties of religion. For

[1] This, of course, is closely related to the old law punishing rebellion against the Colony and to the law of 1750 punishing the levying of war against the King.

[2] In the earlier part of the century a man convicted of mayhem was punished according to the principles of the *lex talionis*, and the court passed sentence of "*membrum pro membro*," in this case castration. *Conn. Col. Rec.*, VIII, 678; see article dealing with it by Simeon Baldwin in the *Yale Law Journal*, VIII, 381 *et seq.*

working or playing on the Lord's Day or day of public fasting or thanksgiving there was a penalty of ten shillings; for convening in companies on the evenings preceding or following the Lord's Day a penalty of three shillings or not over two hours in the stocks; for drinking in taverns on these evenings, five shillings; for standing outside a meeting house and talking during worship, three shillings; for going on the Lord's Day from house to house, other than to church or on some work of necessity or mercy, five shillings; for travelling on that day, twenty shillings; for rude or profane behavior also on that day, forty shillings.[1]

All officers were to restrain people from unnecessarily walking in the streets or fields, swimming in the water, keeping open their shops or following their secular occupations or recreations the evening preceding the Lord's Day or that following. Those convicted of profaning the Holy Day itself and refusing to pay their fines were to be publicly whipped not over twenty stripes.[2]

The deep solicitation of the lawmakers for the moral and spiritual welfare of the people of the Colony is further evidenced by the law requiring all parents and masters to teach the children under their care to read the English tongue well and to know by heart the laws against capital offenders. If this were not possible the latter were to be taught some short orthodox catechism without the Book.[3] Selectmen were especially enjoined to enquire to what extent

[1] *Acts and Laws of Conn.* (1750), p. 139.
[2] *Ibid.*, p. 142.
[3] *Ibid.*, pp. 20-21.

the householders were furnished with Bibles and also with catechisms and other good books, according to the number of persons of capacity to use the same; while constables, grand jurymen, and tithingmen, in the suppression of vice and in promotion of Christian knowledge, were required to make diligent search after all breaches of the laws that related to their office; and the two first-named groups were, moreover, expected to walk the streets on evenings after the Lord's Day and duly to search places harboring people contrary to law.

The underlying feature in this form of community organization was that of interdependence and collective responsibility for individual welfare. The demand above all things was that men should be their brothers' keepers; if possible, keeping one another from falling by the removal of temptations and opportunity for sin and crime through constant scrutiny of the actions of one another and through the severe punishment of breaches of the code. This will explain why for over one hundred years there remained in the Connecticut code the law forbidding an unmarried man to keep bachelor house without consent of the town authorities[1] and why in the eighteenth century no tavern-keeper was allowed to demoralize his customers through the possession of dice, cards, tables, bowls, shuffle-boards, billiards, quoits, and other games of amusement.[2] Such regulations undoubtedly had the effect of producing men not only of great soberness but with a certain rugged severity of char-

[1] *Op. cit.*, p. 152.
[2] *Ibid.*, p. 81.

acter who were scarcely tolerant of the weaknesses of others.

From the foregoing comparison of the codes of 1650 and 1750 the impression comes home to the student that Connecticut at the latter date was in the midst of a great transition, although still powerfully bound by older modes of thought. While still devotedly attempting to hold fast to its seventeenth-century Puritan heritage, the Colony was slowly, probably inevitably, repudiating much of it. The bitter controversies between the Old Lights and New Lights—an aftermath of the Great Awakening—undoubtedly had the most important effects in this direction; also the progress of the Anglicans in western Connecticut and the growing importance of the Baptists in eastern Connecticut. Moreover, the ecclesiastical system and the peculiar ecclesiastical outlook on life that had for a century characterized Connecticut Puritanism were doubtless most adversely affected by the participation of many thousands of the men of the Colony in the wars of the eighteenth century. For they were brought into intimate touch with views that were quite out of harmony with those presented from the pulpit of their local church.[1] Indeed, it is not without significance that during the French and Indian war there appeared in 1755 the first local newspaper, the *Connecticut Gazette*, with its emphasis upon secular interests, to be followed by the *Connecticut Journal*, the *Connecticut Courant* published at Hartford, and the *New London Gazette*.

The influence of these and other forces in under-

[1] See R. J. Purcell's illuminating study, *Connecticut in Transition, 1775-1818*, pp. 5-14.

mining Puritanism is clearly indicated when one turns to examine the Connecticut code of 1784. The old capital laws against blasphemy, false testifying, bestiality, and sodomy that survived in the code of 1750 disappeared from that of 1784. These offenses against individual decency and integrity were otherwise dealt with. The keeping of bachelor house, the entertaining of a young man, and the settlement of strangers within the town without leave were no longer proscribed; nor were the drinking of more than one-half pint of wine at one time, the imbibing of liquors after nine o'clock in the evening, and the use of tobacco. Further, one was no longer liable to a fine as in 1750 for attending a separate church without license nor in danger of the loss of civic rights for maintaining deistic or Unitarian ideas.[1] By the beginning of the new century, so far had the Congregational Church lost ground that it was estimated that not more than one third of the total population of Connecticut was in any way identified with it,[2] whereas, a century earlier an overwhelming majority of the people of this Colony were on its church rolls. But the Congregational Establishment continued in force until the adoption of the Constitution of 1818.

Connecticut succeeded in preserving its Congregational establishment throughout the colonial period largely because it was able to retain its prized charter. Behind this bulwark the Colony was able to lead an existence little disturbed by outside interference. It

[1] See *Acts and Laws of the State of Connecticut* (1784), pp. 206-210.
[2] R. J. Purcell, *Connecticut in Transition*, p. 45.

sought its own counsel and followed an established policy of reticence in its relations with the Mother Country. Only in the face of attacks or other pressing causes did it become really articulate, and then, after the occasion had passed, it sank back into silence. It had little sympathy with the type of government that prevailed in England in the eighteenth century and even less with the Anglican religious establishment, and its best efforts were always given to warding off encroachments on the part of either of these. In this connection it employed with extraordinary effectiveness its so-called London agency. In fact, no colony used this instrumentality of government with greater results, and it is therefore desirable to give some account of its functioning.

In a consideration of the Connecticut London agency, no better way of illustrating its extraordinary effectiveness in protecting the essential interests of the Colony can perhaps be found than in surveying briefly the relations of that Colony with the Mother Country during the first half of the eighteenth century.

As was made clear in an earlier chapter, the permanent London agency of Connecticut came into existence at the time of the English Revolution.[1] When the results of the proceedings of the Convention Parliament became known in the Colony, Colonel Robert Treat, the Governor, and his council, under the newly restored charter government, "saw the necessity of doing something to preserve or [our] standing," and proceeded to draw up an address to

[1] See Volume I, Chapter I for a general account of the London agency.

the King which was sent, together with £50 borrowed for the occasion, to James Porter, a London merchant who was besought to present the address and otherwise to act as the Connecticut agent.[1] Porter, however, was unwilling to assume the responsibility, with the result that in 1693 Major-General Fitz-John Winthrop was sent over. The latter exerted himself to secure a confirmation of the charter. He opposed vigorously not only the commission of Governor Fletcher of New York, which gave him command of the Connecticut militia, but also Randolph's scheme for appointing crown attorney-generals in all the colonies. He sought, in addition, to secure for the Colony the Narragansett country so long in dispute between it, Rhode Island, and Massachusetts Bay.[2] Upon his return to America his place was taken by the Massachusetts agent, Sir Henry Ashurst, a member of Parliament, a Whig, and a leading dissenter who, with all of his self-importance, proved to be one of the most efficient representatives that was ever accredited by a colony to the government of the Mother Country. Ashurst did much to block the very serious attempts made at this period to place royal governors over all the colonies; he also exerted himself in behalf of Connecticut in connection with the Mohegan Indian land controversy which Captain John Mason, supporting the Indians, had referred to

[1] Connecticut Archives (Ms.), "Foreign Correspondence," I, 39a; II, 19-21, 22, 23. The Colony seemed to be ignorant of the fact that Mary was queen regnant.

[2] Connecticut Archives (Ms.) "Foreign Correspondence," II, 64; *Conn. Col. Rec.*, IV, 102, 234, 238; "Winthrop Papers," Mass. Hist. *Coll.* (fifth series), VIII, 327-343; Hinman, *Letters*, 195-203.

the King for settlement.[1] In 1710 he was assisted in his post by the Governor of the Colony, Gurdon Saltonstall, who had been sent over by the General Assembly to care for Connecticut interests in connection with the military problems arising out of the attempted invasion of Canada in 1709.[2] Upon Ashurst's death the following year, the learned but unfortunately rather dissolute Jeremiah Dummer, an expatriated New England man, took up the agency and held it for almost twenty years. But in spite of his masterly *Defense of the New England Charters* written in 1715 and published in 1721, Dummer gradually grew in disfavor with the Colony, especially after surrendering to Bolingbroke's influence and by reason of his failure to guard Connecticut interests in the Winthrop appeal, so that in 1730, when obliged to go into the country for his health, he was rather summarily dismissed from his post.[3]

The famous Winthrop appeal to the King in council against the Connecticut intestacy law, opposed as it was to the English principle of primogeniture, came to a decision in 1728.[4] When the news reached the

[1] *Conn. Col. Rec.,* IV, 469; Hinman, *Letters,* 279-280.

[2] *Conn. Col. Rec.,* V, 140, 122. The cause of the visit related to the unfortunate situation that arose in 1709 when the Queen ordered an expedition against Canada. The Connecticut and New York troops were assembled at Wood Creek where many died of sickness, and toward winter they buried their stores and returned home.

[3] *Conn. Col. Rec.,* V, 188, 190, 300, 303, 305, 362; VI, 133, 226, 318; VII, 307; *Sewall's Letter Book,* I, 305, note.

[4] *Acts, Privy Coun., Col., 1720-1745,* pp. 112, 208; C. M. Andrews, "The Connecticut Intestacy Law," *Select Essays in Anglo-American Legal History,* I, No. XIII. John Winthrop, who made the appeal, was the only son and heir of Major-General Wait Winthrop of Boston; he was also the nephew and heir

Colony that the case had gone against it, steps were taken to send over Jonathan Belcher of Boston, the most successful and influential advocate in New England, with instructions to use every exertion to secure a reversal of the decision, involving as this did the validity of innumerable land titles.[1] Hardly had Belcher settled down to work than the intelligence was received in London of the death of Governor Burnet of Massachusetts Bay. As a result, the former succeeded in securing an appointment, not only to the governorship of this province but also to that of New Hampshire.[2] Before his return to America, however, he had been authorized to transfer the work into the hands of Francis Wilks, another New England man by birth, who had become an influential London merchant and was a member of the East India Company.[3] Wilks was already the Massachusetts Bay agent and possessed such "a great and growing interest at court" that he was retained until his death in 1742, when he was followed in the agency by Eliakim Palmer, Esq., of London.[4] While the latter was agent, the General Assembly voted in 1748, "that Thomas Fitch of Norwalk be appointed agent

of Fitz-John Winthrop, who had been governor of Connecticut; in addition, he was the heir of his grandfather John Winthrop, Jr. He appealed from two decisions of the Superior Court in favor of Thomas and Anne Lechmere, involving the estates left him by his ancestors. For by these decisions the administrator, Thomas Lechmere, was empowered to dispose of them.

[1] Jonathan Law had first been approved but refused. *Conn. Col. Rec.*, VII, 218, 185. The *Talcott Papers* (Conn. Hist. Soc. *Coll.*, IV and V), are especially valuable for the light they throw upon the affairs of the Connecticut agency of this period.

[2] See the *Belcher Papers; Conn. Col. Rec.*, VII, 282.

[3] *Conn. Col. Rec.*, VII, 308; *Talcott Papers*, I, 199, 253.

[4] *Conn. Col. Rec.*, VIII, 361, 440, 506, 517, 578.

and in case of his refusal John Bulkley, Esq., for the purpose of getting reimbursement in the Cape Breton Expedition."[1] Palmer died in 1749, and thereupon the General Assembly selected for this post the distinguished publicist and Unitarian, Dr. Benjamin Avery, who was then Chairman of the Committee of English Dissenters.[2] But Avery could not see his way clear to undertake this work, and upon his refusal the Colony turned, surprisingly enough in light of its historic attitude toward the Society of Friends, to the London Quaker, Richard Partridge, the veteran agent for Rhode Island and New Jersey.[3]

To ward off the serious attempt made at this time in connection with the colonial currency bill to compel Connecticut, Rhode Island, and Maryland to follow the practice of the other colonies and submit all laws to the Crown for approval or rejection, Partridge was reënforced in 1750 by Colonel Elisha Williams from the Colony, a man of the highest intellectual attainments.[4] Again, in 1756 and also in

[1] Ibid., VIII, 506, 517, 578, 579; IX, 185, 217, 264, 418.
[2] Wolcott Papers (Conn. Hist. Soc. Coll., XVI), pp. 40, 69, 41, 102, 199, 187, 190, 218, 237, 262, 313, 316, for letters to and from Avery. Although refusing to accept the agency he nevertheless agreed to take care of the money received by the Colony as reimbursement for the Cape Breton expedition. Conn. Col. Rec., IX, 471, 472, 511; X, 14, 103, 286.
[3] Ibid., IX, 509, 512; X, 6, 14, 17, 61, 214, 484, 566. Wolcott Papers, pp. 516, 517 for his appointment and letter of agency. The Papers also contain a large number of letters to and from Partridge.
[4] Conn. Col. Rec., IX, 512-513; Wolcott Papers, 50, 376, 421. Elisha Williams had a distinguished career. After the dismissal of the Rev. Timothy Cutler from the rectorship of Yale College for his change to Anglicanism, Williams was elected to this office which he retained from 1726 to 1739. Although he met with great success, ill health forced him to resign this work. He

1758, Jonathan Trumbull, later to become Connecticut's Revolutionary War governor, was asked by the General Assembly to go to England in behalf of the Colony in order to deal with the important financial problems arising out of the military operations of the French and Indian War.[1] After his second refusal to undertake the work, the task was turned over to Jared Ingersoll, the most distinguished among the Connecticut lawyers, who gradually gained a great influence with the home government.[2]

In this survey of the Connecticut London agency in the eighteenth century it is to be noticed that only a serious crisis led to the sending of a representative from America to England to take over the work of this office. The Colony felt that under ordinary circumstances a capable resident of London was able to discharge in a satisfactory manner the responsibilities of the agency, which were sometimes very great. In this connection, the point cannot be stressed too greatly, that, while Connecticut and other colonies were not technically represented in Parliament, in practice these dependencies of the Mother Country were undoubtedly given every protection of vital interests, through the efficient work of influential

later acted as deputy for Wethersfield in the General Assembly, was a chaplain with the Cape Breton expedition, and in 1746 was appointed colonel in connection with the expedition launched against Canada. See Francis Parsons, "Elisha Williams, Minister, Soldier, President of Yale," in the New Haven Colonial Hist. Soc. *Papers*, VII, No. 8.

[1] *Conn. Col. Rec.*, X, 484; XI, 108.

[2] For an account of Ingersoll's first and second London agency see the writer's *Jared Ingersoll*. Upon Ingersoll's retirement from the agency in 1760, Richard Jackson, a distinguished London barrister and member of Parliament, took over the office. See *Ibid.*, pp. 77-78.

agents, that could have been expected had they enjoyed the fullest representation in the House of Commons. The crowning achievement of the Connecticut agency, it goes without saying, was the preservation of the charter and with this the freedom of the Colony to walk according to its own light, still the light of seventeenth-century Puritanism, with little hindrance from the Mother Country.[1]

Thus the people of the little commonwealth, free from the heavy financial burdens carried by those of the Mother Country,[2] under a thrifty, almost parsimonious, government, were able with the close of the late war to devote their energies without interference from outside to the improvement of their farms, to the rearing of their families, and—not the least important to them by any means—to the pursuit of spiritual values after their own manner of life.

[1] But two laws affecting Connecticut's fundamental conceptions of social solidarity were disallowed in the eighteenth century: the Act for the Suppression of Heretics, disallowed in 1705, and the Act for the Settlement of Intestate Estates, disallowed in 1728. See C. M. Andrews, *Connecticut and the British Government*, p. 47.

[2] For example, the taxes in England in the middle of the eighteenth century amounted in the neighborhood of a per capita levy of twenty-one shillings sterling per annum; in Connecticut the annual levy did not exceed at the same period three and three-fourths farthings sterling. See the author's "Connecticut Taxation and Parliamentary Act Preceding the Revolutionary War," *Amer. Hist. Rev.*, XXXVI, 729-730.

CHAPTER V

IN TURNING our attention from New England to examine conditions within the Province of New York, one generalization may here be made: whereas within the bounds of the former, landholding was, as a rule, upon a popular basis with the towns still in possession of very considerable bodies of land ultimately to be distributed as need would arise and with individual estates generally of modest proportions; in the latter, aristocratic, even monopolistic, tendencies had been manifested ever since the days of the Dutch patroons. Along the eastern and southern borders of the Colony, like the military marks protecting the frontiers of the early medieval German Empire, stretched a series of great grants. Beyond the Hudson River eastward were Philipsborough Manor, Pelham Manor, Scarsdale Manor, Morrisania, Fordham Manor, the Manor of Cortlandt, Philipse's Patent, Rumbout's Patent, Beekman's Patent, the Great Nine Partners' Patent, the Little Nine Partners' Patent, the Manor of Livingston, Rensselaerwyck and the Manor of Rensselaer.[1] Corresponding to these

[1] For a map of the patroonships and manors that came into existence between 1629 and 1704 see that included in Montgomery Schuyler's *Patroons and Lords of Manors of the Hudson.* The Sauthier chorographical map prepared for Governor Tryon and published in 1779 indicates clearly the bounds of most of the manors and patents in existence at this period. A portion of this map is presented at the end of this volume. See also the *Historical and Statistical Gazetteer of New York,* 1860.

there lay between the Hudson and the east branch of the Delaware, facing New Jersey, the patents of Kakiate, Cheesecock, Wawayanda and Minisink, "enormous grants of two and three hundred thousand acres of land at so small a rent as a beaver skin."[1] Furthermore, in the interior of the Province, up to the Indian country, much of the land was held by great patentees who in many cases had received one hundred or even two hundred thousand acres for a trifling quit-rent of twenty or forty shillings a year. Some proprietors, indeed, such as those controlling the Hardenburgh Patent lying eastward of the Delaware in Ulster County, had claims to great stretches of country containing above a million acres, according to the Surveyor-General.[2]

A number of these vast land grants came into existence as patroonships which the Dutch West India Company offered during the period of its control of the New Netherlands to encourage the planting of settlements. At the time that the Province passed under English control the Dutch patroons were guaranteed the safe possession of their lands. The earlier English governors were fairly cautious in making grants, realizing the evil effects of the Dutch

[1] *A Letter from a Gentleman in New York to his Friend in Brunswick* (September 26, 1750. Broadside, New York Historical Society). For a map of the County of Orange, New York, indicating the limits of these patents see E. M. Ruttenber, *History of the County of Orange*, opposite page 27. The instructions of Sir Danvers Osborne in 1753 refer to "several exorbitant Grants of Lands ... within that part of your Majesty's Province which adjoins to New Jersey. ... " The Governor was to employ all lawful means to vacate these. For this instruction see *Acts of the Privy Council, Col.*, 1754-1766, p. 210.

[2] Cadwallader Colden to Governor William Shirley, July 25, 1749, *Colden Papers*, IV, 123.

policy. Sir Edmund Andros, who administered the Province from 1674 to 1683, was especially careful to see that there was a definite survey before any patent was issued, also that the quit-rent to be paid should be fixed at the time of the grant. It was not, indeed, until the period subsequent to the Revolution of 1689 that there was a marked return to the earlier practice of extravagant allotments. But under Colonel Fletcher "the most extraordinary favors of former Govr's. were but petty Grants in Comparison of his" in giving away parcels containing upwards of one hundred thousand acres and to particular favorites four or five times that quantity,[1] some of which, however, under his successor, the Earl of Bellomont, were vacated by act of the Assembly in the year 1699.[2] Unfortunately, the Assembly on this occasion was actuated by party spirit, with the result that several of the most exorbitant of these patents were, so it was charged, ignored, while others that did not fall within this category were recalled. Under Captain Nanfan so-called ambulatory grants were made, the patentees having liberty to claim lands now in one part of the Province and again in another part, and, following Nanfan, came Lord Cornbury whose gifts of large tracts at trifling quit-rents seem to have equalled those of all of his successors put together.[3] Further, in 1702, during his governorship,

[1] See Cadwallader Colden's "Report on the Lands in the Province of New York" of the year 1732 with addenda of the year 1752. This is printed in E. B. O'Callaghan, The Documentary History of New York, I, 249-255.
[2] The Colonial Laws of New York, I, 412-417; Acts of the Privy Council, Col., Unbound Papers, pp. 59-61.
[3] Among the larger grants made after the Andros administration, Rumbout's Patent came into existence in 1685, the Living-

the Assembly, carried away by the spirit of monopolization, sought to repeal the act of the year 1699. This effort failed only by reason of the disapproval of the Queen in Council.[1]

In 1732 a report was made on the state of the lands by the Surveyor-General, Cadwallader Colden. In referring to the large grants of from fifty thousand to over one million acres lying about in the Province, most of them uncultivated, Colden stressed the point that in the making of these, in most cases no specified quantity of land or number of acres was mentioned, but rather they were designated as lying within certain limits founded by natural features such as streams carrying Indian names, which gave every opportunity to enlarge and explain the patent according to the inclinations of the grantee. Even in cases where the number of acres was specified the tendency, it appears, was to extend it. "I have heard of one instance at least," he asserted, "where the patent Grants 300 acres, and the patentee now claims upwards of sixty thousand acres within the bounds of his Grant."[2]

ston Manor, in 1686, Pelham Manor, in 1687 (based upon the patent of 1666), Philipsborough Manor, in 1693, Kakiate Patent, in 1696, Cortlandt Manor, Morrisania, and the Great Nine Partners' Patent, in 1697, Scarsdale Manor, in 1701, the Wawayanda and Beekman patents, in 1703, the Little Nine Partners' Patent, in 1706, Cheesecock's Patent in 1707, and the Hardenburgh Patent in 1708. A list of manors is to be found in Montgomery Schuyler's *Patroons and Lords of Manors of the Hudson;* see also for additional information the *Historical and Statistical Gazetteer* (1860), p. 258 *et seq.* For Fletcher's grants see the representation of the Board of Trade of July 29, 1707, *Acts of the Privy Council, Col., Unbound Papers,* p. 60.

[1] *The Colonial Laws of New York,* I, 523-525; *Acts of the Privy Council, Col.,* II, 850; *ibid., Unbound Papers,* pp. 59-65.

[2] E. B. O'Callaghan, *Doc. Hist. of New York,* I, 252.

By 1750 many of these great concessions lying along the eastern and southern borders of the Province, as well as unappropriated lands in these regions, were being threatened on account of the pressure then being exerted by the inhabitants of New Hampshire, Massachusetts Bay, and New Jersey. Already in the fall of 1749 Governor Wentworth of New Hampshire, as we have made clear in an earlier chapter, had notified George Clinton, the Governor of New York, of his intention to make certain grants to the west of the Connecticut River and, shortly afterwards, he proceeded to issue his letters patent for the township of Bennington, twenty-four miles to the east of Albany, which Clinton hastened to inform him had already been granted by his own government. Nevertheless, Wentworth proceeded to run a line as an extension of the New Hampshire southern boundary which brought the territorial claims of that Colony now within eight or ten miles of Albany, and covered lands that, according to the Surveyor-General of New York, already paid yearly rents to the Crown.[1]

Thus was inaugurated one of the bitterest intercolonial controversies of the eighteenth century. Although this was finally submitted for adjudication to His Majesty in Council, which resulted in a decision favorable to the claims of New York, it was by no means terminated, but continued until the close of the Revolutionary War. However, during its later

[1] Gov. Wentworth to Gov. Clinton Nov. 17, 1749 and April 25, 1750, Gov. Clinton to Gov. Wentworth, June 6, 1750, The Observations of the Surveyor-General, Oct. 14, 1751, New York Colonial Documents (O'Callaghan and Fernow), VI, 331, 332, 333, 339.

phases it especially involved the conflicting claims of the settlers themselves under titles derived from the two provinces.[1] ·

To the south of this particular region of conflict were those huge grants referred to previously, among them the Manor of Livingston of one hundred and sixty thousand acres. Over the latter Robert Livingston was ruling as proprietor in 1750. It had been granted in 1685 and confirmed by royal authority in 1715 to an ancestor carrying the same name as the incumbent; the successive heads of the family had up to this period enjoyed peace and quiet in undisturbed possession of the great patent. However, early in the '50s, the people of Westenhook, an adjacent township in Massachusetts Bay, began to settle on lands hitherto considered to be within its bounds. By the year 1753 the intruders were threatening most of the eastern part of the estate. Even a considerable number of the Livingston tenants long settled under leases now showed a disposition to unite with the newcomers in ignoring the right of the proprietor by applying for grants of this same land from the Massachusetts Bay government—thereby hoping to be able to escape the payment of rentals. The movement certainly boded no good for the landed magnates of New York as a group, and it is quite natural that there was expressed a fear that the "Infection will very soon be general and then no man that has an estate in this Province or perhaps in North America, will be safe or able to call it his Owne."[2] In the month of

[1] See "Papers Relating to the Difficulties between New York and New Hampshire," *New York Col. Doc.*, VI, 329-624.

[2] Robert Livingston to William Alexander, March 26, 1753, William Alexander Papers, New York Hist. Society.

June the Massachusetts Bay Assembly voted to support the claims of those who had lately established themselves within the borders of the Manor on the assumption that these lands really lay to the east of the boundaries of New York.[1] By July there was open conflict, with the arrest of some of Livingston's loyal tenants who were dragged before the magistrates of Massachusetts Bay. This led in turn to a proclamation by Governor Clinton, who called upon the sheriffs of Albany and Dutchess counties to place under arrest and hold in custody all those implicated in these proceedings.[2] That this proclamation in no way frightened the men of New England is evidenced by the fact that early in 1755, when the high sheriff of Albany County attempted to secure the person of a settler of Claverack within the Manor, not only was the latter rescued, but the former, in spite of his high office, was placed under arrest and conducted to Sheffield, in Massachusetts Bay, where he was confined for a time and was obliged, before receiving his liberty, to give bail for his appearance there at the next sitting of the court of the quarter session. As a result of this, James de Lancey, now Lieutenant Governor of New York, issued a proclamation calling for the apprehension of those parties who thus defied the authority of the Province,[3] which in turn was followed by the killing of a Massachusetts Bay man. Whereupon there appeared as a counterblast a proc-

[1] A transcript of the minutes of the Massachusetts Bay Assembly of June 14 and June 19 relating to these claims is among the Livingston Papers, New York Hist. Society.
[2] For a copy of this broadside bearing date of July 8, 1753, see Broadsides of the New York Hist. Society.
[3] Broadside bearing date of April 2, 1755, *ibid*.

lamation by Governor Phips of that Colony. Finally, there occurred the capture of Livingston's ironworkers and the confining of the sheriff of Albany with others in the Springfield jail, whence they were at length released only as the result of the interposition of Governor Shirley. The latter, again at the head of the government of Massachusetts Bay, was now primarily interested in securing the harmony of the colonies in the face of the great struggle opening up in North America between the English and the French.[1]

The influence of this struggle between New York and Massachusetts Bay, a struggle to be noted also between two different systems of landholding, was also evidenced, it may be said in passing, by the great land riots that broke out in the '60s to the southward of Livingston Manor in Dutchess County in connection with which it was necessary to employ British regulars in restoring peace and good order.[2]

As to the southern boundary, between the Hudson and the east branch of the Delaware, much the same situation existed as along the eastern. Many of the great patents in Orange County, each of which embraced several hundred thousand acres, overlapped grants made by the Province of New Jersey in what are now Sussex and Passaic counties. Even the home government regarded the former as exorbitant. In preparing the instructions for Sir Danvers Osborne in 1753 the Lords of Trade represented that, since

[1] See E. B. O'Callaghan, *The Documentary History of New York*, III, 739, 754, 774, 789, 801-803.

[2] See C. E. Carter, *Correspondence of General Thomas Gage*, I, 95, 99, 107-108; *New York Col. Doc.*, VII, 879.

these had been made without any proper condition attached regarding cultivation and upon trifling and inconsiderable quit-rents "by which your Majesty's Revenue has been injured and the settling and improving the Province greatly obstructed," they had directed him to inquire into the state of all New York patents and to take every lawful means to vacate those that were defeating the desirable ends of government.[1]

As may be imagined, the great landholders occupied a position of decisive influence in the political and social life of the Province of New York and were adept in the guarding of their own interests. This was aided by a system of plural voting which permitted freeholders with estates in several counties to participate in the elections in each.[2] Lords of manors were also aided by the control they exercised over their tenants. The leading aristocratic families of this period, many of whom were intermarried, were the Schuylers, the De Lanceys, the Livingstons, the Philipses, the van Cortlandts, the Bayards, the Heathcotes, the Crugers, the Wattses, the Waltons, the van Rensselaers, the Beekmans, the Bluchers, the Barclays, the Joneses, the Jays, the Verplancks, the Harrisons, the Morrises, the Alexanders, and the Smiths. Some of them were deeply involved in commercial activities, but all of them enjoyed important landholdings, and many controlled immense tracts of land. It was unfortunate that these and a few other families of

[1] C.O. 5: 1128, pp. 60-76.
[2] New York Colonial Documents (O'Callaghan and Fernow), IV, 127-9; VI, 56; C. F. Bishop, History of Elections in the American Colonies, p. 69; A. E. McKinley, The Suffrage Franchise in the . . . Colonies, pp. 215-216.

scarcely less importance tended to monopolize the finest of the lands of the Province up to the Indian country, for, as a rule, they were indisposed to sell any portion of their holdings except at a price that was considered out of all reason by the prospective freeholder, preferring to exploit them by developing tenancies. As a consequence of this policy, the Province—although settled among the first of all the possessions in the hands of the English in 1750 and enjoying many natural advantages over the neighboring plantations, not only as to its situation with respect to trade and commerce, but also as to the quality of its soil in comparison certainly to that of New England—was not nearly so well cultivated or so populous.[1] Indeed, so unfavorable were conditions in the early part of the eighteenth century, especially for the sons of poor people who desired to acquire land and to engage in agriculture as independent small farmers rather than as tenants on the great estates, that many left the Province to establish themselves in near-by colonies, among them, the Palatines.[2] These, ejected from the lands they had squatted upon in the valleys of the Mohawk and the Schoharie, trekked into Pennsylvania and incidentally warned all

[1] See William Livingston's "A Brief Consideration of New York with respect to its Natural Advantages, its superiority in several instances over the neighboring Colonies" (1753). This appeared in the *Independent Reflector* of this year and is reprinted in *Hartman's Historical Series*, No. 39.

[2] In 1710, three thousand of these Palatines were sent to New York for the purpose of producing naval stores. Parliament for this purpose made a grant of £10,000. After two years of effort, Governor Hunter was obliged to give up the enterprise when he had exhausted his own credit. H. L. Osgood, *American Colonies in the Eighteenth Century*, I, 512-513; II, 98.

their fellow Germans seeking homes in the New World to avoid New York.

The attitude of many well-informed colonials not residents of the Province toward the land policy is doubtless reflected in the comment of Secretary Richard Peters of Pennsylvania. "What misfortune has it been to the province of New York," he declared, "that the Land has been monopolized, and 'till lately not the least encouragement ever given, for the poor industrious to settle there." He then suggested a solution that would hardly have met with any favor on the part of New York Assembly, constituted as it was. "I'm vastly surprised that this monstrous monopoly has never been taken notice of when the remedy appears so plain and effectual, nothing more than a Tax upon each one hundred acres of unimproved land which would render it impracticable for any single man to hold a very large tract, and would very soon divide these vast bodies into more useful Parts."[1]

From 1737 to 1746 there was an addition to the population of the province of but 1,153 people, reaching in the latter year a total of 61,589 inhabitants, or an increase of not more than two per cent. In contrast to this, during the same period Pennsylvania was certainly growing at a rate which meant the doubling of her population in a period of twenty years.[2] In spite of the fact that, especially after 1750,

[1] This comment, made, it appears, about the year 1755 was appended to "A Brief Account of Pennsylvania," prepared by Lewis Evans in 1753, a copy of which, with the Peters notations, is in the library of the Historical Society of Pennsylvania.

[2] It is true that the period between the years 1746 and 1776 saw a very rapid increase in the number of inhabitants. This

there was a great increase in the settlement of lands, Governor Tryon reported in 1774 that only one fifth of the acreage of the province was undergoing improvement.[1]

From the foregoing an impression might be gained that the great landowners were attempting personally to exploit much of their vast estates. This, of course, would give an inaccurate picture of the actual situation. While it is true that on Morrisania Manor, there were in the middle of the century some twenty-nine slaves and on Philipsborough Manor some thirty-one[2] who were doubtless usefully employed, yet the prevailing form of agricultural economy favored fairly small farm units. As has already been suggested, a system of tenantry had become well established by the middle of the century on most of the large grants, especially those immediately about the Hudson River, to the eastward of it, and on Long Island. However, certain reserved lands were, of course, worked by the lord of the manor by means of both slave or indentured labor and hired hands. On the reserve a manor house not infrequently impressive in appearance was to be found; there were also, besides the quarters for the workers, usually barns, granaries, a gristmill and a sawmill, both

mounted from 61,589 to 96,775 in 1756 and by 1771 reached 168,007, which indicates that it doubled itself within twenty years. This indicates the existence of a more favorable land policy than during the earlier period. For population statistics see O'Callaghan, *Doc. Hist. of New York*, I, 472-474, and especially Greene and Harrington *American Population before* . . . *1790*, pp. 90-91.

[1] "Report on the State of the Province of New York, 1774," *ibid.*, I, 509.

[2] See the chapter on "Social Classes" by Michael Kraus in the *History of the State of New York*, II, 407.

119

operated by water power, a small cider mill, a brewery, a smokehouse, and a bakehouse, as well as packing sheds where meat, butter, flour, bread, beer, and cider were placed in containers made by the manor coopers. On Livingston Manor there were, in addition, a furnace and a forge which at this period, by means of the available abundant supplies of iron ore and wood for the making of charcoal, were turning out very respectable quantities of pig iron and bar iron. Further, the manor reserve frequently, if not generally, bordered navigable water. In such cases, there was to be found a wharf for vessels and a warehouse where supplies of necessaries were received and disposed of to the tenants and to others living round about. The successful great landowner of New York was indeed not only a landlord, he was an agriculturalist, a miller, a lumberman, a merchant, a banker, a land speculator, a shipowner, and perhaps also an Indian trader and an ironmaster.[1] In addition, if he had manorial rights, he would hold manor courts; not infrequently he also held high provincial office and might be obliged to spend a generous amount of his time in the city of New York on the affairs of the Province.

In the middle of the eighteenth century the city of New York was, as it has always been, the social and commercial center of the Province. It was also the capital. To secure itself from attack it was defended not only by a fort but by palisades and blockhouses that had been constructed in the '40s

[1] For a brief but excellent account of the activities of the people of the Province, see the chapter on "A Century of Labor" by Samuel McKee in the History of the State of New York, II, 285, 290-291.

to connect the North and East rivers, thus giving it something of the appearance of a frontier town.[1]

Peter Kalm, who visited the city in 1748, found an extremely pleasant place. It seemed quite like a garden to him with the streets covered with the shade of beech, locust, lime, and elm trees. The neatness, the substantial quality, as well as the height of the brick houses impressed him, and the cosmopolitan character of the population he noted by the presence of places of worship for Anglicans, Dutch Reformed, Presbyterians, German Lutherans, German Reformed, Quakers, and Jews—without counting the sprinkling of Huguenots and Roman Catholics.[2] Although in size it perhaps gave place to both Boston and Philadelphia,[3] it was a center of opulence with a commerce so extensive as to lead Kalm to declare that it "disputed the preference" with the two latter seaports. Hundreds of brigantines, sloops, and schooners annually left this port for England, New England, the West Indies, the southern continental colonies, and other parts of the world.[4] Already it had become the distributing center of western Connecticut and eastern New Jersey. However, it is of interest to note that in the year 1752 the annual value of the goods shipped to the Province from Great Britain was re-

[1] See the Miller Papers, New York Hist. Society, Vol. I, for the notes of the Rev. John H. Abeel describing New York as it existed in the middle of the century.

[2] Peter Kalm, *Travels into North America*, I, 249-251.

[3] According to the notes of the Rev. John Abeel there were 2,200 houses and 12,743 inhabitants in 1754. See Miller Papers, I, New York Hist. Society.

[4] Much of this commerce was carried on in the ships of Great Britain and New England. See in the present volume Chapter I, "The Heart of New England," pp. 9-10.

ported to be but £150,000 sterling—just equal to the value of the importations of the little island of Antigua from the Mother Country and but one half the value of those of Barbados.[1] In the year 1749 the number of vessels owned by the maritime interests of the Province was but one hundred and fifty-seven, with an average registered carrying capacity of little over forty tons. These were manned by crews that averaged but eight men, which indicates not only that a small proportion of the scanty population of the Province was seafaring but that commercial relations with the Mother Country still continued as earlier in the century to be maintained chiefly by British merchants and by British ships.[2]

Industrially, the Province was not advanced to a point comparable to that of several of the other American plantations. Although there were numerous iron mines, it appears that the only production of crude iron was taking place at Ancram on the Manor of Livingston[3] which smelted in 1751 some six hundred tons of pig iron, one fourth of which was transformed into bar iron.[4] There was, it is true, in the great patent of Wawayanda in Orange County a "plateing mill" with a tilt hammer, but this was not in use during the period under discussion.[5] A good

[1] James Abercrombie's Examination. May 22, 1752. Shelburne Papers, 47: 30.

[2] Gov. Clinton to Board of Trade, May 23, 1749. *Doc. Hist. of New York*, I, 494-495. C. P. Nettels, *Money Supply of the American Colonies to 1720*, pp. 73-74.

[3] James de Lancey to the Board of Trade, Dec. 1, 1757, *Doc. Hist. of New York*, I, 496.

[4] "An Account of Iron Made at Ancram 1750-1756," *ibid.*, I, 496.

[5] "Gov. Clinton's Certificate About Iron Rolling Mills," 1750, *ibid.*, I, 495.

deal of weaving of flax and wool was reported but only in a domestic way for local use; beaver hats also were made, yet the exportation of these after 1732 had been prohibited by Act of Parliament.[1] Lamp black production, however, had assumed some importance,[2] and the baked and refined sugar of the Province was marketed not only in other continental colonies but even in the West Indies, while six distilleries manufactured rum and other spirits used domestically and in both the Indian and the Guinea trade. Further, there were produced very considerable quantities of flour for export, together with other foodstuffs from wheat which had long been one of the great staples of the Province.[3] Unfortunately, as the result of the fraudulent exportation of unmerchantable flour, especially flour mixed with Indian corn, and the false taring of bread and flour casks, these commodities had to a great extent lost reputation abroad which, however, the Assembly of the Province was seeking to retrieve at this period by suitable legislation.[4]

One of the most profitable commercial activities of the Province in the seventeenth century had been the Indian fur trade, although it had employed di-

[1] 5 George II, c. 22.
[2] In 1724 Susanna Parmyter had been granted a monopoly of this commodity for a period of ten years. *The Colonial Laws of New York*, II, 242.
[3] In the seventeenth century the manufacture of flour and bread had been the chief dependence of the town of New York, which enjoyed a monopoly of this business. New York flour at that period was the best produced in America. C. P. Nettels, *Money Supply of the American Colonies to 1720*, pp. 114-116. Governor Crosby to the Board of Trade, Dec. 18, 1732, *Doc. Hist. of New York*, I, 491.
[4] *Ibid.*, III, 788, 883.

rectly comparatively few white men. There had, however, been a great falling off in the receipts of fur, due no doubt largely to the disappearance of beaver in great numbers from the western part of the Colony as the result of continuous trapping, combined with those influences on the "far Indians" that centered not only in the French trading posts of Canada but even in those of the Hudson's Bay Company far to the north; further, the growing importance of the Pennsylvania fur trade on the upper waters of the Ohio adversely affected the New York trade. Nevertheless, Albany was still considered one of the great fur-trading centers of the New World.[1]

The Dutch town of Albany must have presented a quaint appearance in 1750. Most of the houses were so constructed that one of the gable ends faced the street. This end was generally faced with brick while the three other walls presented to view bare unpainted planks. The roofs extended far out into the thoroughfare, and on either side of the street entrance, generally centered, were benches, upon which in fair weather the people would spend the day—when the womenfolk were not scrubbing their floors in good Dutch fashion. One broad street five times the width of the others served as a market place, and at either end of this was a stone church—at the east end, the Dutch Reformed, and at the west end, the Anglican. It would appear, however, that in 1750 there was

---

[1] For the decline of the fur trade see the chapter on "A Century of Labor" by Samuel McKee in *The History of the State of New York*, II, 320-324. The value of furs and skins exported to England in the years 1721 and 1722 was £13,697.10. In 1699-1700 New York sent to England 15,352 skins. C. P. Nettels, *op. cit.*, p. 74, note.

little demand for the latter, except on the part of the garrison, as all of the people spoke Dutch and were particularly attached to the Rev. Theodorus Frielinghausen, the minister of the Reformed church.

Within the town were made great quantities of wampum for the Indian trade. Here also were stored supplies of various commodities in the warehouses of the wealthy merchants who lived on their extensive estates in the country round about. For to Albany came the Iroquois and also, less frequently, those tribes in alliance with them. Here also appeared parties of Canadian Indians carrying on a secret trade in beaver skins. Moreover, from the town each spring there left for Oswego, the English outpost on Lake Ontario, representatives of practically every Albany merchant house to spend the summer bargaining with Indians from many distant tribes, who came with their peltries. In 1749, for example, one hundred and eighty-six canoes arrived there from eleven western tribes; in addition, eight canoes from the Upper Lakes brought French traders. These together carried over sixteen hundred people with fourteen hundred and thirty-five packs of furs which possessed a value that ranged from £14 to £20 per pack, a total value of £21,406.[1]

Limited as it was, the Indian trade was enormously

[1] Report of [John] Lindsay. Commissary at Oswego, August 20, 1749. *New York Col. Doc.*, VI, 538. A recent writer makes the following interesting assertion:

"The pelts exchanged at Oswego in 1749 would today sell for well over $2,000,000. During the period 1750 to 1755, the fur trade reached its peak, causing the British to consider Oswego one of the most important on the continent, and the French to think of it as a place to be destroyed at all costs." F. K. Zercher, in *New York History*, XVI, 310.

profitable, although by no means carried on at all times with absolute fairness to the Indians. Peter Kalm, who visited Albany in 1749 and 1750, wrote, "Many people have assured me that the Indians are frequently cheated in disposing of their goods, especially when they are in liquor, and that sometimes they do not get one half or even one tenth of the value of their goods. I have been a witness to several transactions of this kind. The merchants of Albany glory in these tricks, and are highly pleased when they have given a poor Indian a greater portion of brandy than he can bear, and when they can, after that, get all his goods for mere trifles."[1] It would appear that the methods employed in this commerce were reflected in the general conduct of the people of this region, for Kalm further declares, "The avarice and selfishness of the inhabitants of Albany are very well known throughout All North America. . . . If a Jew, who understands the art of getting forward perfectly well should settle amonst them, they would not fail to ruin him." The good man found an intense hatred of these people, especially by New Englanders, who accused them of having encouraged the French Indians to desolate the New England settlements in the late war in order to bring to them the loot, especially plates, spoons, bowls, cups, etc., for which they paid the Indians good prices.[2]

[1] Joel Munsell, *The Annals of Albany*, I, 262-275.
[2] *Ibid*. This charge was made by Governor Clinton in 1747 in his "Observations on the Representations of the Assembly," C.O. 5: 1085, pp. 265-274. "According to the information I have received, some of those French Indians were lately trading at Albany, when others of them, were at the same time scalping and Butchering his Maj[ty's] subjects on the borders of New Eng-

In 1750 George Clinton was acting as royal governor of the Province. A son of the Earl of Lincoln, he had followed the sea without winning distinction as a naval commander before his appointment in 1741, and in 1743 came to his post, so it is asserted, loaded with debts, hoping by this new situation to recoup his fortunes. By all accounts he was generally complaisant, decidedly indolent, and always inept in the art of governing. Soon after his arrival he began to lean for guidance in the affairs of state upon James de Lancey, one of the most powerful and astute politicians of the Province. Upon de Lancey's advice, it appears,[1] the Governor made the initial fatal mistake of surrendering into the hands of the General Assembly the complete control of public finance, accepting without a serious struggle a reversal of the policy maintained by his predecessors, Governors Hunter, Burnet, Montgomery, and Cosby, of insisting on establishments based on estimates for a five-year period and the granting "in general" of supplies for the support of government.[2] He accepted the act

land, which we can not but look upon with the same resentment as if done to any people of this province; and besides, whatever these Indians Barter these furs for, whether for cloathing, or gunpowder, is so much clear gain to the French, and the strengthening of the hands of his Maj[ty's] enemies." Governor Clinton to the Assembly of New York, Aug. 23, 1745, *New York Col. Doc.*, VI, 372.

For a sympathetic study of Albany in its relations to the larger problem of imperial expansion see A. H. Buffington, "Albany Policy and Westward Expansion," *Mississippi Valley Historical Review*, VIII, 327-367.

[1]*New York Col. Doc.*, VI, 615-616.

[2] "State of Affairs in New York, 1746-1748," C.O. 5: 1095; *New York Col. Doc.*, VI, 615.

It should be pointed out that it was in 1737 under Governor Clarke that the General Assembly first deviated from this practice

of 1744 which provided for specific appropriations and submitted to the creation of a group of officials solely dependent upon the Assembly. Moreover, the latter, through its own committees, purchased and distributed munitions of war, raised, employed, provisioned, and paid the provincial troops, named officers, built fortifications, and supported scouts in the Indian country.[1] Not only did this body employ as its own agent in London a Mr. Charles, Secretary to Sir Peter Warren, but it dismissed the Governor's appointee "as tidewaiter of the colony's imports" and selected one in his place. De Lancey, appointed Chief Justice of the Province during good behavior by the Governor's commission and also designated although not commissioned as yet as Lieutenant Governor, rode on a wave of popularity while the authority of the King's representative was thus being flouted. For a period of almost three years he shaped affairs according to his own desires. However, in 1746 Clinton became convinced that he had been betrayed and,

covering a period of twenty-eight years. The Assembly of course since the days of the notorious Cornbury had been striving to establish an absolute control of the finances. This was in line with a general movement on the part of the royal colonies. Richard Bradley, writing from New York in 1729, complained, "I doubt not, but Y^r Grace is or soon will be convinced that the General Assemblys of these Countrys'; Seem to Aim at an Arbitrary, and Independent power, by their Assuming the sole appropriation of money raised for the publick Service, Their usual insisting on passing of bills hurtfull to his Majesty's Prerogative and interest, at the same time they pass Money bills, And by refusing to give any salary, at all to some officers of the Crown, and lessening those of Others, when, at the same time, they Augment the Salary of such as they appoint; and that without any apparent application of it." C.O. 5: 1086, folio 13.

[1] See Governor Shirley's "View of the Situation in New York," C.O. 5: 1095; New York Col. Doc., VI, 615-616.

repudiating this masterful man, now turned to the Surveyor-General, Cadwallader Colden, for advice.

Colden, a man of means, was a native of Scotland; he had been educated at Edinburgh and in London, and for a time was a Philadelphia merchant; he was certainly one of the most distinguished among British colonials, the friend of many of the world's most famous scientists, a philosopher, a student of botany, astronomy, and physics, a physician, and a historian. He looked with abhorrence upon the recent usurpations of the Assembly and dedicated himself to the task of extricating the Governor from his embarrassing situation. This brought down upon him the hatred of the popular leaders. "We esteem it a great Misfortune to the Country," declared the Assembly in addressing the Governor in October, 1747, "that you have fallen into such ill Hands, that the Fate of this Colony should in this time of eminent Danger, depend entirely upon the Advice and Caprice of a Man so obnoxious; who by the whole Course of his Conduct seems to have only his own Interest in view without any Regard to the Safety or Welfare of the Colony."[1] But Colden returned their odium with interest. "You know Sr What Kind of a Creature an American assembly is," he declared in writing to Governor Shirley in 1749, "& yet you cannot have a sufficient conception of the Ignorance & mean Spirit of the Dutch members here, most of them of the lowest rank of Artificers."[2]

Colden's case against the Assembly, and also against

[1] *Ibid.*, VI, 618.
[2] *Colden Papers*, IV, 120. At this time the Assembly was composed of but twenty-seven members.

a majority of the Governor's Council, was based upon
what to him was indubitable proof that the members
had been influenced in their opposition to the Governor by a group of powerful men who, for sinister
purposes, sought to strip Clinton of his power and to
preserve the neutrality of the Province of New York
in the war then being waged between England and
France. He charged that this conspiracy had taken
place in order that, among other advantages to be
gained by this neutrality, the French Indians might
make Albany a rendezvous, in connection with their
savage incursions into New England across the Hudson. To him, de Lancey had largely won his popularity in the promotion of this scheme of neutrality.[1]
Further, he defended strongly the conduct of Clinton.
To the accusation that the Governor had drawn out
public money for private use he declared,

"I have been near 30 years in the Council of this
Province and longer conversant in the publick affairs
of it and in all that time I do not remember that any
publick money was drawn by any Govr from the
Treasury and applied to any other use than what it
was design'd for by the Assembly that granted it."

He then went on to observe,

"If Govr Clinton had made use of his power in
drawing the least sum out of the Treasury contrary
to the interest of the grantors it cannot be doubted
this Assembly could have pointed it particularly out
but no such thing has so much as been attempted. On

[1] *Op. cit.*, IV, 34-44. For the connection of the de Lancey
family with the Canada trade see Professor C. H. McIlwain's Introduction to Peter Wraxall's *Abridgment of Indian Affairs*,
p. xxvii, note 4. Respecting the question of neutrality, see *The
History of the State of New York*, II, 227.

the contrary, I am persuaded that there has been more of the publick money converted to private use since the Assembly assumed the whole power of issuing it than has been done in any shape by all or any of the Governors since I came into this Province. I am so much persuaded of the truth of this that I could but [put] the whole contraversy upon this single issue."[1]

Clinton, after his break with de Lancey, spent the remainder of the period of his administration in attempting to strip the latter of influence and to win back the powers that had slipped into the hands of the Assembly. He sought, among other things, to prevent the confirmation of de Lancey's appointment to the office of Lieutenant Governor and exerted himself to secure that honor for Colden, especially in the late '40s when he saw that his own tenure of office was drawing to a close. The ministry, however, could not be prevailed upon to incur the hostility of this leader of the popular group.[2] The Governor also threw down the gauntlet to the Assembly and, for a period of two years after peace was restored, refused to sign bills which made yearly specific appropriations. However, in 1750 he yielded under great financial pressure.

It may be well to point out that in the course of the struggle between Clinton and the Assembly of New York the issues involved finally came before His

[1] Cadwallader Colden to Governor William Shirley, July 25, 1749, *Colden Papers*, IV, 122.
[2] It, however, seems to be true that Lord Halifax in 1749 expressed the hope that de Lancey would not be allowed to serve as deputy in case Clinton returned. Gov. Clinton to Cadwallader Colden, Nov. 6, 1749, *ibid.*, IV, 148-149. De Lancey, however, had powerful friends at court, among them, the Archbishop of Canterbury and Admiral Sir Peter Warren.

Majesty in the form of a report upon the state of that Province prepared by the Board of Trade in the spring of 1751. This was strongly adverse to the Assembly. As a result, when Osborne was appointed to office in 1753 the 39th Article of his instructions called upon him to secure a permanent and fixed revenue for the support of government as a means of restoring peace and tranquillity and preventing encroachments upon His Majesty's authority and prerogative within the Province. When this instruction came before the Assembly it was voted that His Majesty should be addressed with the assurance that the imputations contained therein were groundless and had been most falsely and maliciously represented. The address, however, was dismissed, and the Privy Council went on record to the effect that as the result of exigencies of the service in time of war the Assembly had taken to itself not only the disposal of the public money, but had wrested from the Governor "the nomination of all officers of Government ... and in short almost every other executive part of Government, by which unwarrantable Encroachments and Invasions of your Majesty's just and undoubted authority, Order and good Government were subverted, Your Majesty's Service obstructed, and the Security of the Province endangered."[1]

As to Clinton's plan for circumventing his enemies by securing the appointment of Colden as Lieutenant Governor, it was argued by the Lords Commissioners when the proposal came before the Board of Trade that "if a man of Quality & Gov. in Chief could not,

---

[1] *Acts of the Privy Council, Col., 1745-1766*, pp. 209, 246-247.

with the assistance of Mr. Colden bring the Assembly to terms, how could Mr. Colden expect to do it in his absence?"[1] In fact, the Board came to the conclusion to disappoint both groups by sending over to New York an Englishman of weight. As a result, Sir Danvers Osborne, a kinsman of the Earl of Halifax, was made Governor in place of Clinton. Unfortunately, when he arrived in the Colony his mind was clouded and soon after assuming office he took his own life. As a result, De Lancey, who had now received his commission as Lieutenant Governor, realized his ambition, and in his own person combined that office with those of Chancellor and Chief Justice of the Province.

[1] Extract from the letter of John Catherwood to Governor Clinton without date, *ibid.*, 1745-1766, 305.

CHAPTER VI

PLOWMEN OF THE JERSIES

HOW CAN he get wisdom that holdeth the plow and that glorieth in the goad, that driveth oxen and is occupied in their labor and whose talk is of bullocks?"[1] asked rather caustically Governor Lewis Morris of New Jersey in replying to the popular branch of the General Assembly which had in its address to him in the spring of 1745 confessed with an air of mock humility that most of the members of the same were farmers and plowmen.[2]

While farming, it is true, occupied the attention of the overwhelming majority of the people of the Province, it cannot be forgotten that during the period under consideration lumbering went hand in hand with this activity and represented a rather important economic interest. The population, which totalled 61,383 in the year 1749,[3] was settled largely on the rich alluvial soils in the eastern and the western parts of the Colony. Between these sections, and especially in the northern part, comparatively few people were living, for in this region lies a wide tract of hilly, almost mountainous, land, then valued chiefly for its pine and cedar trees. Nevertheless, out of the

[1] Ecclesiasticus 38: 25-26.
[2] *Papers of Governor Lewis Morris, 1738-1746*, pp. 237, 277-278.
[3] *New Jersey Archives*, first series, VII, 245; Greene and Harrington, *American Population before ... 1790*, pp. 106-107, for other figures.

134

labor of the plowmen of the Jersies came abundant supplies of grain, beef, and pork. The annual surplus of these commodities beyond the local needs, together with the timber from the hills valued at £30,000 sterling, was exported to the West Indies, Lisbon, Madeira, Ireland, and England. According to Governor Belcher, writing in 1749, these exports were shipped abroad mostly in New Jersey vessels that numbered twenty with a total displacement of fifteen hundred tons.[1] At the same time it seems to be true that the people of the Province were supplied with European commodities almost entirely from New York and Pennsylvania, and that there was but little direct commerce between the former and the people of the Mother Country.[2]

[1] Governor Belcher to the Board of Trade, April 21, 1749, *New Jersey Archives* (first series), VII, 244. In 1742, according to Governor Morris, there were only three brigantines and four or five sloops that traded to the Madeiras and the West Indies. Lewis Morris to the Board of Trade, December 15, 1742, *Papers of Governor Lewis Morris*, p. 156.

[2] *Ibid.*, p. 156.

The efforts on the part of East New Jersey to assert an economic independence of the port of New York is indicated in the early part of the century when, in the surrender of their political powers in 1702, the proprietors reserved the right to retain Perth Amboy as a free port. This was granted but at the same time the Crown insisted that the same duties should be paid on articles entering New Jersey that were paid in entering New York. See Governor Hunter's Instructions, Dec. 27, 1709, C.O. 5, 995, 53-4, quoted in C. P. Nettels, *The Money Supply of the American Colonies before 1720*, p. 118.

It appears that with respect to money standards East New Jersey continued to be differentiated from West New Jersey. That of the East, which was the official standard, conformed to that of New York, that of the West, to Pennsylvania. *(Ibid.,* p. 122). During the period under discussion a Spanish-milled dollar was worth in West Jersey 27 shillings, in East Jersey but 26 shillings. Board of Trade *Journal, 1741-1749*, p. 439.

All of the accounts of this period point to the fact that the great majority of the inhabitants of New Jersey were living comfortably. Indeed, it was stated in 1742 by one who knew them well that they regarded themselves "the most easie and happy people of any collony in North America."[1] And well they might congratulate themselves. Conditions were generally favorable. No foreign foes or menace from native Americans lurked along their borders. No extensive expenditures were required for fortifications and none to secure the friendship of powerful Indian tribes. In peace men plowed their fields and went about in pursuit of their personal interests. There was a remarkable absence of public burdens. According to a report sent to the Board of Trade in 1749 it was stated that " 'tis 17 years since any Tax was raised on the people for support of the Government,"[2] the expense of which was entirely met by the loan of bills of credit of the Colony to the inhabitants for the improvement of their lands, which operation in the early '40s yielded some £3,000 in the form of interest. Surprisingly enough, this manner of financing the provincial government was never apparently subjected to grave abuses. In other words, the history of public finance in colonial New Jersey is in marked contrast to that, for example, in Rhode Island where, as has been noticed in an earlier chapter, the scandal of inflation had by 1750 given the latter Colony a very unsavory reputation. Nevertheless, in

[1] Lewis Morris to Peter Collenson, May 24, 1742, *Papers of Governor Lewis Morris,* p. 147.
[2] Governor Belcher to the Board of Trade, April 21, 1749, *New Jersey Archives* (first series), VII, 246.

connection with even the fairly conservative practice of the former of issuing money on land security
and utilizing the interest thereon to meet the charges
of government there developed an issue of great importance which it would be well to consider at this
point.

The issue referred to grew out of the practice of
the Assembly in course of the eighteenth century—a
practice by no means limited to New Jersey—of
issuing bills of credit to circulate for a limited period
as a legal tender for all debts incurred either "for
Sterling Money, Silver Money of America or any
other Species of Gold, Silver, or any other quantity of
Plate or Gold."[1] Upon this basis £40,000 had been
issued in 1723, £20,000 in 1730, and £40,000 in 1733,
all of which had been loaned to the inhabitants with
interest at five per cent.[2]

When some of the colonies had turned to the use
of paper money at the end of the seventeenth century
and early in the eighteenth in connection with war-
time emergencies, the government of the Mother
Country had not been unsympathetic with their efforts to furnish aid.[3] As time went on, however, the
demand for paper money, even in time of peace, was
intensified, and also, as a consequence, the tendency to
inflate the colonial currency. An opposition very

---

[1] *Acts of the Privy Council, Col., 1745-1766*, p. 26. For a
discussion of the hostile attitude of the Board of Trade toward
the Barbados and New York legal tender acts of 1706 and 1709,
respectively, see C. P. Nettels, *Money Supply of the American
Colonies before 1720*, pp. 269-275.

[2] *Acts of the Privy Council, Col., 1745-1766*, p. 25.

[3] By 1715 the use of bills of credit had become quite general,
although Virginia, Maryland, Jamaica, Barbados, and the Leeward Islands were not involved. C. P. Nettels, *op. cit.*, p. 275.

naturally developed to making this a tender for all debts. As a result, in 1720 an instruction was sent to all royal governors to restrain them from giving their assent to any act for striking bills of credit without a clause to prevent the same taking effect until approved by the Crown, except in the case of acts designed to secure a revenue for meeting the charges of government.[1] It was under the shadow of this instruction that New Jersey had felt free to erect her system of provincial finance. This was done in spite of the fact that the Lords of the Committee of the Privy Council showed their hostility in 1731 to "a Most pernicious practice" on the part of several of the colonies of issuing bills of credit "in lieu of Money in Order to Discharge their public Debts and for other purposes."[2] In fact, the Colony in 1734 was singled out for special commendation by the Board of Trade when a group of Bristol merchants strongly voiced their opposition to the Crown's approving the act of the Assembly of the preceding year providing for the printing of £40,000 in bills of credit. The measure was not only accepted but in this connection the Lords Commissioners pointed out that there was no essential difference between this and a former New Jersey law and that the latter had been executed with good effect and had proved to be beneficial to the Province.[3]

Nevertheless, one can detect a growing opposition in England to colonial paper money, especially to the practices of the New England colonies. For ex-

---

[1] *Acts of the Privy Council, Col., 1720-1745*, pp. 329-330.
[2] *Ibid.*
[3] *Ibid.*, p. 424.

ample, in 1736 the Privy Council desired the Board of Trade to lay before it a state of the paper currency in New England, having been informed that bills of credit to a great value had been issued there.[1] The following year while approving certain supply acts of Massachusetts Bay, it was decided to send to the governor of that Province a peremptory instruction not to give his assent in the future to any paper money bill without a suspending clause.[2] It is therefore not surprising that in April, 1740 the House of Commons should resolve,

"That the Creating and Issuing Paper Bills of Credit in the British Colonys and Plantations in America by Virtue of Acts of Assembly there and making it obligatory in all Persons to take such Bills of Credit in payment for Debts Dues and Demands hath frustrated the good Intentions of an Act . . . Entituled, An Act for Ascertaining the Rates of Foreign Coins in Her Majesty's Plantations in America, and hath been a great Discouragement to the Commerce of this Kingdom by occasioning a Confusion in Dealings and lessening of Credit in those parts."[3]

Close upon the heels of this resolution the Board of Trade prepared two additional instructions for the governors of those colonies obliged to submit their laws to the King for approval. The first provided for the enforcement of the act of Parliament passed in the sixth year of the reign of Queen Anne for ascertaining the rates of foreign coins;[4] the sec-

[1] *Ibid.*, p. 507.
[2] *Ibid.*, pp. 561-562.
[3] *Ibid.*, 1746-1766, pp. 24-29.
[4] *Statutes of the Realm*, VIII, 792.

ond, for the introduction into all laws that related to the issuing of bills of credit in lieu of money, a clause suspending the operation of the same until the pleasure of His Majesty had been made known. These were approved in July of that year and were forthwith sent to America.[1] With respect to Maryland, Connecticut, and Rhode Island, the three colonies not obliged to submit their laws, it may be said in passing that the Lords of the Committee recommended the sending to these a circular letter containing the address of the House of Commons and directions to be observed regarding acts providing for a paper currency, which was ordered.[2]

When, therefore, the New Jersey House of Representatives in 1744, after the receipt by Governor Lewis Morris of the additional instructions referred to, desired him to sign a bill for the printing of £40,-000 in bills of credit of the same type as the three that earlier had been approved, he was obliged to face the wrath of the popular chamber by refusing to do so unless it should carry a clause suspending its operation until approved by His Majesty.[3] He also proceeded to censure that body for resolutions it had entered into at this juncture when the news had arrived that a bill was about to be introduced into Parliament to regulate the colonial paper currency. This resolution declared, "That if the said Bill, or any Bill of that Tendency should pass into a Law, it would not only be an Encroachment upon the fundamental constitution of this Colony, and the Concessions made

[1] *Acts of the Privy Council, Col., 1720-1745,* p. 677.
[2] *Ibid.*
[3] *Ibid.,* pp. 24-25.

to the First Settlers thereof by His Majesty's Royal Ancestors, but also Destructive of the Liberties and properties of his Majestys Subjects now Inhabitants of the same."[1]

However, the opposition of Governor Morris to the money bill referred to was not the only obstacle to its enactment. The Governor's Council sitting in its capacity as the upper chamber of the Assembly was bitterly opposed to the measure and described the emitting of large sums of bills of credit as similar in its effect to cold water to a man in a high fever, "the more is given, still the more is called for . . ."[2] In rejecting the bill the fear of inflation with its attendant evils was emphasized by this body. To the majority of the House of Representatives, however, the attitude of the Council was due to influence of the Governor upon them. There was a feeling, in other words, that could the supposed basis for the opposition of the latter be removed, the desired legislation would pass the Council, little as that assumption was later to be fulfilled.

Thereupon, an attempt was made without success not only to bribe Morris to consent to the passing of the money bill by promise of suitable financial support of the government—which was not being maintained in even a tolerable manner—but to secure from the Crown permission for the Governor to sign it without the objectionable reservation.

[1] *New Jersey Archives*, XV, 396-397. The same sentiments were at this period expressed in the New York and Pennsylvania Assemblies. *New York Col. Doc.*, VI, 613 and *Penna. Col. Records*, IV, 152.
[2] *New Jersey Archives*, XV, 385-388.

At this juncture occurred the death of Morris and the appointment of Jonathan Belcher, ex-governor of Massachusetts Bay and New Hampshire, to fill the vacancy thus created.[1] Belcher in 1748 not only signed a bill—carrying, however, the necessary suspending clause—which provided for an issue of paper money similar in amount to the preceding bill and to be current for sixteen years, but also urged His Majesty to give it favorable consideration.[2] The following year it came before the Board of Trade, at which juncture Richard Partridge, the New Jersey London agent of the Assembly and Belcher's Quaker brother-in-law, strongly urged its acceptance, and Ferdinand Paris, London agent for the East New Jersey Proprietors, "in behalf of himself and other Creditors ... of the Province," as vigorously opposed it.

The New Jersey agent argued that a further supply of paper currency was absolutely necessary for purposes of trade. This was especially so in light of the fact that all of the bills emitted by the acts above referred to had been redeemed, with the exception of one half of the last £40,000, all of which would be called in in 1754. The New Jersey bills, he declared, were the most highly esteemed of those issued by any of the colonies, and were actually considered better than silver or gold by the inhabitants who were accustomed to demand these rather than specie in all transactions. Indeed, when the time came to redeem

[1] The nineteenth article of Belcher's instructions directed him not to give his assent to any acts for issuing money bills unless a draft of the bill had previously been submitted to His Majesty for directions or carried a suspending clause. *Acts of the Privy Council, Col., 1720-1745*, p. 372.
[2] Board of Trade *Journal, 1741-1749*, p. 343.

them at the Loan Office the premium, he affirmed, rose to as much as seven per cent. His testimony was supported by that of a Captain Ware who had recently come from the Province.[1]

Paris, on the other hand, pointed out that although the preamble of the act set forth specious pretenses, yet nowhere did the bill authorize the interest arising from the loan of the bills to be applied to the service of government, but left its disposition to the legislature. He further declared that the exchange on the old bills was at 175 and new emissions would lessen their credit and that the direction of the act that all contracts already made should be paid in these bills was unjust and unreasonable, as was the clause providing that those accused of counterfeiting the bills, although residing in another province, were triable by a jury of two counties in New Jersey. A further argument against the countenancing of further issues was that a burden was laid upon the poor who were the only borrowers and, as a consequence, plunged themselves into greater difficulties; as a result, debtors were thereby led to go deeper into debt. Finally, he insisted that the legal tender feature of the act was contrary to a resolution by the House of Commons passed in 1729.[2]

In representing the bill for disallowance the Board of Trade followed the line of argument of Paris, making clear, among other objections, that by experience the issuing of bills of credit for loan had had very pernicious effects by tempting persons in low and desperate circumstances to borrow beyond their

[1] *Ibid.*, p. 439.
[2] *Ibid.*, pp. 438-439.

ability; another objection was that upon the shoulders of these poor people consequently fell the burden of public taxation while the more wealthy "do not contribute in any Degree to the Charges and Support of Government."[1]

Not to be discouraged, in 1753 a petition of the New Jersey House of Representatives was presented to His Majesty to permit the Governor to give his assent to a bill for making current £60,000 in bills of credit upon a like footing as those heretofore emitted within the Colony. After mature consideration the Board of Trade prepared a report which was embodied in a royal instruction. This instruction seemed to accomplish a number of desirable things in light of the very anarchic political conditions within the Colony to be described and the unwillingness of the popular chamber to support the efforts of the Governor to uphold the law and to reëstablish order. It first of all made clear that in light of the effect and operation of bills of credit formerly issued in the Province, a moderate quantity of these when based upon good security with a proper fund for redemption within a limited time might be of advantage in promoting trade and settlement and in offering the least burdensome method of levying money for the support of the government. No objection, therefore, would be raised to the emission of the above sum by the Assembly, provided that three conditions were satisfied. First, that the bills were not to be declared legal tender; second, that the interest arising from the loan of these should be definitely appropriated to

[1] *Acts of the Privy Council, Col.*, 1745-1766, pp. 27-28.

the services of government and should be issued by warrant from the Governor and Council only; third, that Governor Belcher should be instructed not to execute such an act as was contemplated in the bill until all of the older bills had been called in and destroyed.[1]

The New Jersey lower house, however, persisted in its demand for paper money in spite of the fact that the Board of Trade plan was far from acceptable to it. In 1755 the draft of a bill for printing £70,000 in bills of credit was presented to the Privy Council for approval, although "drawn contrary in every respect to his Majesty's aforementioned Instruction."[2] This was followed in 1757 by still another which was not any more acceptable to the Crown than the previous drafts, although it provided for the issuing of the sum of £79,000 in bills of credit for the use of His Majesty, or if not needed, for the relief of the Colony, and was accompanied by another calling for the printing of an additional sum of £60,000, to be loaned out, with a provision that the interest arising thereon should be used to sink the former issue.[3]

Meanwhile the Empire had become involved in war. The demand for immediate action was therefore so great, especially in the case of the exposed colonies, that at last the governors of the neighboring provinces of New York and Pennsylvania, who had also been forbidden by royal instructions, as has been noticed, to approve bills for the printing of paper money without the suspending clause, felt

[1] *Ibid.*, pp. 228-229.
[2] *Ibid.*
[3] *Ibid.*, p. 361.

under necessity to violate not only the same in permitting this to be done as an emergency measure, but also another instruction as to the length of time such paper should be current.[1] While the people of New Jersey were considered to be in no immediate danger, yet in the course of time an appeal was made to them as well as to the inhabitants of other colonies to support the war. In light of this altered situation the Privy Council at last decided to change the Governor's instructions in line with an alteration that had already been made in those of the Governor of New York. Therefore, when Francis Bernard in 1758 took Belcher's post, the twenty-second article of his instructions permitted him, in case of emergency in time of war, to assent to bills for the issuing of paper currency under the same conditions and regulations as were prescribed by the act of Parliament in 1750 for the New England colonies.[2]

In its essence the struggle just described over the legal-tender acts was between the creditor, English mercantile and New Jersey land proprietorial groups on the one hand, favoring deflation, and on the other, the debtor, quit-rent paying groups, supporting inflation. The British government, firmly committed to a policy of enforcing throughout the colonies a system of sound public finance, was therefore strongly arrayed against the latter. It, nevertheless, felt impelled as a war measure to make the desired concessions with respect to bills of credit, under the prescribed limitations.

Although in 1750 there were few people living

[1] *Op. cit.,* pp. 362-363.
[2] *Ibid.,* pp. 371-372.

within the borders of New Jersey, outside of Bergen County, who did not employ the English language—and in this respect the Colony was in marked contrast to its neighbors, New York and Pennsylvania—no great degree of provincial solidarity existed. The old historic political divisions of East New Jersey and West New Jersey were evidenced. In the former section of the Province to the south of the Dutch settlements on the Hudson were a number of transplanted New England towns such as Newark, Elizabethtown, Woodbridge, Middletown, and Shrewsbury, where the local institutions of New England had been reproduced with greater or less degree of fidelity, but where by the middle of the eighteenth century, doubtless as the result of the influence of such institutions as the "Log College" and Princeton, the Presbyterian Church had apparently become the dominant religious organization, rather than the Congregational Church.[1] Large numbers of Scots were also to be found in East New Jersey, living especially in Somerset, Middlesex, and Monmouth counties, where they had established their kirks.[2] In West New Jersey, on the other hand, the Quaker influence was the leading factor not only in the religious life but in governmental matters. On account of the existence of sectional jealousies the Province could boast of no single capital. The General Assembly met alternately at Perth Amboy on the Eastern Shore and at Burlington

[1] W. A. Whitehead, *East Jersey Under the Proprietary Government*, pp. 295-331; F. B. Lee, *New Jersey as a Colony and as a State*, I, 343-345; H. J. Ford, *The Scotch-Irish in America*, pp. 110-114, 413-436.

[2] See George E. Pryde, "The Scots in East New Jersey," New Jersey Hist. Soc. *Proceedings*, XV, 1-39.

on the Delaware. The influence of ideals maintained by both the Puritan and the Quaker groups had resulted in the development of a powerful spirit of individualism among the people. This spirit was heightened by the appearance, especially in northern New Jersey in the '40s, of large numbers of Ulstermen who brought with them from Ireland not only their Presbyterianism but also a certain attitude toward government typical of border peoples.

The history of New Jersey for the period under consideration illustrates how a people may live in the midst both of economic prosperity and political conditions that border on anarchy, with a government powerless to function in the direction of establishing even the semblance of law and order. The explanation of this lies in the temporary break-down of all authority when an effort was made to maintain a policy toward the land of the Province that was in harmony with legal rights as against widespread and determined opposition.

Although New Jersey since 1702 had been a royal province, it was peculiar with respect to the fact that all ungranted lands within its borders belonged, not to the Crown, but rather to those who were the proprietors or their heirs or assigns, either of East New Jersey or of West New Jersey, at the time of the transference of the government.[1] These two proprietary groups and their patentees became involved in the most serious difficulties. Lands from time to time had been surveyed, patented to others, and subsequently subdivided. Individual proprietors

[1] E. J. Fisher, *New Jersey as a Royal Province*, p. 171.

such as James Alexander and Robert Hunter Morris had also received important concessions. It was asserted by the antiproprietorial groups that the disposal of the land had been done in such a manner that it involved many irregularities and led to confusion in land titles and rights.[1]

As was suggested, Ulstermen were pouring into the vacant northern portion of the Province, many of them coming without invitation and settling down without invitation. Having once squatted on land it was a problem of the greatest difficulty to persuade them to leave. In resisting the claims of the proprietors they would frequently secure Indian deeds. The influence of the presence and example of these people upon those already living within the Province was indubitably profound, and the practice became general for families to squat upon any favorable body of land in defiance of the legal rights involved, and to resist efforts at removal.

The year 1745 saw the beginnings of a decade of violence as the result of efforts on the part of the Proprietors of East New Jersey[2] to survey and allot certain of their lands occupied by intruders in the "Van Gesin" and "Horseneck" purchases in upper Essex County not far distant from Newark. When one of the leaders among the occupiers was placed in the Newark jail to await trial he was rescued by his fellows who, after making a breach in the wall of the jail, most thoughtfully mended the same before

[1] Petition of the General Assembly of October 19, 1749, Board of Trade *Journal, 1749-1753*, p. 69.

[2] For an account of the activities of these proprietors, see D. McGregor, "The Board of Proprietors of East New Jersey," New Jersey Historical Society *Proceedings* (new series), VII, 177-195.

dispersing. A large part, if not most of the settled population of New Jersey, including the New England townships, were expected to pay rentals for their lands. These people expressed an intense sympathy with the squatters and other intruders openly resisting the proprietorial claims and apparently were encouraged by many of the local magistrates. In face of this situation, the arm of the law was paralyzed. The antiproprietorial elements were described in 1748 as "A Torrent bearing down all before them, Trampling on all law and authority."[1] According to certain depositions that were made in the year 1749, about one third of the people of Essex County were rioters and a much larger number were "favourers" of them, with most of the people of the county related either by blood or marriage to at least some one of the disaffected. As a consequence, it was utterly impossible to find a jury which could be depended upon to stand for impartial justice. Among these rioters themselves, three fifths, it was estimated, held their lands by patents and surveys under the proprietors, one fifth had squatted upon lands and later acquired Indian deeds, while the remaining fifth had no pretense whatsoever to any land and made a living by plundering the timber from the property of others.[2] All that was needed apparently to bring together a mob numbered by hundreds was the infor-

[1] "Journal of the Provincial Council, December 1, 1748, *New Jersey Archives* (first series), XVI, 15-19.

[2] Deposition of Daniel Pierson, Justice of the Peace, *ibid.*, XVI, 192-193. For an extended report of the quit-rent riots see *Acts of the Privy Council, Col., Unbound Papers*, pp. 274-275, 277-293, 310, 312, 315; see also B. W. Bond, *The Quit-Rent System*, pp. 105-108, and H. W. Osgood, *The American Colonies in the Eighteenth Century*, IV, 24-31.

mation spread among the resisters to proprietorial claims that one or more of their number were within the clutches of the law. Although none of them were imprisoned at Perth Amboy, on one occasion a great body of rioters, under the impression that some of their sympathizers were imprisoned, entered that seaport and, having broken open the jail, loosed all prisoners. Between 1745 and 1748 twenty riots are recorded, and many occurred subsequent to the latter date.

From Essex County in the east the uprising against the proprietors spread northward into Bergen, south to Middlesex and westward to Morris, Somerset, and Hunterdon counties, thus including, finally, all of the northern part of the Province. In Hunterdon County, the West Jersey Society, possessed also of patents in East New Jersey as well as in West New Jersey, had one tract of one hundred thousand acres under cultivation as a result of numerous assignments. In 1735 the tenants living upon this had numbered but one hundred, but by 1745 there were several times that number. Although previously these had been quiet and attentive to their obligations, they now joined with the Essex County rioters and refused not only the payment of rentals but any recognition of their landlords. In Morris County the lands belonging to the Penn family were brazenly stripped of the valuable timber in spite of everything that the Penn representatives could do, including appeals to the local authorities. Hardly less serious was the situation in the other counties just mentioned.

In the course of time the rioters to protect their interests finally organized themselves after a fashion,

took common oaths to uphold what they chose to
call their rights, and appointed committees which
were empowered to levy upon the members and to do
all of those things necessary to defeat the demands of
the Proprietors. At first they urged, as a defense of
their lawless acts, frauds and abuses committed by
the Proprietors or their patentees, whereby the same
lands had been sold to people two or three times, thus
imposing upon multitudes of innocent people.[1] The
proprietorial groups, however, denied the truth of
this and challenged their opponents to prove that
more than six people had been imposed upon since
the year 1665 by reason of any willful or inadvertent
duplication of grants and insisted that they had
always stood ready to grant compensation to those
who had received injury as the result of this. In the
midst of the struggle, it may be pointed out that an
appeal was made to the natural rights of man to
vindicate the claims of the squatters:

"No man," declared a correspondent to the *New
York Weekly Post-Boy*, in June, 1746, manifestly a
resident of New Jersey, "is naturally entitled to a
greater proportion of the earth than another; but
tho' it was made for the use of all, it may nevertheless
be appropriated by every individual. This is done
by the improvement of any part of it lying vacant,
which is thereby distinguished from the great common of Nature, and made the property of that man

---

[1] This argument was used particularly with respect to the
Elizabethtown Purchase and the Monmouth Purchase which
had been secured by settlers from Governor Nicolls before the
latter learned of James, Duke of York's deed of lease and release
to Berkeley and Carteret. See E. J. Fisher, *New Jersey as a Royal
Province*, pp. 171-209.

who bestowed his labour on it, from whom it cannot afterwards be taken without breaking thro' the Rules of Natural Justice; for thereby he could be actually deprived of the Fruits of his Industry."[1]

Later on in the course of the conflict, it is interesting to note that the claims of Connecticut to the northern portion of New Jersey were actually set up by the antiproprietorial group when a number of the rioters in Hunterdon County and their sympathizers signed a memorial to the government of the former Colony praying that they and their lands should be taken under its protection and that a Connecticut county be set up in those parts.[2] But Connecticut had on foot much more ambitious plans than meddling with a situation that offered small prospects of large gains. Her eyes were turned in the direction of northern Pennsylvania.

It was not until the year 1755, in the midst of war, that the resisters lost at least some confidence in their ability to make good their pretensions. In that year, with the coming of the British regulars to North America and the subsequent spreading abroad of a rumor that after these troops had finished with the French and Indians they would carry fire and sword into northern New Jersey and thus reduce the country to peace, numbers threw themselves upon the mercy of the court.[3] It may be added that the judges

[1] New Jersey Archives (first series), XII, 308-309.

[2] Ibid., XVI, 545-546, 552-556. It is of interest that Thomas Fitch, who in 1751 was Deputy Governor of Connecticut, had been the legal adviser of the Elizabethtown rioters. E. J. Fisher, New Jersey as a Royal Province, p. 184.

[3] For the use of British regulars to put down land rioters in Dutchess County, New York, in 1766 see C. E. Carter, Correspondence of General Thomas Gage, I, 96, 99, 107-108.

treated them with unexampled leniency, at most fining them but small sums of money while requiring them to furnish recognizances for their future good behavior. Others, feeling a greater confidence in their position, banded together to secure a favorable decision from the provincial court of chancery.

Added to the confusion within New Jersey was the controversy with New York over the boundary between the two provinces. While this was of long standing, it had now reached an acute stage which led to clashes between the settlers of the borderland, each setting forth claims based upon conflicting grants of land. A proper solution of this problem was a matter of the most vital importance to New Jersey, for to admit the claims of Lieutenant Governor de Lancey of New York meant the loss of much of her most valuable land. Under the terms of the grant made to Carteret and Berkeley in 1664, it was stated that the northern boundary should be as far as the "northernmost branch of the said Bay or River of Delaware, which is in forty-one degrees and forty minutes of latitude, crossing over thence in a straight line to Hudson's River to the forty-first." What did this mean? The New York government emphasized the word "Bay," seeking to ignore the stated latitude which would carry the line beyond Delaware Bay well up the course of the Delaware River; New Jersey stressed the specific latitude and explained away the previously mentioned term. While a somewhat informal understanding was reached in 1684 by Governor Dongan and Deputy Governor Lawrie, no definite formal solution of the problem was found. In 1719, as the result of an agreement between the two provinces, a line was run which, however, was not accepted by the Council of New York by reason of the opposition of the patentees of some of vast land grants in what was then considered to be parts of Ulster and Orange counties, New York. In vain the Proprietors of East New Jersey, and those who had received allotments from them for lands in this disputed region, sought a settlement of the matter. Apparently owing to the powerful influence exerted in London by the great New York land magnates, especially the de Lancey family concerned in the "great Minisink Patent"—the grant of which was so worded as to extend far into New Jersey—for many years nothing further was done. This policy of delay was followed in spite of the fact that the Proprietors of East New Jersey stood ready to assume half of the total cost of making a definite survey. At last, in the year 1748, the General Assembly of New Jersey passed a law providing for the running of the line *ex parte* in case New York would not agree to participate in running it. This was submitted for the sanction of the Crown and, after an extended hearing before the Board of Trade, failed to secure the royal approval.[1]

However, the situation of affairs now demanded imperatively an agreement. Hundreds of families were moving into the northwest part of New Jersey and settling upon lands in the very region subject to dispute. This movement brought dismay to those who had established themselves in these parts under the New York patents. Many New Yorkers, losing

[1] E. J. Fisher, *op. cit.*, pp. 210-235; *Acts of the Privy Council, Col., 1745-1766*, p. 214.

faith in the ability of their government to protect their interests, now turned to that of Connecticut, as did the Hunterdon County inhabitants of New Jersey. In 1751 a memorial in their behalf came before the General Assembly of that Colony asking for a grant "to Any or All the lands they now have ... that Lyeth to the westward of Hudson River."[1] One outcome of this was the organization of the so-called Delaware Company by Connecticut men to prosecute the westward claims of their Colony. While most of the activities of this company were concerned with lands to the westward of the Delaware River, nevertheless it may be mentioned here that late in 1754 an Indian deed was secured to a great body of land to the eastward of the Delaware, not, however, in Orange County, the boundaries of which were the center of dispute between New York and New Jersey, but to the northward in Ulster County just to the south of the great Hardenburgh Patent.[2] Little relief, therefore, was obtained by this interesting appeal to Connecticut.

As to the activities of the New Jersey people in the disputed region, it may be pointed out that to provide them with a local government, there was erected in 1753 out of the older County of Morris, the new County of Sussex, magistrates of which determined to defend the rights of New Jersey men against the hostile acts of the New York patentees. The following year witnessed a series of border disturbances in which the New Yorkers seem to have fared second best.

[1] This memorial and the report of the committee of the Assembly upon it are printed in *The Susquehannah Company Papers* (ed. J. P. Boyd), I, 3-5.
[2] *Ibid.*, I, 196-200.

It now became apparent that the issue must be settled without delay. In 1754 the New York Assembly passed an act which called upon the Privy Council to terminate the controversy. This, however, was disallowed. The reason assigned was that the procedure was contrary to constant practice since questions of disputed colonial boundaries had never been determined in the first instance by the Crown, as the bill called for, but by commission with, of course, the right of appeal reserved. The act was also obnoxious since it sought to determine, to an extent at least, the rights of certain of the New York patentees.[1] In place of this the Council recommended that a commission should be appointed, in line with the wishes of the East New Jersey Proprietors. However, it was not until the year 1764 that the Crown approved of acts of the two provincial legislatures making provision for this and moved to appoint a commission of fifteen eminent colonials.[2] The decision of this body was announced late in the year 1769 and was ratified by the agents of the two provinces under the provision that the rights of the occupiers of lands on either side of the line should be confirmed.[3] In the main the claims of New Jersey were vindicated.

[1] The Act of 1754 was entitled, "An Act for submitting the Controversy between the Colonys of New York and New Jersey ... to the final determination of His Majesty." *Acts of the Privy Council, Col., 1745-1766*, pp. 301-302.

[2] *Ibid.*, pp. 214, 301, 686-687.

[3] W. A. Whitehead, *Northern Boundary Line; The Circumstances Leading to the Establishment in 1769 of the Northern Boundary Line between New Jersey and New York;* E. J. Fisher, *New Jersey as a Royal Province*, pp. 210-239.

If anything beyond the disputes over lands and boundaries were needed to insure the existence of political chaos in New Jersey in the year 1750, this was supplied by the deadlock that existed between the executive and legislative branches of the provincial government. The truth is that underneath a cloak of formal courtesy that usually characterized the relations of the Governor and the Assembly, there had long been confirmed if latent hostility, which occasionally came to the surface in bitter denunciations and equally cutting retorts. Much of this friction was doubtless caused by an inherited attitude on the part of the people of New Jersey toward their executives. Previous to 1738, and after the surrender of the political authority by the proprietorial groups in 1702, the governor of New York had also been commissioned for New Jersey. Most of these itinerant executives were intensely unpopular. Consequently, there were repeated and insistent demands for a separate establishment with assurances at the time given to the home government by the General Assembly that the Colony would provide a liberal support for a resident governor. As a result, in 1738 Lewis Morris, native-born colonial with important interests within the Province as well as in New York, was so commissioned. It was doubtless hoped that this would be a happy choice. Morris possessed great political experience in the affairs of both New Jersey and New York. In the council of the former he had opposed the notorious Lord Cornbury and, as the Chief Justice in the latter, had taken a popular stand in the struggle against Governor Cosby. Morris, however, was distinctly an aristocrat with great land interests and confirmed in what might be called the official point of view with reference to all public issues. He was extremely skeptical also of the moral and intellectual capacity of the people among whom he was living to participate in public affairs, although he had no doubts as to the determination of their representatives to control the provincial government. The year after taking over the administration he felt impelled to declare that there was "much Insincerity and Ignorance among the people ... with so rooted a jealousy of their Governors and ... an Inclination in the meanest of the people (who are the majority and whose votes make the Assembly) to have the sole direction of all the affairs of government."[1]

The first and only outburst of popularity that Morris enjoyed died away when he indicated his disappointment that the Assembly had provided for his support but one half the amount that he had every reason to anticipate. Before the close of his administration, which ended with his death in 1746, his relations with the House of Representatives had become so strained, especially over questions of the Governor's salary and of the printing of the additional bills of credit for loans previously considered, that that body finally refused to appropriate money for his office and even denied, upon his widow's subsequent application for the receipt of the back salary due, that New Jersey was under the slightest obligations to his estate.[2]

[1] Governor Morris to Sir Charles Wagner, May 10, 1739, *Papers of Governor Lewis Morris*, pp. 40-41.
[2] For the House's defense of its conduct see the *New Jersey Archives* (first series), XVI, 149-156.

As for Governor Jonathan Belcher, who succeeded Morris,[1] he sought to avoid the difficulties faced by the latter and to win the confidence and favor of the popular branch of the legislature, by his nominations to the Council, by his attitude toward money bills, and otherwise. His position was, however, one of great delicacy.[2] In the midst of the land riots he was impelled to apply to the Assembly for funds necessary to enlist soldiers who, at least, he felt, could be counted upon to guard the jails from the attacks of the mobs. The House of Representatives while outwardly condemning the violent conduct of the squatters and other disturbers of the peace, nevertheless, could not be persuaded to make any appropriation except upon a basis which the upper chamber, dominated by the proprietorial interests, considered was in plain violation of the royal instructions to the Governor respecting the taxation of the unprofitable lands of the Province. Belcher, although willing to run the risk in this emergency of approving the bill of the representatives, was helpless during this period. In fact, the Council had grasped the whip end and, supported by the general attitude of the home government toward New Jersey affairs, exercised an unprecedented influence for some years in the affairs of the Province. As a result of this deadlock the provincial treasury was destined to remain empty for years, with the provincial authority held up to mockery.

In the course of this struggle, Governor Belcher was accused of seeking to win favor with the antiproprietorial group by the recommendation of Wil-

[1] John Hamilton and John Reading were each in charge, as of the council, before Belcher appears.

[2] H. L. Osgood, *American Colonies in the Eighteenth Century*, IV, 31-32.

liam Morris of Hunterdon County to a seat in the provincial council, who, according to Robert Hunter Morris, testifying before the Board of Trade in 1750, was not only identified with the rioters but on several occasions had spoken publicly in their favor and was also connected with a group in the General Assembly that had "endeavored to pull down or trample upon the authority of the Crown."[1] Later he recommended Samuel Smith, Clerk of the House of Representatives, for another place on the Council. The latter also was accused before the Board of being sympathetic with the resisters and it was further charged that his "family were the most active persons in that faction."[2] As a result, the Lords Commissioners ordered the drafting of a letter reprimanding Belcher for nominating persons of that type for such responsible posts. Further, taking the advice of Morris, who was not only Chief Justice of the Supreme Court of the Province but perhaps Belcher's most vigorous opponent on the Council, they proceeded in 1751 to recommend that mandamuses be granted to David Ogden and to Lewis Morris Ashfield, grandson of the late governor, both of whom were agreeable to the great proprietorial interests.[3] All this was in the nature of a rebuke to the Governor who, in spite of his extreme reluctance to seat Ashfield, was, after a delay of some two years, compelled to do so.[4]

Such were the Jersies of the plowmen in the middle of the eighteenth century.

[1] *New Jersey Archives* (first series), XVI, 91 and 357; Board of Trade *Journal, 1749-1753*, p. 153.

[2] *Ibid.*, p. 174. *New Jersey Archives* (first series), XVI, 314.

[3] *Acts of the Privy Council, Col., 1745-1766*, p. 791.

[4] *New Jersey Archives* (first series), XVI, 315-317, 324-327, 346, 365, 385, 402.

CHAPTER VII

THE NEW WORLD PARADISE OF THE SECTS

THE LAST of the continental plantations to come under consideration in this present study is the proprietary colony of Pennsylvania, truly at this period the New World paradise of Europe's persecuted sects. "Coming to speak of Pennsylvania," declared Gottlieb Mittelberger, in describing his journey to the Province in the year 1750, "that colony possesses great liberties above all other English colonies, inasmuch as all religious sects are tolerated there. We find there Lutherans, Reformed, Catholics, Quakers, Mennonites or Anabaptists, Herrnhuter or Moravian Brethren, Pietists, Seventh Day Baptists, Dunkers, Presbyterians, Newborn, Freemasons, Separatists, Freethinkers, Jews, Mohammedans, Pagans, Negroes and Indians. The Evangelicals and Reformed, however, are in the majority. But there are many hundred unbaptized souls there that do not even wish to be baptized."[1] He then, however, proceeded to describe the trials of a preacher of the gospel in this land of liberty. Most preachers, he affirmed, were hired by the year like the cowherds in Germany, and the most exemplary were often "reviled, insulted, and scoffed at like the Jews by the young and old, especially in the country.... I would, therefore," he affirmed, "rather perform the meanest herdsman's

[1] See his *Journey to Pennsylvania in the year 1750* (translated by Carl T. Eben), p. 54.

162

THE NEW WORLD PARADISE OF THE SECTS

duties in Germany than be a preacher in Pennsylvania. Such unheard-of rudeness and wickedness
spring from the excessive liberties of the land, and
from the blind zeal of the many sects. . . . There is a
saying in that country: Pennsylvania is the heaven of
the farmers, the paradise of the mechanics, and the
hell of the officials and preachers."[1]

Out of a population estimated at between two and
three hundred thousand[2] it was asserted in 1755 that
one half were Germans and that of the remainder
some two fifths were Ulster Presbyterians, two fifths
were Quakers, and the rest were members of the
Anglican Church with some few Baptists.[3] These
figures are remarkable as indicative of the numerical
but not the political submergence of the Quaker
group, which as late as 1721 still constituted, it was
estimated, three fourths of the entire population.[4]

The inundation of German-speaking peoples which

[1] *Ibid.*, p. 63.
Mittelberger further illustrates the freedom in religious matters that existed at this period in Pennsylvania. "I was well
acquainted with an old German neighbor, who had been a
Lutheran, but had re-baptized himself in a running water; some
time afterwards he circumcised himself and believed only in the
Old Testament; finally, however, shortly before his death, he
baptized himself again by sprinkling water upon his head."
Ibid., p. 110.
[2] It was given as upwards of three hundred thousand in 1755
by Governor Morris in a letter to General Braddock. *Pennsylvania
Archives* (fourth series), II, 372. This figure seems too high.
See C. A. Herrick, *White Servitude in Pennsylvania* (pp. 179-
180), for various estimates; also Greene and Harrington, *American Population before . . . 1790*, p. 115.
[3] William Smith, D.D. *A Brief State of the Province of
Pennsylvania* (1755), p. 10 (Sabine *Reprints*); W. J. Mann,
Life of Muhlenberg, p. 377.
[4] Representation of the Board of Trade upon the State of His
Majesty's Plantations, Sept. 8, 1721. Shelburne Papers, 45: 236.

had its beginning toward the end of the seventeenth century, when the modest stream of immigration widened gradually into a flood, is one of the most notable aspects of American colonial history.[1] While this flood spread itself rather widely it had its greatest effects upon the civilization of provincial Pennsylvania and was at its height in the period under consideration. "Last week arrived here Captain Haveland from Holland," wrote a Philadelphia correspondent to an English paper in 1750, "the fourteenth ship ... from Holland this year, on board of which [ships] have been brought 4,317 Germans."[2] Indeed it would appear that an average of something over eighteen ships came loaded each autumn to the Port of Philadelphia with these precious cargoes.[3] It is asserted that from 1750 to 1754, for a period, that is, of some four years, at least twenty-five thousand Germans were brought to the Province, while numbers went directly to other plantations, especially to

[1] In this connection see a recent important publication, S. B. Strassburger and W. J. Hinke, *Pennsylvania German Pioneers* (Pennsylvania German Society *Proceedings*, Vols. XLII-XLIV), giving the original lists of arrivals in the port of Philadelphia from 1727 to 1808; also consult L. F. Bittinger, *The Germans in Colonial Times*; A. B. Faust, *The German Element in the United States*; F. R. Diffenderfer, *The German Immigration into Pennsylvania*; "Pennsylvania, the German influence in the Settlement and Development" in the Pennsylvania German Society *Proceedings*, VII-XVII; J. F. Sachse, *The German Sectarians of Pennsylvania, 1708-1747.*

[2] Gottlieb Mittelberger, *Journey to Philadelphia*, p. 37; Frank R. Diffenderfer, *German Immigration into Pennsylvania through the Port of Philadelphia 1700-1775. Part II: The Redemptioners*, pp. 45, 209.

[3] R. B. Strassberger and W. J. Hinke, *Pennsylvania German Pioneers*, I, xxix. From 1727 to 1755, two hundred and thirty-four of these ships came. *Ibid.*, I, xlvii-lii.

Maryland, the Carolinas, and Nova Scotia.[1] In view of the indescribable hardships sustained by many of these newcomers in attempting to get a footing in the New World, reports of which did not fail to reach Germany, one is impressed with the deep-lying dissatisfaction with conditions at home that led so many, in spite of some knowledge at least of the hazards involved, to risk family, freedom, and even life itself for the prospect of expatriation and existence under new conditions.[2]

In the case of the *Unitas Fratrum or* Moravian Brethren who in the early '40s established the town of Bethlehem, numerous edicts had, it appears, been launched against them by various authorities in Europe, among them the King of Prussia, the Tzarina of Russia, the King of Denmark, the Duke of Gotha, and the city of Basel in Switzerland.[3] Even the Elector of Hanover, who was incidentally the King of England, issued a proclamation against them which declared, among other things, "We therefore Order that all Herrenhutter Books which are already Known as their Hymn Book and the Sermons of the Count Zintzendorff, and all other that for the future may be printed, shall not be tolerated in our Dominions." The people were warned not only to give up their books but also to bear in mind that the Ordinance of 1734 permitting private devotions did not give permission to meet with such people as were the Mora-

[1] Diffenderfer, *op. cit.*, II, 209; W. J. Mann, *Life of Muhlenberg*, p. 377; Strassberger and Hinke, *op. cit.*, I, 1-676 for lists for the years 1727-1754.

[2] For a brief discussion of conditions that led to German emigration see Lucy F. Bittinger, *The Germans in Colonial Times*.

[3] See the *Pennsylvania Journal* for December 20, 1750.

vians.[1] However, while not tolerated by George, acting as Elector of Hanover, this kindly people with pacifistic principles were received with open arms by the same George, in his rôle of King of England. Parliament, in fact, passed a special act at this period which guaranteed the Moravians an asylum,[2] with the result that many of them joyfully seized the opportunity and in coming to America became not only loyal but valuable subjects whose influence with the Indians was as great as it was wholesome. In sailing to America in ships chartered for the purpose, they came with a full knowledge of conditions and with the way prepared for them by their leaders, and therefore suffered little hardship.[3]

On the other hand, many thousands of distressed Germans, quite ignorant of all the hazards, were lured by agents of the Dutch "man-stealers," known as Newlanders, to depart from their homes without adequate provision for establishing themselves independently. The music master Mittelberger, to whom reference has already been made, declared that, when in 1754 he was about to return to Württemberg from Pennsylvania, "many Wurtembergers, Durlachers and Palatines, of whom there are a great number there who repent and regret it while they live that they left their native country, implored me with tears and uplifted hands, and even in the name of God, to make this misery and sorrow known in Germany, so

---

[1] *Loc. cit.*

[2] For the history of the act of 1749, see J. T. Hamilton, *A History of the Moravian Church*, pp. 135-137.

[3] *Transactions of the Moravian Historical Society*, I, 33-51, 107-125.

that not only the common people, but even princes and lords might learn how they fared. ... "

It is hard to realize today how great an effort it was to make the trip from the region of the upper Rhine, where many of those prospective emigrants were living, to the port of Philadelphia. The weary, heartbreaking journey frequently if not generally lasted from about the first of May to the end of October. From Heilbronn to Rotterdam the Rhine boats were obliged to take from four to six weeks, on account of the existence in the middle of the eighteenth century of thirty-six custom-houses between those two towns at each of which the ships were examined; in Holland there was a month's or six weeks' delay; then from Holland to England, if the winds were contrary, another month was consumed. In addition, there might be two weeks spent at some port of the latter country, generally at the Isle of Wight, before the ship was examined and the customs duties paid, when the long voyage, lasting from six to twelve weeks, began. Under modern conditions the trip, in spite of its length, made as it was in the summer, might be far from unpleasant; but on the emigrant ship grim tragedy lurked. On a two-hundred-ton vessel there might be four hundred passengers together with a heavy cargo of household goods and farm implements.[1] Each individual received a place scarce two feet wide and six feet long for sleeping quarters. There was an absence of privacy. The drinking water was black, thick, and likely

---

[1] The average number of passengers on a ship of two-hundred-tons' burden was, according to Diffenderfer, almost three hundred. *German Immigration into Pennsylvania*, p. 51. Not until

to be full of worms; the ship biscuits were frequently rotten and alive with creatures; there were indescribable stenches with scurvy and other loathsome diseases, accompanied with starvation, thirst, and scenes of death. Few women in confinement, it was asserted, escaped with their lives. The crews did not always wait for death. "One day, just as we had a heavy gale," Mittelberger recorded sadly, "a woman in our ship who was to give birth and could not, under the circumstances, was pushed through a loop-hole [port hole] in the ship and dropped into the sea, because she was far in the rear of the ship, and could not be brought forward!" He further declared, "Children from one to seven years rarely survive the voyage; . . . I witnessed such misery in no less than thirty-two children in our ship, all of whom were thrown into the sea."[1] Only too frequently the despair of the disillusioned people caught in these man-traps beggars description.[2]

The sight of land raised in the hearts of the survivors great joy, accompanied by prayer and singing. But alas! In most cases the private funds of these Germans were too limited to pay the passage, which for adults varied from six to ten pounds and for chil-

the year 1750 did the Pennsylvania Assembly act to limit the number of people that could be crowded into an immigrant ship. *Statutes at Large*, IV, 382-388; C. A. Herrick, *White Servitude in Pennsylvania*, pp. 161-162. The act was highly commended by the Board of Trade. *Acts of the Privy Council, Col., 1745-1766*, pp. 115-116.

[1] Mittelberger, *Journey to Pennsylvania*, pp. 22-23.

[2] For an account of the sufferings of the passengers on board the *Love and Unity* which brought Palatines to Philadelphia in 1731 see F. R. Diffenderfer, *German Immigration into Pennsylvania*, pp. 62-63.

dren was half of that fare.[1] As a result, they were obliged to agree to the sale of their labor by the ship captain to those who would pay these fares and other expenses incurred during the voyage, which meant that they were bound out to service for periods of from two to seven years, if over fifteen years of age, and if from five to fifteen years of age, till they were twenty-one years old. Consequently, many parents were compelled to "sell and trade away their children like so many head of cattle."[2] To the ship, until as a rule the cargo was disposed of, came prosperous, land-owning Englishmen, Dutchmen, and Germans, many from a great distance, to purchase their labor, which they secured at prices ranging from £10 to £14 for an adult. However, on occasions those not thus disposed of were led about the country until a purchaser could be found. "It often happens," declared a witness, "that whole families, husband, wife and children are separated by being sold to different purchasers, especially when they have not paid any part of their passage money."[3] And, should a husband or wife die at sea when the ship had made more than half the voyage, the survivor was obliged to serve for the deceased as well as for himself or herself.

The character of the service to which these redemptioners were bound depended upon the inclinations of the master and his occupation. As most of the people of means had estates and as much of the land was still wild in native forest,[4] the need of laborers

---

[1] C. H. Herrick, *White Servitude in Pennsylvania*, p. 186.

[2] *Ibid.*, pp. 176-177; Peter Kalm, *Travels into North America*; Gottlieb Mittelberger *Journey to Pennsylvania*, p. 28.

[3] *Ibid.*, p. 28.

[4] "This Country is all a Wood, where not artificially cleared,

was very great for clearing this of trees, or if it had been cut over, of the stumps of the oak and other hardwoods, brush, and rocks. Therefore, most of the bondsmen were purchased to perform this arduous labor and were occasionally forced to work side by side with negro slaves, who were fairly numerous within the Province. Should they attempt to escape by running away, upon being returned, the penalty for each day's absence, according to Mittelberger, was an additional week, for each week, a month, and for a month, half a year.[1] It is perhaps surprising that there were many among these German immigrants who, according to Peter Kalm, had the means to pay their passage but who voluntarily entered into the indentures for the purpose of having, when once they had gained their freedom, not only knowledge of the methods of land cultivation peculiar to the New World, but funds for the purchase of a farm upon which they thereupon settled and prospered. It may be added that as the lands in the region of the lower Delaware were by the middle of the eighteenth century mostly in private hands and held at a high price, those wanting to secure good but cheap allotments were obliged to look westward and northward. As a rule, therefore, the German redemptioners left the region where they had labored as bondsmen to acquire

but the Timber will not answer the expense of bringing many miles to Philadelphia. . . . " Lewis Evans, "A Brief Account of Pennsylvania . . . 1753" (Historical Society of Pennsylvania).

[1] Gottlieb Mittelberger, *Journey to Pennsylvania*, p. 29. The law provided that there could be exacted five days' labor for each day the servant was absent without permission. *Penna. Statutes at Large*, II, 54-56. For an extended treatment of this see C. A. Herrick, *White Servitude in Pennsylvania*, Chapter XI.

homes along the frontier.[1] In this region, as the result of their industry and economical methods and the fruitfulness of the lands, they generally prospered.[2]

From the figures that have been previously given, it is obvious that the farmers of Pennsylvania in the middle of the eighteenth century looked to German immigration for the principal supply of indentured labor. In contrast to this, during the first quarter of the century, reliance was placed chiefly upon the arrival of sufficient numbers of British and especially Irish servants. In 1729 out of some 6,208 immigrants only 243 apparently were Palatines while 276 were English and Welsh, 43 were native Scots and the remainder Ulstermen.[3] By 1750 the relative impor-

---

[1] Lewis Evans wrote in 1753: "In Pennsylvania the Land is too dear to be engrossed and yet cheap enough to anybody that will improve it. Our Surveys have been very regular almost all adjoining one another. This keeps up good Neighbourhood, and husbands the Proprietaries' Interest. The people there are thick settled, have easy intercourse, and need not want Mills, Schools, or Churches." Op. cit.

[2] Lewis Evans in referring to the spread of settlements into the interior declares that "The Œconomy of the Germans has since taught us the method of bringing their produce to Market, from the remotest part at a small expense. The Method is this, ev'ry Farmer in our province almost, has a Waggon of his own, in the Service of his Plantation, and likewise horses for Tillage; in the Spring or Fall of the year (when it is here a Vacation from farming), They load their Waggon and furnish themselves and beasts, and provender for the Journey. The Waggon is their Bed, their Inn, their Everything. Many will come one hundred and fifty miles without spending a shilling. It is pretty to behold our back Settlements, where the farms are large as pallaces, while the Owners live in log hutts; a sign tho of thriving Farmers." Ibid.

[3] Writers in the eighteenth century did not distinguish between the native Irish and the Ulstermen. The latter contributed most of the emigrants from Ireland during this period. See Volume I of this study, especially pp. 257-262.

tance of the supply from Ireland and Great Britain had declined so that out of some 5,317 immigrants who arrived in that year but one thousand came from the British Isles while 4,317 were from Germany.[1] It would appear that the Ulstermen were not so highly esteemed as servants for they were combative and not overindustrious and it is certain that they were much more inclined to run away from their masters than were the Germans.[2] However, whatever may have been their defects as servants, they were hardy, adventurous men who courted the vicissitudes and dangers of the western Pennsylvania frontier. In the course of the eighteenth century they succeeded in establishing some one hundred and thirty communities within the Province and Lower Counties on the Delaware. In the process of this very significant colonization movement they boldly seized and squatted on lands, asserting that it was "against the laws of God and of nature that so much land should remain idle while so many Christians wanted it to labor on," defied those who attempted to eject them, and doggedly resisted the payment of quit-rents.[3] As a people they demanded aggressive action against hostile Indians and were bitterly opposed to the pacifistic policies of the Quakers and other noncombatant sects.

[1] William Douglass, *British Settlements in North America,* II, 326; C. A. Herrick, *White Servitude in Pennsylvania,* pp. 165-166.

[2] *Ibid.,* pp. 166-167.

[3] For a discussion of this, as it relates to western Pennsylvania, see "Squatters and Titles to Land in early Western Pennsylvania," in the *Western Penna. Hist. Mag.,* VI, 165-176; also W. R. Shepherd, *History of Proprietary Government in Pennsylvania,* pp. 48-53, 111-112, 547; C. H. Lincoln, *The Revolutionary Movement in Pennsylvania,* p. 33.

If by means of a map one were to illustrate the location of the various racial and religious groups within Pennsylvania in the year 1756 it could be shown that with respect to the three old counties of Philadelphia, Chester, and Bucks, the first was inhabited largely by Quakers; they also played the leading rôle in the two latter where, however, Ulster Presbyterians, Welsh Baptists, and Presbyterians were to be found in considerable numbers, with a sprinkling of Germans. To the west and north of the old counties were the five newer counties of Berks, Lancaster, York, Cumberland, and Northampton.[1] As to Berks, it was the fourth county where the Quakers were ordinarily in control but where Germans, divided into several religious groups, were massed; in both Lancaster and York, while the Germans were predominant, mixed with them were numerous Ulstermen; Cumberland was settled almost entirely by the latter; on the other hand Northampton was a mixture of German, English, and Ulstermen.[2] The Anglicans, constituting less than one tenth of the total population, were numerous and influential in the three old counties, especially in the City of Philadelphia and in Berks County. Thus, the tier of Delaware River counties was inhabited largely by people of British

[1] Lancaster County was taken out of Chester in 1729; York County out of Lancaster in 1749; Cumberland County out of Lancaster in 1750; Berks County out of parts of Philadelphia, Chester, and Lancaster counties in 1752; Northampton County out of the unsettled portions of Bucks County also in 1752. *Penna. Statutes at Large*, IV, 131-134; V, 70-77, 87-94, 133, 140, 141-146.

[2] See a report prepared October 14, 1756 analyzing the returns to the Pennsylvania Assembly and the constituent elements of the counties, Pennsylvania Historical Society.

ancestry. There the Quakers and Anglicans were busy contending for political supremacy. To the west of this region up to the Susquehanna was planted the great body of the German people, interspersed with the Ulster Scots, while the latter were also living in scattered communities along the extreme western frontier.

The very numerical preponderance of the German element might well have placed political control in its hands without the coöperation of any other group; yet a very large proportion of these people who had entered Pennsylvania previous to 1750 probably had not as yet submitted to naturalization.[1] Only slowly, indeed, did the race become politically conscious. Nevertheless, the laws of the Province encouraged the change in nationality, as illustrated by the act of the year 1742 that gave to foreign Protestants with religious objections to oaths the right to affirm, a right already enjoyed by the Quakers.[2] Consequently, with the growing realization of the value of participation in government, the Germans increasingly availed themselves of the opportunity of becoming British subjects, especially those living in the more settled part of the Province. This is evidenced by the reports on naturalization sent to the Board of Trade from time to time.[3] As a result of this tendency, by the

[1] An act passed in the thirteenth year of the reign of George II provided for naturalization of those foreign Protestants who had resided seven years or more in any of the American colonies and who would take the prescribed oaths and make a required declaration. Ruffhead, *English Statutes at Large*, IX, 384.

[2] *Pennsylvania Statutes at Large*, IV, 391-394.

[3] For lists of those naturalized from the year 1743 to 1753 see C.O. 1271: 28, 47, 48, 57; 1273: 90-92, 93-95, 98-100, 119-120.

middle of the century the German-speaking electo-
rate was fast becoming a powerful and active element
in political life. It was with this group that the
Quakers, now in a minority, were allied in their opposition to the participation of Pennsylvania in warlike
activities, an alliance perfectly understandable in view
of the principles of public policy espoused by the
Mennonites, Dunkards, and Moravians and the powerful influence exerted by Christoph Saur, who at
this period was editor of the *Pennsylvanische Berichte,*
a newspaper, which with some changes in title, was in
existence from 1739 to 1777.[1] Saur, bitterly opposed
to the proprietorial interests, moulded the opinions of
many who were not of these pacifistic sects. At the
approach of war between the English and the French,
he warned his fellow Germans that there was a design
to enslave them, that a military service law was
planned, and that all the miseries they had suffered in
Germany with heavy aggravations, would be their
lot.[2] This warning did not fail of its effect for most
of these people were peaceably inclined.

In fact, the atmosphere of the Province was, in the
main, one of good will toward all men. In view of
the circumstance that numerous religious and racial
groups existed side by side there was remarkably little
friction, all of which appealed to those who had left
their ancestral abodes because of intolerance, persecution, and the existence of military despotism.[3] "To

[1] The elder Saur died in 1758, and his son with the same
name took his place as editor. J. O. Knauss, *Social Conditions
Among the Pennsylvania Germans,* pp. 3-6.
[2] William Smith, *A Brief State of Pennsylvania,* p. 39. J. O.
Knauss, *op. cit.,* pp. 38-39.
[3] Saur reported a conversation in which a native of Württem-

speak the truth, one seldom hears or sees a quarrel among them," declared Mittelberger in describing the people of Pennsylvania, "even strangers trust each other more than acquaintances in Europe. People are far more sincere and generous than in Germany; therefore, our Americans live more quietly and peacefully together than the Europeans, and all this is the result of the liberty which they enjoy and which makes them all equal."[1]

The Quakers had laid the foundations of this spirit of good will by their treatment of the Indians. Germans such as Mittelberger, coming from the oppressions of the Old World, attributed this humanity to liberty and to lack of compulsion in measures involving hostile relations of peoples. It is therefore not surprising that there was a strong inclination on the part of all those Germans not exposed to the actualities of frontier warfare to rally to the support of the Quaker political principles and to vote for Quaker candidates to the provincial assembly. For as yet there was little demand on the part of this group for the responsibilities of office. Indeed, so decisive was the aid that these newcomers were able to bring to the Friends that Dr. William Smith, a political opponent, elected Provost of the College of Philadelphia in 1755,[2] declared in that year in an open letter to a friend in England that the only remedy for the

berg, on being asked why so many Germans risked the long and dangerous voyage, replied that they had scarcely been able to live in Germany due to governmental oppression. Although Prussia welcomed them, he declared, there they would be slaves and vassals. *Pennsylvanische Berichte*, December, 1754. Quoted by Knauss, *op. cit.*, pp. 141-142.

[1] *Journey to Pennsylvania*, p. 113.

[2] Chartered as "The College, Academy, and Charitable School of Philadelphia," in 1755.

evils of the situation facing the commonwealth—then in the midst of war with French Indians harrying the frontiers—was the suspension of the right of voting for members of the Assembly by naturalized Germans. The latter he described as "A Body of ignorant, proud, stubborn clowns (who are unacquainted with our Language, our Manners, our Laws, and our Interests) indulged with the Privilege of Returning almost every Member of the Assembly."[1]

It may be pointed out in this connection that the three old counties returned eight members each to the Assembly; the City of Philadelphia two members, making twenty-six out of a total of thirty-six members with Lancaster returning four, York and Cumberland two each, and Northampton and Berks one each.[2] As late as 1756, there were sixteen Quakers in the Assembly, eleven Anglicans, six Ulster Presby-

[1] William Smith, *A Brief State of Pennsylvania*, p. 40.
[2] For purposes of the annual election of members of the General Assembly, each county was divided into eight election districts, each of the latter consisting of a number of townships. Each township in September by vote of the freeholders nominated one person as the district inspector for the election, who was thereupon chosen by lot at the county seat from these district nominees. These eight inspectors received by written ballot "rolled up" the votes of all freeholders possessing either at least fifty acres, "well situated," twelve of which were in cultivation, or fifty pounds current money, who had been residing within the Province for two years. If the circumstance of the voter were known to the inspector, the ballot was without question deposited in a box; otherwise, he was obliged to swear or affirm as to his qualifications. Clerks were present to record the names of voters. With the close of the election, the votes were tabulated by the judges and inspectors and the names of those elected proclaimed from the courthouse door. Assemblymen received five shillings a day from the provincial treasury during the session with mileage from and to their places of residence. Lewis Evans, "A Brief Account of Pennsylvania . . . 1753."

terians, one Lutheran, one Moravian, and one Baptist. This may be taken as a typical display of strength on the part of the various groups under the circumstances of the Quaker-German combination. However, as the four Quakers elected for Bucks and Chester counties resigned in that year out of loyalty to the principles of their society in face of threats from the Mother Country to require all in the service of the Province to take the usual oaths rather than affirmations, the strength of the Anglicans was thereupon increased to fourteen and the Ulstermen to seven. At last a Quaker control that had been really continuous from the beginning of the life of the Colony gave way, at least temporarily, to the militant policies of the latter groups.[1]

Granted the fact of this dominating position of the Quakers in the Pennsylvania Assembly down to 1756 and their influence in the shaping of public policy, it may be of interest at this point to raise the question: How far was the public law of the Province an embodiment of the peculiar conceptions of this sect? For here alone in the New World was Quakerism able to develop a sufficient control of legislative processes to give sustained direction to its ideals.[2]

When William Penn took over the lands embraced within the Province, the Swedish and Dutch settlers were living under the protection of the so-called Duke of York laws adopted in 1664 at Hempstead on Long

[1] Report of October 14, 1756 on the Pennsylvania Assembly Hist. Soc. Penna.

[2] It is, of course, true that both in West New Jersey and later in East New Jersey the Quaker influence was felt and that in the former the Friends were numerically and politically the dominant group down to the middle of the eighteenth century.

Island and extended in 1676 to this district. These laws, based largely upon the New England codes, especially those of Massachusetts Bay and of the former Colony of New Haven, reflected the Puritan conceptions of statecraft. Among the capital laws, that is, laws entailing the death penalty, were: the law against the denial of the true God, that against false witnessing, another directed against any child over sixteen years of age guilty of smiting a parent unless under proper provocation, as well as others against unnatural sexual acts, kidnapping, the slaying of a defenseless man with a sword, and the killing of a man while lying in wait. This code provided also for such penalties as branding on the forehead, the boring of the tongue with a red-hot iron, whipping, and other, milder punishments.[1] All this was swept away, at least so far as Pennsylvania was concerned, when on December 10, 1682 at a popular assembly held at Upland, Penn secured the ratification of a body of laws which he and those assisting him had drawn up in England the preceding May. This Great Law, as the code was designated by contemporaries and by subsequent lawmakers, became the basis of the later provincial law. It fully reflected the spirit of humanity and toleration of the Friends and their horror of bloodshed. One crime alone, that of murder, was punishable with death;[2] mutilation quite disappeared; on the other hand such comparatively mild penalties as the forfeiture of goods, the wearing of a badge of

[1] See the writer's "The Criminal Codes of Pennsylvania," *Journal of the American Institute of Criminal Law*, VI, 323-325; also his "Crime and its Punishment in Provincial Pennsylvania," *Pennsylvania History*, II, 3-4.

[2] Under the charter treason also carried the death penalty.

shame, and gagging were introduced. Like many another great soul, Penn must have been convinced that men would react in harmony with their environment and that if the social order to be created by his Holy Experiment dealt with the individual in mercy and kindness, these qualities would be reflected in the acts of the latter. But, as the years passed, he became very much alarmed over reports of confusion and lawlessness that reached him from the Province, which was described in 1698 as "the greatest refuge and shelter for pirates and rogues in America."[1] As a result, he journeyed again to his proprietary where in 1701 the Great Law was profoundly modified by a code drawn up under his direction and which was ratified at New Castle. Mutilations, branding and whipping once again stand out prominently among other sanctions.[2] This code, when submitted to the Privy Council, was criticized for embodying unusual penalties, with the result that out of a total of one hundred and four acts fifty-three were disallowed.[3] Although many of the laws thus annulled were repassed in 1705 with the objectionable features eliminated, there seems to have been a growing conviction that the comparative mildness of the New Castle code had as a chief effect the attracting of men of lawless tendencies into the Province where, without serious risk to life and limb, they committed many enormi-

[1] *The Colonial Records of Pennsylvania*, I, 519.
[2] See the *Pennsylvania Statutes at Large*, II, 1-140. In this code castration was provided for in the case of certain acts violating the moral order of nature.
[3] For a discussion of the royal disallowance of Pennsylvania laws see W. T. Root, *The Relations of Pennsylvania with the British Government*, Chapter V.

ties. Consequently, in 1718 the General Assembly passed "An Act for the Advancement of Justice and More Certain Administration Thereof," in which it was stated that the unhappy situation confronting the people was due to the fact that the statutes of Parliament did not extend to Pennsylvania. To remedy this difficulty it was thereby expressly declared that certain offenses such as arson, burglary, mayhem, petit treason, and misprision of treason were felonies of death punishable according to the laws of Great Britain.[1] As a result, the number of offenses involving the death penalty now mounted to twelve, while five offenses made those guilty liable to branding on the forehead.[2] Finally, an act passed in 1722 declared that anyone convicted of counterfeiting the money of the Province should be placed upon the pillory, have both ears cut off, be whipped thirty-one lashes and, in default of the payment of damages that his acts might have caused, should be sold into servitude for seven years.[3] One may assert that the Pennsylvania criminal law after 1722 down to the outbreak of the American Revolution was one of the harshest bodies of law in North America. In spite of this fact, it may be further stated that there was a steady growth in the number of crimes of a serious nature. Nor were the severe measures allowed to remain mere threats on the statute books of the Province.[4] The Quakers, indeed, confronted by a situation

---

[1] *Pennsylvania Statutes at Large*, III, 199.

[2] These offenses were adultery, burglary, house-breaking, rape, and robbery.

[3] *Ibid.*, III, 331.

[4] See the author's "Crime and its Punishment in Provincial Pennsylvania," *Pennsylvania History*, II, 10-16.

not of their own creating or choosing had been impelled to rule the Province by means other than brotherly love and a merciful spirit. In other words, fundamentally they were Englishmen with all of the practical-mindedness of that race. Faced with the actual responsibilities of government they felt obliged to make some compromises in applying their conceptions of human relations in their efforts to reconcile theory and practice.[1]

Whatever may have been the nature of the problems facing the agencies of law enforcement, the happy condition of the Province from a material standpoint cannot be questioned. The climate was temperate and healthful, the soil rich, varying from the light and sandy lands near the rivers to the rich and deep black mould of the interior woodlands. Two great rivers, the Delaware and the Susquehanna,

---

[1] Referring to the government of Pennsylvania in the middle of the eighteenth century, Lewis Evans has the following rather caustic comment:

"The present Form is extreemly defective; 'tis upon a Supposition that all Mankind are virtuous. Nobody need to be told that that is a Mistake. 'Tis a Government without Rewards or Punishments, adequate to Merit or Iniquity. The Inhabitants of American Birth are not very eager in Pursuit of Learning except where it be a trade. At this time, nine tenths of the justices of the Peace: have never read fifty Pages of Law before they had their Commissions tho' they are also judges of the Court of Common Pleas; but they are mostly trading People, and if they don't understand Law, they do Expediency. There are several who remember to have seen Men raised to Posts, where both natural and acquired Abilities were necessary, whom the World judged to have scarce Wits enough to keep them out of a well. But who does not rejoice to see it otherwise?" "A Brief Account of Pennsylvania . . . 1753."

Richard Peters commenting on the above says, "Our Author is pretty severe upon our Magistrates, but he is conscious that the Veracity of Assertion will hinder any Contradiction." *Ibid.*

with their tributaries, afforded means of transportation. As a result of the labor of an industrious population under these favorable conditions, there was a surplus of food each year sufficient on an average, it was asserted, to feed at least one hundred thousand people other than those living within the Province.[1] It appears that the inhabitants were generous with this abundance. At least one traveller at this period declared, "In Pennsylvania one might travel about a whole year without spending a penny; for it is customary in this country that, when one comes with his horse to a house, the traveller is asked if he wishes to have something to eat, whereupon the stranger is served with a piece of cold meat which has been left over from dinner; in addition to this he is provided with fine bread, butter and cheese, also with plenty to drink. If one wishes to stay over night, he and his horse are harboured free of charge."[2]

The farms of provincial Pennsylvania, averaging in size from one hundred to four hundred acres, were devoted to the raising of a variety of field crops and live stock. The chief agricultural products were wheat, Indian corn, cattle, swine, horses, rye, barley, and oats. The beef and pork were exported in large quantities as were wheat and Indian corn, the first-named cereal largely in the form of flour and bread. From the hard woods of the Province large numbers of barrels and other wooden containers were likewise manufactured for export. Pig and bar iron produced in excess of local needs, in bloomeries, furnaces,

[1] Governor Morris to General Braddock, March 12, 1755. *Penna. Archives* (fourth series), II, 372.
[2] Mittelberger, *Journey to Pennsylvania*, p. 97.

and forges were also exported. Moreover, Indian traders brought to Philadelphia a wealth of skins and furs, most of which were sent to England. Finally ships, built at Philadelphia and sold in Great Britain, made a considerable return,[1] although it was asserted by Peter Kalm that hulls made of Pennsylvania oak were not so lasting as those of the oak of New England or of Europe.[2] It is of interest that coal had apparently not as yet been discovered in a commonwealth now famed the world over for that article, although some of those who went among the Indians higher up in the country claimed to have seen it.[3] As to importations, during the twenty years preceding 1750 the merchants of the Province bought from England commodities valued, according to the custom-house books, at over one million pounds, one fourth of which were foreign-made goods landed in England before transhipment to America. In 1747, goods to the value of £82,404 were received from

[1] Answer of the Lieut. Governor of Pennsylvania and counties of New Castle, Kent, and Sussex on Delaware to the Queries from the Board of Trade, March 15, 1731. Shelburne Papers, Vol. 45.

[2] *Travels in North America*, I, 105, 180.

A contemporary offers an explanation for the fact that ships built in Pennsylvania were not long lived. "The Timber used here for Shipbuilding is Oak; and that called White Oak is esteemed the best, and is the only sort used for Plank. Our Ship Carpenters never season a Stick, whence you may know the short duration of Ships built here, and indeed Forrest timber is never so durable as that which grows openly in Parks and Fields; New Jersey furnishes us with Pines for the Deck and Masts as well as for all our house building." Lewis Evans, "A Brief Account of Pennsylvania . . . 1753."

[3] Kalm, *Travels in North America*, I, 85.

Lewis Evans, the surveyor, writing from Philadelphia in 1753 says, "But there is no Sea Coal, Chalk, or Cinnibar yet discovered. . . . " *Op. cit.*

the Mother Country of which but 8,585 pounds' worth were produced abroad. These figures indicate that the total value of the imports of that year were double their value twenty years earlier.[1] The growth of commerce is also evidenced by the fact that in 1730 it was computed that about one hundred and seventy ships, most of them sloops and small brigantines averaging about sixty tons, cleared from the ports of Philadelphia, New Castle, and Lewes each year;[2] in 1745, there were over three hundred,[3] and in the year 1755, from Philadelphia alone, according to Governor Morris, some five hundred vessels sailed, and these, moreover, were mostly owned by merchants of that town.[4]

It would not be far from the truth to describe Pennsylvania in 1750 as among the most prosperous of all parts of the British Empire. One of its most eminent men, in fact, called it the most flourishing in North America.[5] Philadelphia was perhaps the most populous town in all the English settlements in the New World.[6] Peter Kalm speaks of its "grandeur and perfection." He declares that "its

[1] For tables of imports for the years 1723-1747 inclusive, taken from the London Custom-House books, see Kalm, *op. cit.*, I, 50-52. See *ante* p. 10, for estimates in the year 1743.

[2] Answers of the Lieut. Governor of Pennsylvania to the Queries of the Board, 1730. Shelburne Papers, Vol. 45.

[3] Kalm, *op. cit.*, I, 53.

[4] Gov. Morris to General Braddock, March 12, 1755. *Penna. Archives* (fourth series), II, 372.

[5] William Smith, *A Brief State of the Province of Pennsylvania*, p. 10.

[6] The population of American towns in the eighteenth century is difficult to ascertain with accuracy. Richard Peters, in the early years of the French and Indian War in comparing New York and Philadelphia, declared: "The city of New York is

fine appearance, good regulations, agreeable situation, natural advantages, trade, riches and power, are by no means inferior to those of any of the most ancient towns in Europe" and that it is the capital of a province which "now vies with several Kingdoms in Europe, in number of inhabitants."[1] It was a great seaport, although ninety miles up the Delaware, and the largest ships sailed to its wharves where they rode in five fathoms of fresh water. Its single great disadvantage as a port was owing to the fact that for a month or longer in winter the river was frozen over and navigation, therefore, was suspended— something that did not happen to saltwater ports.[2]

In 1749 the City[3] measured over a mile in length, in breadth, a half a mile or more, and possessed, it seems, something over two thousand dwellings.[4] The streets running north and south and east and west were regular and attractive with a width of fifty feet, with the exception of Market Street which was nearly one hundred. The houses, several stories in height and generally provided with plate-glass win-

much more advantageously situated than Philadelphia, and yet how surprisingly has the latter risen to that superiority, which it at present undoubtedly has, not only over the former, but over all the cities in the British colonies." See his annotation of Lewis Evans' "A Brief Account of Pennsylvania... 1753," Penna. Hist. Soc. Boston enjoyed a population almost if not quite equal to Philadelphia. See E. B. Greene and V. D. Harrington, *American Population before the Federal Census of 1790*, pp. 22 and 118.

[1] *Op. cit.*, I, 59-60.
[2] "It is not safe attempting this coast in January or February in inward bound ships." Lewis Evans, *op. cit.*
[3] For the incorporation of Philadelphia as a city in 1691, see the *Pennsylvania Magazine of History and Biography*, VIII, 504.
[4] *The Maryland Gazette*, June 7, 1749.

dows and French chimneys, were mostly built of brick[1] and covered by cedar-shingle roofs. This cedar had in the past been procured from trees growing in near-by swamps and was esteemed for its lightness and durability.[2] However, by the middle of the century the scarcity of this material for roof covering had created a serious problem. When the time had come for renewal of the roofs it was necessary to change to tile or slate. But in doing so the houses had to be provided with stouter walls to carry the additional weight, which in itself entailed the reconstruction of many of the buildings, a task that was then proceeding.

Twelve churches adorned the city. There were two credited to each of the larger religious denominations, that is, to the Quakers, Presbyterians, German Reformed, and Lutherans; while the Anglicans, Baptists, Roman Catholics, and Moravian Brethren each supported one.[3] Philadelphia could also boast of a fine lending library, a newly founded academy in 1753 out of which finally came the University of Pennsyl-

[1] "The whole world cannot afford better bricks than our town is built of, nor is the Lime which is mostly brought from White-Marsh inferior to that wherewith the old castles in Britain were formerly built." Lewis Evans, *op. cit.*

[2] Evans, referring to the white cedar of Pennsylvania, declares that "it is excellent where duration, and not strength is wanting, for which Reason we use it for the Pannels of our wainscotting, Pails, Tubs, Brewers and Distillers, Cisterns, Coolers, and Tubs, likewise for Shingling Houses and for Fences. The Cultivation of this wood would be the most beneficial of any thing that could be introduced into Europe from America: for they grow very fast, and so close together that there is scarce Room in some places for a man to squeeze between them, and the Swamps where they grow are the greatest curiosity in America." *Ibid.*

[3] Peter Kalm, *op. cit.*, I, 36-43.

vania, a philosophical society, and two printing establishments. Here Benjamin Franklin, editor of the *Pennsylvania Gazette*, was attracting attention with his electrical experiments and with his suggestions as to their significance.[1] The chief architectural ornament of the city, one may mention in passing, was a new, impressive town hall where not only the city fathers, but the deputies of the Province gathered to deliberate.

One may think perhaps in terms of sober dress as well as sober speech in this center of Quakerism in 1750. But it is related that the apparel of the men, especially of Englishmen, was very costly, even among the farmers. "Every one wears a wig, the peasant as well as the gentleman," declared Mittelberger. He also found that the women's apparel was "very fine, neat and costly. . . . All wear dainty fine white aprons, on their shoes usually large silver buckles, round their throats fine strings of beads, in their ears costly drops with fine stones, and on their heads fine white hoods embroidered with flowers and trimmed with lace and streamers."[2] This honest and not unsusceptible man found the English-speaking women "very beautiful, generally gay, friendly, very free, plucky, smart, and clever but also very haughty," who wore over their shoulders scarlet or blue cloaks when walking and riding and, on their heads, beautifully colored "bonnets" of taffeta, which "serve instead of parasols, but are much prettier."

[1] For example *The Scots Magazine* of January, 1750, gives much space to these experiments and the propositions laid down as a result of them.

[2] *Journey to Pennsylvania*, pp. 113-117.

Even the English servant woman, he declared, dressed as elegantly as an aristocratic lady in Germany.

From everything that has thus far been said we are able to infer that while there was a certain political equality among the people of the Province, at least among those of Protestant faith who could take the required oaths or affirmations for the purpose of naturalization and for holding office, there were fairly definite social lines and barriers separating English-speaking from non-English-speaking people, freemen from redemptioners, and bondsmen from slaves. A certain racial pride on the part of the English settlers was apparently exhibited too frequently in an objectionable fashion. "In this Country there exists (what we do not find in Old England), among the English settlers, a supreme contempt for the Germans," wrote a German gentleman from Philadelphia in 1747. "This may be owing," he declared, "to the fact that the former see numbers of lowly and poor German immigrants in comparison with whom they entertain an exalted opinion of themselves."[1] As to the existence of slavery in Pennsylvania, it may be said that there was some little sentiment against it in the middle of the eighteenth century, but not so much as one might expect, in light of the famous Germantown protest as early as the year 1688. It is true that the number of slaves was not large, at most from two to three thousand, and that not only the Quakers "but likewise several Christians of other denominations sometimes set their Negroes at liberty."[2] Nevertheless, Peter Kalm affirmed in the year 1749

[1] *Pennsylvania Magazine of History and Biography*, XVI, 120.
[2] Peter Kalm, *op. cit.* I, 394.

that while the Quakers once scrupled to receive slaves "they are no longer so nice and they have as many Negroes as other people."[1] Slavery, however, was in nowise a fundamental element in the economy of the Colony. Rather, it was an excrescence of provincial aristocracy.

The keynote of eighteenth-century Pennsylvania was fruitful activity on the part of all groups with a consequent abundance of the material things of life. There was, as has been suggested, plenty of good food at low prices, with the farmer and the mechanic comfortably housed and clothed and the merchants prospering as a result of a ready sale of the surplus commodities of the Province in the West Indies and in other markets. Doubtless the production of wealth was stimulated by the fact that the government was able to aid industrious farmers to improve their lands by advancing funds from the Loan Office created for that purpose, while at the same time it refrained from placing public burdens on the people at large. For not only were the inhabitants of the Province not obliged to render military service but under ordinary circumstances were quite freed from levies on their possessions. "Liberty in Pennsylvania extends so far," observed a contemporary, "that every one is free from all molestations and taxation on his property, business, house and estates. . . . A peculiarity, however, is that unmarried men and women pay from two to five shillings annually, according to their income, because they have no one but themselves to provide for. In Philadelphia this money is applied to the purchase

[1] *Op. cit.*, I, 390. For a detailed discussion of slavery in the Province see E. R. Turner, *The Negro in Pennsylvania . . . 1639-1861*, especially chapters II, III and IV.

of the lights which burn every night in the streets of the city."[1]

What has just been stated may well lead to the question: How then were the charges of government met if not by direct taxation? Lieutenant Governor Patrick Gordon, in reporting to the Board of Trade in 1730 on the provincial revenues, declared that it came from two sources: the first was from the interest secured on public loans which was brought about as we have seen in the case of New Jersey by the emission of paper currency; further, there was a small excise on the sale of spirits. The former brought in three thousand pounds Pennsylvania currency and the latter a thousand pounds—"a sufficiency to answer all the present exigencies of this Government."[2] By 1752 the income from the excise had mounted to the sum of £3,519.6.8, of which total £2,224.12.8 came from Philadelphia County, with less than one hundred pounds from each of the counties of Northampton, York, and Cumberland, which paid in respectively £77, £54, and £40, in round numbers.[3] In that year it was also calculated that the Province was entitled to receive interest amounting to £8,460.12 on sums advanced on land mortgages by the Loan Office, with a net revenue, after necessary deductions, of £7,381.1. The happy situation of the Province was summed up by Governor Morris in a letter to

[1] Mittelberger, *op. cit.*, p. 55.
[2] Shelburne Papers, Vol. 45.
[3] See statement of excise collected 1752-1753. Penna. State Archives (Ms.), Doc. 607. In the year 1752 there were 120 taverns in Philadelphia with licenses and 118 other establishments which were privileged to sell rum and other strong liquors by the quart. Lewis Evans, "A Brief Account of Pennsylvania . . . 1753."

Braddock early in 1755, "We are burthened with no taxes and are not only out of Debt, but have a Revenue of Seven Thousand a year and Fifteen Thousand in Bank, all at the Disposal of the House of Assembly."[1]

Maryland, the Lower Counties on the Delaware, and Pennsylvania were, by the middle of the eighteenth century, the surviving proprietary colonies within the British Empire out of all those that came into existence in the seventeenth century. Over the last named Thomas and Richard Penn, the sons of the first proprietor, sought to exercise jointly the powers and to enjoy the privileges embodied in the royal charter of the year 1681.[2] These had been limited, however, by subsequent parliamentary enactment, such as the statute requiring the royal approval of those appointed by proprietors to act as governors, that also placed restrictions in America on the sale of lands to aliens,[3] and especially the acts regulating trade and industry which were binding upon all the plantations. Under the terms of the charter, the Proprietor, with the assent of the freemen of the Province, was empowered to pass such measures as would meet the needs of the settlers, provided that these were in

[1] *Pennsylvania Archives* (fourth series), II, 372-373. Governor Hamilton in communicating with the House of Representatives in August, 1751 declared that not one shilling was levied on the people for the service of Government (*ibid.*, II, 156) and in 1754 said in a veto message, "You cannot be insensible, Gentlemen, that the Funds you are now possessed of, which are to continue for several years, without Demunition, are greatly more than sufficient for the support of Government." *Ibid.*, II, 227-228.

[2] The Delaware Counties came to Penn by a lease and release from James, Duke of York, after 1681.

[3] 7 and 8 William III, c. 22, Par. 16.

harmony with the laws of England. In fulfillment of this, William Penn, after much experimenting with idealistic schemes of government and under some compulsion, issued his "Frame" of 1701, which became the basis of government throughout the remainder of the colonial period. It established a legislature composed of the governor, appointed by the Proprietor, and an assembly chosen annually by the freemen.[1] In other words, the Council of the Province was no part of this legislature.[2]

[1] Referring to the difficult position of the Governors of Pennsylvania Lewis Evans declared:

"If they disobey the Proprietors they are in danger of losing their places, and if they disoblige the Assembly they lose their Salaries. But the late Governor Mr. Thomas, after quarreling with the Assembly, found means of supplying himself without their Help. He turn'd out the Magistrates in the Assembly's Interest, and put in others of his own; these recommended so many for Licences to keep public Houses, that we have seen a grand jury make a present to the very Court that granted them." "A Brief Account of Pennsylvania ... 1753."

[2] William Smith, *Brief State of the Province of Pennsylvania*, p. 10.

"The Governor for the better execution of his Office has several able and experienced Gentlemen to advise with in an Emergency call'd his Council tho he nominates and superceds at his pleasure; they are not limited to numbers but generally consist of 10 or 12; they are only his privy Council during his Administration. In Case of a Lieutenant's Death or removal, the oldest Councellor if another is not Chosen, becomes President of the Council, who with 4 Councellors at least can exercise all the Powers of a Governor except Legislation. This defect of Power in the President of Council is one of the greatest in our Constitution. In President Palmer's late Administration when our Coast was annoy'd with six or seven Privateers at one time, we had no power to make an Act for The Public Utility and Safety, tho the whole Province had been at Stake ... whether this Exception of Legislation was accidental as some suppose, or design'd as others imagine for the Sake of securing the proprietary Interest, I cannot tell, But this I venture to say, the Proprietary Interest will Suffer most, if extremity shou'd oblige the As-

It may be asserted that in no other British colony, outside those that were corporate, was the power of the deputies of the people more aggressively employed in the direction of controlling government than in Pennsylvania in the '50s. These representatives boldly asserted even their right to sit on their own adjournment as a body, denying thereby the authority of the governor to prorogue or dissolve them.[1] Since 1723, they had claimed, upon the basis of a law passed in that year and assented to by Sir William Keith, "in manifest Contempt of all the Instructions of the Proprietary Familey," the sole right to dispose of the public money. Further, they had wrested from the governors the appointment of a number of officers in possession of lucrative posts, such as the provincial treasurer, the trustees of the Loan Office, the collectors of the excise, the health officer, the brander of flour, and the brander of beef and pork. "The Powers they enjoy," stated a contemporary, "are extraordinary and some of them so repugnant that they are a Source of greatest Confusion in the Government."[2] Moreover, one unique provision of the charter which was granted

sembly with the President of Council to pass Acts of Assembly. It is the Opinion of some of the most eminent Lawyers and Statesmen on the Continent that they may pass Laws, tho' an Act of Assembly be expressly to the contrary." Lewis Evans, *op. cit.*

[1] "But what most distinguishes the Assembly of this Colony from all others in America is to meet on a Set day, and sit upon their own Adjournment and during their own pleasure, without its being in any Body's Power to disolve or prorogue them ... But those Priviledges would not suit any Assembly, who are not elected yearly, on the Expiration of a year is a certain Dissolution." *Ibid.*

[2] William Smith, *A Brief State of the Province of Pennsylvania*, pp. 10-11.

to Penn aided the establishment of a virtual legislative independence of Great Britain; this was the clause providing that the Proprietor had five years within which to transmit to the King's Council for acceptance or rejection, all acts after the same had been passed, with the provision that rejection must take place within a period of six months, otherwise the measures thus transmitted would be considered laws. As a result of this, complained the Board of Trade in 1721, "it frequently happens that several Laws unfit for the Royal Assent continue in force for five years and after being disallowed by the Crown are enacted again, and by this practice become in a manner perpetual."[1]

In 1746 an issue arose over the right of the Crown to pass on certain acts which had long been before the Privy Council. The statute directly in question was passed by Pennsylvania in the year 1742 and was based upon an earlier act, that of the year 1729-30, imposing an import duty of five pounds on persons convicted of heinous crimes who were being brought into the Colony from the Mother Country.[2] The earlier act was not called into question, but in September, 1746, Fane, the legal counsel for the Board, reported adversely against the act of the year 1742. This led the Proprietors to petition the King in Council rela-

[1] Representation of the Board of Trade, Sept. 8, 1721. Shelburne Papers, 45: 235. For the reports of the legal advisers of the Board of Trade on the Pennsylvania laws from 1745 to 1753 see C.O. 1269: 15, 18, 33; 1273: 58, 59; 1274: 51, 61-63, 67-68, 78, 83, 108-110, 116. For a discussion of this see W. T. Root, *The Relations of Pennsylvania with the British Government*, Chapter V.

[2] *Pennsylvania Statutes at Large*, IV, 164, 366.

tive to the calling into question of old acts that had long been before the Commissioners for Trade and Plantations.[1] In spite of this, an order in council dated December 17, 1746 approved a representation of the latter proposing the repeal of the Act of 1742 as not warranted by the laws of Great Britain.[2]

Evidence is not lacking that the Crown was concerned to observe a disposition on the part of the people of Pennsylvania to render themselves autonomous and, in the words of a critic, to set up "a pure Republick," as it were. There was much, it is true, not clear in the legal relations between His Majesty and the Province, especially as to the degree to which the former could, under the charter, interfere in the government of the latter. For example, in 1752, in response to orders of the Lords of the Committee of the Privy Council, the Board of Trade laid before the Attorney-General and the Solicitor-General certain queries for their opinion, which shows a strong desire on the part of the Mother Country to exercise over the law-making processes of this plantation a much stricter control than previously. These were, first, whether, consistent with the charter, the Crown could give to the Governor instructions of any kind, other than such as relate to the laws of trade and navigation; secondly, whether the Crown could give instructions to the Governor relating to the passing of laws in general; thirdly, whether the Crown could give instructions to the Governor not to give his

[1] C.O. 1271: 33, 38. In Feb., 1744-45 the Board took into consideration a body of laws passed in 1725-1726 and reported on by Fane in 1727. *Ibid.*, 1271: 15-16.
[2] *Ibid.*, 1271: 44.

assent to any particular law, unless a clause be inserted suspending its execution till His Majesty's pleasure could be known thereupon; fourthly, whether the Crown could give instructions to the Governor to endeavor to obtain a clause to be inserted in any act suspending its execution until the King's pleasure can be known thereupon.[1] The nature of the reply of the legal advisers, if one were sent, is unknown to the writer. The question, however, in a general way had arisen in the year 1744 when the law officers of the Crown had been requested by the Board to give an opinion as to what the legislature of Pennsylvania might be obliged to do and what appropriate means were in order to provide for the security of that Province, and received a reply that there was little that could be done outside an act of Parliament.[2]

The true state of the government of Pennsylvania in the middle of the eighteenth century is indicated by a letter of Governor Morris of the year 1755. In referring to the Assembly of the Province, he wrote, "You are sensible, they have been most remarkably indulged, both by the Crown and Proprietaries, and are suffered to enjoy Powers unknown to any Assembly upon the Continent, and even such as may render them a very dangerous Body hereafter; but not content with Privileges granted to them by Charter they Claim many more and among others an ab-

[1] See the Board of Trade *Journal, 1749-1753,* pp. 283-284. C.O. 1273: 101.
[2] For the report of D. Ryder and W. Murray, October 19, 1744, see *ibid.,* 1271: 12. This opinion follows closely that of Attorney-General Northey, delivered February 22, 1714. For this see "Edward Northey's Legal Opinions," Library of Congress Accessions.

solute exemption from the Force of Royal and Proprietary Instructions."[1] Such was Pennsylvania, not only a land of religious sects but where men were most aggressively reaching out to grasp all of those powers which they identified with a system of self-government.

Reference has been made to the fact that in the middle of the eighteenth century Thomas and Richard Penn were joint-proprietors of Pennsylvania. They were the surviving sons of William Penn, the Founder, by his second wife, Hannah, and together with their elder brother John succeeded under the terms of their father's will of 1712, supplemented by one drawn up by their mother six years later. By the latter John received one half of the proprietary; the remainder was divided equally between his two younger brothers.[2] After the termination of a suit in chancery which sustained the earlier will and also after a release of the claims of the descendants of William Penn's first wife in 1731, the three sons of Hannah administered their propriety without interference and with unusual unanimity until the death of John in 1746. His undivided portion by his own desire thereupon went to Thomas, who now had rights to three fourths of the total; for under the terms of a formal agreement executed in 1732, the brothers had determined that the estate should be reserved to their male heirs, under condition that if any of the three should die without such issue, his

[1] *Penna. Archives* (fourth series), II, 352-353.
[2] See *Pennsylvania Colonial and Federal, A History, 1608-1903* (H. M. Jenkins, editor), I, 372-3.

estate should go to the surviving brothers or brother as the case might be, "as he might appoint."[1]

What manner of men were these sons of the great Founder? We may dismiss Richard as rather a nonentity. He had neither business capacity nor ambition. His sole concern with respect to the proprietary was to secure an income sufficient to keep his growing family out of debt. A recent historian has described John and Thomas as not possessed of "an atom of William Penn's goodness of heart or breadth of character. They were sordid, unscrupulous, overbearing and dishonest." As to Thomas, he was "little better than a common blockhead" and "was greedy, stingy and cruel, and withal dull, repellent and morose."[2] These charges are difficult to sustain unless one is prepared to rely upon the opinions of the enemies of these men.[3] For it appears to be true, as indicated by their correspondence, that John and Thomas were not unworthy successors to William, in spite of the fact that they were less idealistic than the latter. On the other hand they certainly far surpassed him in common sense and gave to the Province a businesslike administration, putting an end to a world of confusion —something that he could not do. They were, of course, not unmindful of the potential value of their propriety in the support of the Penn family and

[1] *Ibid.*, I, 374.
[2] A. C. Buell, *William Penn* (1904), p. 348.
[3] The author at this point desires to acknowledge his indebtedness to Muriel Louise Wilson, one of his former graduate students, whose unpublished master's thesis, "Thomas Penn, Chief Proprietor of Pennsylvania: A Study of the Proprietarial Activities as Evidenced by the Penn Letter Books," has been of great assistance to him at this point.

sought to draw the largest possible revenue from it. However, down to the '60s of the eighteenth century they were so burdened with debts, partly on account of William Penn's negligence and incompetence, that little progress was made in establishing the family fortunes. "People imagine because we are at the head of a large Province we must be rich," declared Thomas in a letter written about the year 1750, "but ... I tell you that for fifteen years from 1732 to 1747, I laid by but about one hundred pounds a year."[1] One chief problem was the difficulty involved in the proper collection of the quit-rents from the lands. For the quit-rent rolls were in chaotic condition upon the death of the first Proprietor. Even in 1755, Thomas complained that "not one-fifth of our quit-rents are paid."[2] So late as 1764 rents from the appropriated lands of Northampton County amounted to but £161.15.6.[3]

In the middle of the century, the terms of granting lands as fixed by the Proprietors was the payment of £15.10 Pennsylvania currency on each one hundred acres with an annual quit-rent payment in addition of a penny an acre, in place of earlier terms which in 1736 had been nine pounds and ten shillings, Pennsylvania currency, and a quit-rent of one-half penny an acre. This payment was subsequently reduced to £5 sterling or £8.10 Pennsylvania currency.[4] The Pennsylvania land system was apparently well regulated

[1] Letter Books (Ms.), quoted by Miss Wilson in her "Thomas Penn, Chief Proprietor."
[2] Ibid.
[3] Ibid.
[4] For the variations made by the Penns in the terms upon which lands were granted in the course of the seventeenth and

and sensible and seems to have met with general approval.

"What the world has imputed to the Happiness of our Constitution, is with more justice to be ascribed to the happy management of the Land Offices," affirmed Lewis Evans, the surveyor, in 1753. He thereupon described the method employed for the sale of land. The individual desiring a piece of land applied to the provincial Secretary for a survey warrant and at the same time paid £5 for each one hundred acres with six months' credit for the payment of the remainder, amounting to £10.10 or a total of £15.10. The warrant was thereupon sent to the Surveyor-General. After the deputy surveyor of the district had surveyed the land, a detailed description was prepared by the Surveyor-General, and this was returned to the Secretary's office. The patentee, after payment of the sum still due to the Receiver-General, then received a patent which passed under the great seal of the Province and was recorded in the Rolls Office. The fees incidental to this for a tract of two or three hundred acres did not exceed a couple of guineas, "and not a Guinea more on 1,000 Acres."

"The Correct Management of the Proprietaries's Affairs," Evans asserted, "has prevented all Disputes, and Law Suits between the Planters, so frequent, in the other Colonies. Every man is glad of holding immediately under the Chief Lord of the Soil. And if we add to this the great Ease, and Dispatch that Business has been done with in our Offices we need

eighteenth centuries, see B. W. Bond, *The Quit-Rent System in the American Colonies*, p. 134; and W. R. Shepherd, *Proprietary Government in Pennsylvania*, pp. 17-18, 34.

not wonder to see so many strangers flock thither to partake of our Happiness."[1]

By the year 1774, owing to the most constant attention to the details of business on the part of Thomas, now the surviving son of William, the revenue had become large. For example, in June of that year, the Proprietor acknowledged remittances amounting to £12,700.[2]

As to the Proprietors and the Holy Experiment, it may be pointed out that William Penn remained in the Quaker faith until his death. This was also true of John, although he was a "fighting" Friend who further believed in compelling settlers suspected of Roman Catholicism to take oaths to clear themselves. However, Richard, early in his manhood, joined the Established Church of England. As to Thomas, it may be said that he remained a member of the Friends' communion until after his marriage in 1751 to Juliana Fermor, daughter of the first Earl of Pomfret. He, however, had an ambition to act as governor in person of Pennsylvania. In fact, during the years from 1732 to 1741 he was in the Province giving personal supervision to various matters pertaining to the proprietorial business, and until about 1755 was constantly expecting to have matters so arranged, especially the vexatious boundary dispute with Lord Bal-

[1] Lewis Evans, "A Brief Account of Pennsylvania ... 1753."
[2] These are figures for the year 1774. In 1776, the total revenue was £10,204 and 7¼ d. In that year 1,627,279 acres paid a penny an acre quit-rent, while 1,385,219¾ paid a halfpenny an acre, and 856,895¼ acres paid a shilling per hundred acres. "Account of Pennsylvania Land Grants, 1681-1766," Penna. Mss., II, 113. Friends' Library; "Land Grants," Penn-Physick Mss., IV, 95; these are quoted by Bond in his *Quit-Rent System*, p. 134, note 3.

timore, as to permit him to return to spend the rest
of his years there. During the period before the death
of John he might have had the coveted appointment
had it not been for the opposition of the Friends in
England who insisted that as a Quaker he must live
up to the professions of his religion and therefore
must not allow himself to take the oaths required of
all governors. This may have influenced him in his
decision to break with that sect. By 1743 he had
discarded the Quaker garb, due, as he wrote to Governor Thomas, to his position in favor of the proper
defense of the Province, with war existing at that
time between Great Britain and Spain, and also as he
adds, because he might yet become governor himself.
His repudiation of Quakerism, together with his zeal
in promoting the family interests within Pennsylvania, however, brought upon him so much criticism that
by 1755 he had come to the conclusion that he was
not prepared to subject his family to the disagreeable
treatment sure to follow should he go there to live.
As a result, from 1748 to 1754 with which period this
volume is concerned, James Hamilton, a member of
a powerful Pennsylvania family and a capable man of
good character, acted as chief executive. Although
he enjoyed the confidence of the Chief Proprietor he
insisted on resigning during the last-named year, because he was involved in continuous disputes with
the Assembly and also because he was obliged to
neglect his own important business interests in the
filling of a position that he did not find particularly
profitable. Such was William Penn's Holy Experiment in 1750.

CHAPTER VIII

THE IRON MEN

BEFORE turning from the continental colonies to describe the activities of the British people upon the Island and Banks of Newfoundland as well as in the region of Hudson Bay, it is desirable for the fulfillment of the purposes of this survey to take into consideration the circumstances that led to the passage of one of the most criticized of all of the acts of Parliament relating to America: the Iron Act of 1750. This statute placed the colonies under severe restrictions in the production of iron and struck at an industry that was assuming great importance by the middle of the eighteenth century, not only in parts of New England, but in a number of the colonies to the south of the Province of New York and to the north of the Carolinas, with Pennsylvania even at this period in the lead.

The Act has been repeatedly cited as a classical instance of British stupidity and selfishness in the relations of the Mother Country with her dependencies. Be that as it may, it does at least illustrate effectively both the motivations of those who were responsible for the guidance of imperial economic policy and the enormous complexity of the problem of applying wise remedies to conditions then present in order to rectify the maladjustments of the mercantile system. It should be made clear at the outset that Englishmen in the middle of the eighteenth century were persuaded that they were witnessing, in the astonishingly rapid development of the American iron industry, the beginnings of a rapid decline of their own. Unless this decline were checked they were convinced that it would inevitably be accompanied with dire economic and social consequences. For already, as will be seen in the course of this chapter, the manufacture of iron had become of vast significance in the life of the population of the Mother Country.

Here is a picture of industrial England left by a traveller in the year 1747. "I forgot to tell you," he declared in a letter to a friend, "that yesterday we saw smoaky Birmingham or (as most people pronounce it Brunigam), on our Left; though the Spires appeared very handsome above those artificial Clouds. I believe the Hardware of this Place travels farther over the World, than any Commodity Britain produces."[1] Ten years preceding this statement it was asserted by Abraham Spooner, an ironmaster of this town, that at least one hundred and thirty-five thousand people living there or within a radius of ten miles of it were dependent upon iron manufacturing for a living.[2] In fact, by 1750 the whole region round about the town was dotted with furnaces, forges, slitting and rolling mills, and the establishments of fabricators of various types of hardware. And, what was true of Birmingham was almost

[1] *A Tour through Ireland by Two English Gentlemen* (1745), p. 22.
[2] "Report of the Committee of the House of Commons," 1738. Penn Papers Relating to Iron, Doc. 45 (Historical Society of Pennsylvania).

equally true of many other places. Indeed, next to the production of woolens, the manufacture of iron employed. the largest number of people engaged in industry in England with ironworks and coppice woods for iron-making in about half the counties of England and Wales.[1]

The working of metals was undoubtedly one of the earliest of the skilled occupations established in the Island. The cruder direct process of converting the ore into wrought iron had since the fourteenth century been displaced by the method of producing cast iron through the process of smelting. This cast iron was subsequently turned into the wrought iron that supplied the needs of the trade.

It should be mentioned in this connection that English iron ore consisted of various qualities, each adapted to special purposes. For example, the Clee Hill iron of Shropshire was the most famous in the world at this period for the making of gun barrels. In fact, those produced in Birmingham for the Tower Arsenal were all of this iron, which was malleable and yet was exceedingly strong. The iron from the Forest of Dean in Gloucestershire was, on the other hand, convertible into highly tempered steel and was used chiefly in making edged articles such as scythes. An iron that was easy to work when hot and could be easily punched and bent but became extraordinarily

---

[1] Testimony of William Rea, an ironmaster of Monmouth, before a Committee of the House of Commons, *ibid.*

It appears that in 1717 there were 116 forges in England; in 1736 the number had risen to 135; in 1750 the number had dropped to 114. See E. W. Hulme, "Statistical History of the Iron Trade in England and Wales, 1717-1750," *Transactions* of the Newcomen Soc. Study Hist. Engin. and Tech. 9: 12-13.

tough when cold was secured in Shropshire to the west of the Severn and also in larger quantities in Cumberland, where existed a mine held to be inexhaustible,[1] from which the furnaces of Lancashire, Hampshire, Yorkshire, Cheshire, Staffordshire, Gloucestershire, Worcestershire, and Shropshire were supplied. The ore that produced "cold short iron," excellent for nails came from the east of the Severn in Shropshire and from the counties of Staffordshire, Yorkshire, Nottinghamshire, Cheshire, and Derbyshire.[2]

Six things were considered essential to the production of iron advantageously in the middle of the eighteenth century: accessibility to an inexhaustible supply of ore, an abundance of wood, coal, water power, and skilled labor, and convenience of transportation. By means of a millrace and waterwheel, power was secured for the operation of the great wood and leather bellows which forced the blast through the ore and fuel laid in juxtaposition in the "high furnace." This power was also essential for the use of the great hammer at the forge and for both the slitting and rolling mills in the later processes. Where power did not exist, the more primitive nonblast or air-furnace method was still extensively employed.

Although in the seventeenth century attempts had been made to use coal in the smelting of iron, and the Dudley Furnace had established the possibilities of

[1] At Millom are to be found today the highly productive mines of red hematite ore, conveniently located for transportation by way of the Duddon and the sea to the various blast furnaces.

[2] *Some Considerations Showing that the Importation of Iron from America will sooner put a stop to the Importation of Iron from Sweden and Russia.* Undated. Penn Papers on Iron.

this utilization, it was apparently not until the days of Abraham Darby in the early part of the eighteenth century that coke was accepted by any of the furnace men as a possible suitable substitute for charcoal. But even then the change came very slowly so that in 1750 the age of coke was still in the future.[1] One strong argument in favor of this change, however, was the wastage of the wood resources of England in the processes of iron and steel production. In fact, this was becoming acute in parts of the Kingdom as early as the middle of the sixteenth century and in 1584 Parliament actually forbade the erection of any additional ironworks in the three southeastern counties, Kent, Surrey, and Sussex.[2] Toward the end of the seventeenth century there were within ten miles of Dudley Castle nearly twenty thousand smiths and yet, on account of the lack of fuel due to this wood wastage, many of the ironworks, it is stated, were decayed.[3] The shortage of this commodity finally, among other reasons, led to the gradual shifting of

[1] The writer of *The State of the Trade and Manufacture of Iron* (1750, p. 2), referring to iron ore declared, "It is not to be converted with Advantage into good Malleable Iron with any other Fire, that we know of, but what is made of Wood, Charkt, or Charcoal." Wagner Collection, Yale University. However, in Staffordshire, the use of coke in the making of malt had become well established by 1730. John Pinkerton, *Voyages and Travels*, II, 22.

[2] In the year 1552 it was actually proposed to Parliament that the iron mills be abolished out of the realm. In favor of this it was argued that, 'whereas wood was formerly sold at the stock for one penny a load, by reason of the iron mills it is now at two shillings a load; further, that Spanish iron formerly sold for five marks per ton now there are English iron mills ... iron is sold at nine pounds per ton.' *Calendar* of the Mss. of the Marquis of Salisbury, Hist. Mss. Com. Part I, p. 164.

[3] H. Scrivenor, *History of the Iron Trade*, p. 38.

iron smelting from the West Midlands in the direction of the Severn and the forests of Wales.[1]

It must not be inferred by what has been said that coal was not widely used in the iron industry by the middle of the century. In fact the rise of iron manufacturing in Worcestershire and adjacent counties was owing, not only to the presence in this region of inexhaustible supplies of iron ore, the Forest of Dean, and the Severn River which afforded easy transportation of materials, but also to the possession of great deposits of pit-coal.[2] This was commonly used in the working of the iron after the initial treatment of the crude ore in the charcoal blast. For example, in the turning of pig iron into bar iron it was customary with each ton of iron to utilize one and a half loads of coal and three cords of wood.[3] Indeed, the extension of the use of pit-coal in manufacturing processes in the seventeenth century was doubtless the leading factor in the expansion of iron fabrication during the same period.

In light of the situation with respect to wood shortage it is therefore not surprising that before the beginning of the eighteenth century the demands for bar iron on the part of the fabricators had far outrun the supply of the forges just as the demands of the forgemen for sows and pigs had far outrun the supply

[1] G. C. Allen, *The Industrial Development of Birmingham and the Black Country*, p. 15; Pinkerton, *Voyages and Travels*, II, 10, 11, 14.

[2] See "The Petition of the Iron Merchants, Iron Masters and Iron Mongers to Parliament," March 3, 1736, Penn Papers Relating to Iron.

[3] Report of the Committee of the House of Commons on the Iron Trade, *ibid.*, Doc. 27.

of the furnaces with the result that producers of English hardware became increasingly dependent upon importations of iron from Sweden, Russia, and Spain. In fact, an act of the reign of William III recognized the scarcity and dearness of bar iron within the Kingdom and, to meet this situation as well as to encourage industry in Ireland, permitted the importation of this metal from that island free of duties.[1] It was estimated in 1736 that at least twenty thousand tons of iron had to be secured from abroad each year to meet the demands of the trade.

The explanation of the inability of the furnacemen to produce an adequate supply of pig iron lies of course in the rising cost of its production whenever unusual demands were made upon the proprietors of wood lots. Unlike pit-coal, the charcoal could be secured within the Kingdom only in measured quantities, based usually upon the anticipations of those who many years previously had either planted trees for this end or had preserved their coppices. But the landowner was obliged to balance the advantages of utilizing his lands in one or more of several possible ways; he naturally hesitated to devote to coppices, acres that might be more profitably employed during the period of the growth of the trees. In other words corn, wool, and wood, each having its own peculiar economy, were in a sense competing for his fields, and the selling price of his timber would therefore necessarily be based to a greater or less degree upon the value of the lands to him during the years of the slow maturing of this crop. This last-named factor could

[1] 7 and 8 William III, c. 10, Sec. 17.

operate due to the fact that growing trees are not a perishable crop such as corn and could therefore be held indefinitely for a favorable market.

The intimate relationship between the existence of an adequate supply of wood and the production of iron may be illustrated by the statements of a writer whose "Thoughts on the Iron Trade" was published in *Aris's Birmingham Gazette* in 1750. He declared that forty years previous to the time of writing there was neither iron furnace nor refining forge between Lancaster and Cumberland, with the result that many persons grubbed up their trees growing even on poor land. About the year 1711 two furnaces and a number of forges were built in this region. During the first twenty years there was not wood sufficient to make five hundred tons of bar iron in any year. Nevertheless, due to the encouragement that these and other works subsequently built gave to owners of lands, there now existed a supply of wood adequate to produce fifteen hundred tons of iron and it was calculated that in twenty years more there would be wood enough to make two thousand or even twenty-five hundred tons yearly. "More Endeavours are now used to improve and Enlarge their Woods than ever, several Persons planting Wood on Arable ground, tho' Arable Ground is Scarce, nothing like sufficient to supply them with Bread."[1]

It is true that there existed the possibility of supplying almost any quantity of timber to the burners of charcoal or to the furnace men in the various parts of England, so as to allow the latter an amount suf-

[1] See *Aris's Birmingham Gazette,* Nov. 19, 1750.

ficient for producing the quantity of pig iron that would meet adequately all the needs of the home market. But the price that the furnace men could pay for their wood was fixed by factors that they themselves could not entirely control. For they were producing their iron in competition in the home market with both Swedish and Russian iron. This foreign-produced metal paid a duty of but forty-one shillings and sixpence per ton if imported in British ships.[1] In fact, the increased demands of English fabricators for iron seems to have had the curious effect of decreasing the demand for the domestic product in the course of the eighteenth century. In 1718 it was estimated that eighteen thousand tons of bar iron were made in England; it was also estimated that in less than twenty years the amount had dropped to between twelve and fifteen thousand tons with the result that some of the forges had actually suspended operation and the price of wood had fallen, undoubtedly owing to the large importations of foreign Iron."[2] This importation of bar iron could easily

[1] Henry Saxby, *The British Customs*, p. 177. This gives the duty at £2.8.6 per ton but certain deductions brought the duty down to the figures given above. The duty on pig iron if produced in the plantations was three shillings and ninepence per ton. See "Report of the Committee of the House of Commons" (1737 ?). Penn Papers Relating to Iron, etc., 1712-1817, Doc. 27.

[2] "Report of the Committee of the House of Commons" (1737 ?), Penn Papers Relating to Iron, Doc. 27. Other figures differing rather widely from these are 13,300 tons in 1717, 12,-000 in 1720, 18,800 in 1750. E. W. Hulme, "Statistical History of the Iron Trade in England and Wales, 1717-1750," *Transactions*, Newcomen Soc. Study Hist. Engin. and Tech. 9: 12-35. The writer stresses the unreliability of the registers of the total output of pig iron for England and Wales.

have been cut off by prohibitive duties, but that would have resulted in the loss of important foreign markets won by the hardware trade and the throwing of thousands of people out of employment and was therefore opposed to sound mercantilistic principles. As a result of these factors, by the year 1738, out of a total of thirty-five thousand tons of bar iron used annually by the ironmasters it was asserted that but twelve thousand tons of this was made in England, a little over one third.[1] Under these circumstances it was felt that the vastly important iron trade of the Kingdom was largely at the mercy of foreign powers, especially of Sweden, and it is true that in 1717, upon a rupture of relations with the latter country, the price of bar iron advanced from £13 to £22 per ton and continued at this almost prohibitive price level during the period of trade interruption with that kingdom.[2]

The question naturally was raised as to the possibility of securing adequate supplies of iron within the Empire which might serve as a substitute for that from foreign countries. There were also other questions raised at this period even more pressing for an answer. For the English ironmasters and ironmongers had been made to realize that something was happening to their former great markets in America. In place of the brisk demand in that quarter for various types of ironware, there was a falling off of orders; stocks were therefore accumulating in ware-

[1] *Ibid.*, Doc. 31.
[2] See a broadside, undated but of this period, entitled *Reasons for Encouraging the Importations of Iron in Bars from his Majesty's Plantations in America, ibid.*

houses that had filled these orders, and many of the weaker furnaces and forges in the '30s that had supplied iron for American consumption were obliged to suspend operation. Of the one hundred and twenty-five forges scattered through England and Wales at this period, thirty of them or almost one fourth were standing idle while the others were running at not more than two-thirds capacity, according to testimony presented before a parliamentary committee.[1] At Stourbridge and Wolverhampton great numbers of artisans, previously employed in making nails, scythes, and such articles for exportation, sought work in vain, and it was stated that many in desperation had deserted their families. At Dudley, another iron center, the poor-rates, owing to widespread unemployment, mounted from two to three shillings on the pound to the appalling level of twelve and thirteen shillings. Abraham Spooner, Birmingham ironmaster, declared "that already our manufactures are in a miserable condition occasioned ... for the want of a demand from the plantations for the several sorts of wrought iron-ware" which formerly he himself could not make fast enough but now had great quantities lying by him.[2] Doubtless one source of the difficulty was owing to the fact that one half of all the iron produced in England and three fourths that of Staffordshire and Worcestershire was made into nails, "a trade which has decayed," it was declared, largely as a result of a lessening of the demand on the part of the colonies.[3]

---

[1] See the "Committee Report of the House of Commons" (1738 ?), *ibid.*, Doc. 45.
[2] *Ibid.*   [3] *Ibid.*

The iron industry in America to the north of the Carolinas was in truth gradually assuming very great importance. Although attempts had been made in the seventeenth century to establish works both in New England and Virginia, the real development dates from the beginning of the next century.[1] It appears that by the end of the second decade sufficient progress had been made in some of the colonies to alarm the English iron manufacturers. In 1719 a bill was introduced into Parliament by which it was provided that no one in any of the plantations should fabricate any ironware out of sows, pigs, or bars.[2] Nothing came of this attempt at restriction. However, in 1721, to aid in meeting the competition of American ironworks, all export duties on British iron were removed.[3]

Among the earliest of the American iron men was former Governor Spotswood of Virginia, who was interested in pig iron production and in the early '20s was exporting this metal from the old Dominion to London and to Bristol. For example, to the latter city he sent twenty tons in 1723 in the form of ballast in the loaded tobacco ship, the *Greyhound*.[4] Gradually

[1] A. C. Bining, *British Regulation of the Colonial Iron Industry*, p. 14.

[2] D. Macpherson, *Annals of Commerce*, III, 72; G. L. Beer, *Commercial Policy of England Toward the American Colonies*, p. 85.

[3] 8 George I, c 15, Par. 7.

[4] Jefferies Manuscript No. 19. Bristol Reference Library. It is of interest that this shipment, perhaps the first iron that he sent abroad, took place the year after he resigned from his governorship. See Bining, (*op. cit.*, pp. 20-21), on Spotswood's activities.

Professor Kathleen Bruce in her scholarly study, *Virginia Iron Manufacture in the Slave Era*, presents a picture of the beginnings of iron manufacturing in the Chesapeake Bay region.

to the north and south of the Potomac there appeared ironworks—such as the Principio Works in Maryland established in 1715—until by the middle of the century within that Province and Virginia there were at least ten blast furnaces making annually on an average five hundred tons of pig iron each, which totalled five thousand tons.[1]

Special inducements, moreover, were offered to colonials to engage in the iron business. Virginia, for example, to encourage the erection of ironworks, in 1748 exempted people thus employed from working on the roads other than those necessary for bringing iron ore or iron to some navigable river; they were also exempt from the requirements of attending muster and were permitted to take timber for the building of necessary bridges and for seven years were freed from colonial levies.[2]

By the year 1718 it appears that Massachusetts Bay had laid the foundations for iron manufacturing and had among her people those skilled in the production and fabrication of this article. In that year the Prov-

She suggests that as early as 1716 Spotswood began his iron industry; by 1732 there were three blast furnaces and one air furnace operating, the first three at Germanna and the latter near Fredericksburg. He was undoubtedly the first in Virginia to engage in "the Mystery of Making Iron." She gives 1724 as the date of the actual founding of the Principio Company in Maryland. See her "Introduction," pp. 9-17. For interesting items regarding the ironworks in Stafford County, Virginia for the years 1725-1726, see *Tyler's Quarterly Historical and Genealogical Magazine*, Oct., 1934, pp. 89-93.

[1] *A Short Account of Iron made in the Colonies of Virginia and Maryland*. Without date. Penn Papers Relating to Iron.

"There are three furnaces for melting iron ore, one furnace for making bar iron and a furnace for casting iron posts, etc.," wrote Colonel Lee, President of the Council, to the Board of Trade, September 29, 1750. Shelburne Papers, 45: 169-185.

[2] Hening, *Laws of Virginia*, V, 137-138.

ince provided bounties upon various types of ironware produced locally, that is, forty shillings per ton
on all bar iron equal in quality to Spanish iron, five
pounds per ton on rod iron or faggots of a suitable
fineness to work into nails, with twenty pence per
thousand on various sizes of nails and twelve shillings
per ton on all Holland ware cast from iron of equal
quality to English or Dutch ware.[1] By 1722, as a result of this encouragement, it was exporting to South
Carolina, among other manufactures, axes. By 1733
New England could boast of at least six furnaces and
nineteen forges.[2] It appears that the New England
ironmasters were so successful in the development of
a market for their products that they turned to importing considerable quantities of bar steel from
England to manufacture into implements, and soon
set up furnaces here and there for the production of
steel, with the result that by 1736 they and the ironmasters to the southward had succeeded in driving
from the American market to the north of the Carolinas not only English axes but many other tools, according at least to the testimony of British ironmongers. Moreover, quantities of nails were being
turned out from American slitting mills in successful
competition with the English product, and Rhode
Island was providing herself and neighboring colonies
with anchors.[3] Although New York was slow in

[1] Minutes of the Council of Massachusetts Bay, June 6, 1718,
Mass. Archives.

[2] See *Considerations on the Bill now Pending before the House
of Commons for Encouraging the Importation of Pig and Bar
Iron from America* (1750 ?), Penn Papers Relating to Iron.

[3] John Banister's testimony before the Committee of the
House of Commons 1738 (?), *ibid.* See also *The State of the*

developing iron production and iron manufactures and by 1750 had but one furnace in operation and a forge that was idle, New Jersey by the late '30s had a number of furnaces and forges[1] as had Pennsylvania.[2] Indeed, the latter province by 1750 had become the greatest iron producer of all the British plantations.

As to the quality of the American iron, there is little doubt. In 1737 Henry Calvert, writing from New York in July, states that there had arrived in the city a large consignment of American-made scythes stamped with the name "Hazard" which sold for six and seven shillings and were actually preferred by the country people to the best imported article;[3] while William Bole, a Philadelphia merchant, declared on August 1 of that year in a letter to his English correspondent that he had no need for garden spades, axes, carpenter tools, and nails as "these they make here."[4]

It is not surprising in light of the facts just recited, that in the year 1736 and even slightly earlier Parliament was deluged with petitions for the relief of the iron trade. One came from the ironmasters and iron-

Trade and Manufacture of Iron in Great Britain Considered (1750), p. 11.

[1] See C. D. Boyer, *Early Forges and Furnaces in New Jersey.*

[2] In 1750 there existed besides numerous furnaces and forges, a slitting and rolling mill, a plating forge with tilt hammer and two furnaces for making steel. Letter of Gov. Hamilton to the Board of Trade, Oct. 18, 1750. Hist. Soc. of Penna. Transcripts. See also A. C. Bining, "The Iron Plantations of Early Pennsylvania," *Pennsylvania Magazine of History and Biography*, April, 1933, and his *Colonial Iron Industry*, pp. 19-20.

[3] Gov. Hamilton to the Board of Trade, Oct. 18, 1750. Hist. Soc. of Penna. Transcripts.

[4] *Ibid.*

mongers of Lancashire, another from the same groups
of Worcestershire, still others from Bristol and Staffordshire with various petitions from those trading in
America. Among the latter was the "Humble Petition of the Merchants, Iron Masters, and Iron Mongers of this Kingdom in behalf of themselves and
many others trading to His Majesty's Plantations in
America."[1]

The last-named petition recited that, while premiums had been provided by act of Parliament for
the importation from America of tar, pitch, turpentine, hemp, masts, yards, and bowsprits, there
was no encouragement given to iron, although it
could be produced there in quality equal to the best
Swedish iron. Several furnaces and forges had already been erected in America and by means of these
and others to be built, Great Britain could be so adequately supplied with iron as to be rendered independent of any foreign country for a commodity so
essential to the support of the navigation of the Kingdom. However, it would be necessary, it was emphasized, to offer encouragement for the importation of
American bar iron, pigs, and sows and at the same
time to lay restraints on iron manufacturing in the
colonies.

The petitioners thereupon emphasized the disadvantages of so great a dependence upon Swedish iron.
It was well known, they declared, that the government of Sweden had laid high and severe duties upon
British manufactures which alone could be exchanged

[1] This is the first of the original manuscripts among the "Penn
Papers Relating to Iron." It is dated March 3, 1736. Hist. Society of Pennsylvania.

for iron.[1] This commodity, nevertheless, under prevailing conditions had to be purchased abroad "while your own subjects . . . lye unemployed and starving."

The other petitions referred to above all stressed the point that the erection in New England within the past few years of forges and slitting mills had already led, not only to the making of bar iron and the manufacture of axes, nails, and sundry other things for themselves but to the exportation of great quantities of these articles to many of the other plantations, and that, unless these slitting mills were destroyed and some stop put to American manufacturing, the iron trade of England would soon be utterly ruined.[2] The Worcestershire petition especially stressed the fact that the iron trade of this region had increased and flourished until lately, but now had greatly declined for want of the usual demands for iron products. This the petitioners ascribed to nothing but the mak-

[1] On December 11, 1734 the King of Sweden issued an edict prohibiting the importation of certain types of English goods and placing a very high duty, amounting almost to prohibition, upon all other imports, woolen hose and yarn alone excepted. A William Axtell, in testifying before a parliamentary committee at this period, asserted that England was obliged to purchase from that country iron to the value of one hundred and fifty thousand pounds sterling and yet, owing to these prohibitions, was unable to sell goods in return beyond the value of twenty or thirty thousand pounds at the highest. Report of the Committee of the House of Commons on the Petitions Relating to Iron, 1736-37, ibid., Doc. 27. In 1735, according to the records of the London Custom-House, there were exported to Sweden 14,030 pounds of glassware, 3,074 dozen beaver hats, 216 hundredweight of tin, 324 gross of tobacco pipes, 3,320 yards of flannel, 800 pieces kersies and 28,732 hundredweight of stuffs. P.R.O. T. 64. 273.

[2] "Humble Petitions of the Merchants, Iron Masters and Iron Mongers," March 3, 1736. Penn Papers Relating to Iron.

ing of iron and ironware in America. The petitioners saw the decline of their industry, especially
since many of the artificers and workmen had of late
left and it was feared had removed themselves to
America. Any encouragement, however, to import
bar iron from America, they felt, would not mend
matters but would increase the evils of which they
were complaining.[1]

It seemed clear that could America be induced to
give up iron manufacturing and in place send its
pigs and sows to England the general situation of the
industry in England would be greatly improved, even
should this mean nothing more than the substitution
of American iron for that produced abroad. Yet, was
it possible to make this substitution?

Certain writers insisted that American iron was of
the same composition as the "cold short" of England
and quite unlike that of Sweden and Russia. Were
this true and should it be freely imported would it not
continually depress the local product without re-
lieving Great Britain's precarious dependence upon
the foreign markets for Oregrund[2] and other types
of bar iron?[3] This question, with others affecting the
iron industry, was referred to a committee of the

[1] *Ibid.*
[2] The best quality of Swedish iron.
[3] The arguments contained in three pamphlets on the subject
are summarized in "The Petition of the Merchants, Iron Masters
and Iron Mongers." The titles of these are, *Reasons Against the
Making and Manufacturing of Barr Iron in America; Reasons
Against the Importation of Sow and Pig Iron from America into
Great Britain under the Present low Duty;* and *Some Considerations Showing that the Importations of Iron from America will
Sooner put a Stop to the Making of Iron in England than the
Importation of Iron from Sweden and Russia.*

House of Commons. Fortunately the testimony presented before it was preserved and is among the manuscripts and printed papers on the iron industry secured by Paris, Proprietorial Agent for Pennsylvania, for Thomas Penn. This may well be briefly summarized.

Joshua Gee, ironmaster of Shrewsbury, who was importing Virginia and Maryland pig iron, presented figures to prove that this iron could be produced more cheaply and advantageously in America than in England and warned the committee that if forges and manufactures were suffered to increase in the colonies these would eventually drain the Kingdom of its workers and would lead to the decline of ironworks of all kinds. Abraham Spooner of Birmingham likewise declared that if America were encouraged to make bar iron it would certainly end in the destruction of all ironworks in England.[1] According to the Custom-House report, in the year 1736 there was shipped to America and the West Indies 43,921 hundredweight of wrought iron. By this it appeared that Jamaica required a much larger quantity than the combined demands of Pennsylvania and New York. Nevertheless, it indicated that the chief iron-producing regions of New England and of the Chesapeake Bay were the largest customers, New England purchasing 8,491 hundredweight of wrought iron and Virginia and Maryland 8,983 hundredweight.[2] It was, however, asserted before the committee by one of the ironmasters, William Parkin, that there should

[1] "Committee Report of the House of Commons" (1737 ?), Penn Papers Relating to Iron, Doc. 45.
[2] P.R.O. T. 64. 273.

really be a demand for four times the amount of iron now sent to the plantations which could be attributed only to the quantity of ironware manufactured in America.

As a result of the agitation thus raised there was framed "A Bill for Promoting the Exportation of the Woollen and other Manufactures of this Kingdom and for Encouraging the Importation of Iron from America and for Restraining the Increase of Iron Manufactures there," bearing date of January 31, 1738.[1] The bill provided that there might be imported from the Plantations, in British and Irish ships, pigs, sows, and bar iron, unwrought and discharged of all poundage, subsidies, and other levies; that in turn for this encouragement after February 1, 1738 no mill or other engine for slitting or rolling iron or any furnace for making steel should be set up in any colony on pain of forfeiting one hundred pounds lawful money for each month wherein such mill would operate. Further, that after May 1, 1739 all foreign steel exported from Great Britain and Ireland to the Plantations should carry a duty of ten pounds a ton and, that after September 1, 1739, it would be unlawful to transport out of any of His Majesty's colonies to any other plantation or to Great Britain or Ireland any iron which shall be wrought up in America into nails, tools or other manufactures, under pain of the seizure of the cargo and the payment by the offender of fifty pounds for such offense.[2]

[1] An annotated copy of this bill is among the Penn Papers Relating to Iron, Doc. 35.

[2] On the margin of the manuscript copy of the bill among the Penn Papers, apparently in the hand of Ferdinand John Paris,

The time, however, was unfavorable for so serious a challenge of the right of the colonies to develop their own industrial life, although it is true that they already labored under restrictions with respect not only to the exportation of their wool and woolen manufactures and those articles on the enumeration but also in the making and exporting of hats. War with Spain appeared on the horizon and this demanded a united front. The war finally became merged in that of the Austrian Succession. It was therefore not until after the Peace of Aix-la-Chapelle that the British iron interests again turned to Parliament with appeals for relief. As a result a bill to encourage the importation of pig and bar iron from America was drafted.

According to a writer of the year 1749, the bill just referred to came most opportunely "when the nation [Sweden] which hitherto chiefly supplied us with Iron is laying farther dutys in order to raise the Price upon us and when our own Iron seems to be falling off and decreasing both in quantity and quality." He then went on to declare, "A few years since it was computed that about two-fifths of all Iron manufactured in Great Britain was first made and produced here; it is believed by those who are most conversant therein that Great Britain does not now Furnish above One Fifth Part of the Quantity here manufactured and a great deal of such fifth is

opposite the last clause is written this comment: "This is an ugly clause in its Consequences." According to the writer it might prevent the sending of a ship to Great Britain for sale because it contained American bolts.

so coarse and bad in quality as not to be fit for nail or small work."[1]

In spite of the above testimony relative to the decline of iron production, probably not less than six hundred thousand individuals, including women and children, were dependent for a livelihood upon the iron industry in England, according to an estimate of two hundred thousand workers actually employed in the middle of the century at an average weekly wage of seven shillings.[2] These people must be kept at work, it was felt. The nation had come out of the War just concluded heavily burdened with obligations, with taxes that had mounted upwards to a sum that averaged one guinea for every man, woman, and child within the Kingdom. Were half of the workers, as the result of unemployment, thrown upon the parish for relief, it was estimated that at the rate of twelve pence per week per individual this would bring an addition of £260,000 to be raised yearly by the taxpayers, besides the pauperization of a large percentage of the population.

In light of the above situation, one is not left in doubt why the conviction came home to thoughtful Englishmen that the time had come to throw off, if possible, the dangerous dependence upon Sweden for iron as had been done earlier in the century with respect to certain of the naval stores and ship timber procured from that country and Norway. It was felt at the same time with equal earnestness that the

[1] *Some Considerations on the Bill to Encourage the Importations of Pig & Bar Iron from America* (March 6, 1749).

[2] *Considerations on the Bill now Depending before the Honourable House of Commons for Encouraging the Importation of Pig and Bar Iron from America* (1749 ?).

plantations should not be allowed to overthrow one of the greatest of the industries of the Mother Country, bringing with it dire consequences to the laboring classes. Even those interests in England most sensitive to anything that would strike at American prosperity seemed to recognize the justice of placing restrictions upon colonial iron production, provided that concessions corresponding to these restrictions were provided. The Bristol Merchant Venturers, deeply involved in American trade, doubtless reflected this solicitous attitude when in their petition of March, 1749 to the Commons they argued in favor of a bill to embody these ideas.

"That your Petitioners humbly apprehend," they declared, "that a permission of Importing Pig and Barr Iron into Great Britain from the American Plantations Duty free will be attended with many valuable Consequences to the Nation in general, as it will greatly promote and encourage our Colonys abroad and thereby our own Manufacturers of various Kinds at Home, will considerably relieve us from the necessity we are now under of being supply'd with these Articles from Foreigners who prohibit many of our Manufactures, receive great sums in specie every year from us & are strictly united with our Rivals in Trade.

"That with regard to our own Manufacturys of Small or fine Iron ware, Your Petitioners are of opinion that there should be a restriction to prevent any Persons abroad from erecting any Slitting or Rolling Mills, or any Forges for Plating of Iron, whereby that valuable manufactory here will be preserved to us."[1]

[1] Merchants Hall, Bristol, Book of Charters (1749), p. 315.

The culmination of all this agitation extending over a period of fifteen years or more was the passage of the famous Iron Act of the year 1750.[1] This statute did away with the duty on both pig iron and bar iron imported from the plantations and produced there, with the restriction that bar iron to enjoy this exemption should be carried alone to the Port of London and should not be conveyed, subsequently to being stamped, more than ten miles from the city limits. The act then declared that in order "that Pig and Bar Iron made in his Majesty's Colonies in America may be further manufactured in this Kingdom, Be it further enacted by the Authority aforesaid, that from and after the twenty-fourth Day of June one thousand seven hundred and fifty, no Mill or other Engine for Slitting or Rolling of Iron, or any Plating forge to work with a Tilt Hammer, or any Furnace for making Steel, shall be erected, or after such Erections, continued, in any of his Majesty's Colonies in America; and if any Person or Persons shall erect, or cause to be erected, or after such Erection, continue, or cause to be continued, in any of the said Colonies, any such Mill, Engine, Forge or Furnace, every Person or Persons so offending shall ... forfeit the Sum of two hundred pounds lawful Money of Great Britain."

This measure all governors or acting governors were called upon to enforce under penalty of forfeiting five hundred pounds lawful money and of being disabled to hold any office of trust.[2]

[1] 23 George II, c. 29.
[2] See circular letter of May 29, 1750 signed by Thomas Hill, directed to the Governors of His Majesty's Plantations. C.O. 324: 13, pp. 244-77.

The reaction of some colonials to the Iron Act is doubtless well indicated by the views of the Pennsylvania surveyor and map-maker, Lewis Evans. Writing in 1753, he says:

"I cannot omit here doing justice to the British Parliament in their Act relating to the Admission of our Iron to the port of London only for sale. They knew that thus under a popular appearance, they would effectually damn it. The vicinity of Sweeden to London will always make the freight and insurance low, and notwithstanding the duty upon their Iron, it can be afforded cheaper than ours. But freights from Sweeden to Bristol, Liverpool, and other parts of the West Coast of Britain, would in War time be nearly as dear as from the British plantations; and they have taken care to prevent our enjoying the consumption of Iron on that side which is very considerable by reason of Pontipool, Birmingham, or Sheffield, so that for any benefit Britain may receive in case of a war with the northern Powers, by being supplied from her own Plantations, the Act had as well never been made, because not a man in America will set up an Iron Works, for the sake of the benefit of it. Supposing our Iron could be afforded in London within twenty shillings as cheap as the Sweedish, we might afford it as cheap as theirs at Bristol in case of a War with France. Oh! the Piety! feed our Enemies."[1]

The Act unhappily did not fulfill the rosy expectations of its supporters. Previous to this the importation of pig iron from the colonies amounted to something over two thousand tons. During the year 1750, 2,924 tons of American pig iron and five tons of bar iron were imported; in 1751, the amount was

[1] "A Brief Account of Pennsylvania," Hist. Soc. of Penna.

3,220 tons of pig iron with 23 tons of bar iron; in 1755, it reached 3,389 tons of pig iron and 389 tons of bar but dropped in 1757 to 2,699 tons of pig iron and 69 tons of bar.[1] It is of interest to note that Virginia and Maryland were the leading exporters of this iron; for 1750 their total was 2,508 tons of pig iron; for 1751, 2,950 tons and for 1752, 2,762 tons.[2] These figures indicate that American ironmasters generally found it to their advantage to manufacture the product of their furnaces and forges rather than to ship it to England. "There is indeed a necessity for their manufacturing," wrote the author of *The State of the Trade and Manufacture of Iron in Great Britain*, in 1750, "but of a quite different nature from what has been represented. A necessity that will not be removed by the importation of Bar-iron from thence; but will subsist as long as there are Forges there, and increase upon the Erection of more Forges. It is a Necessity of the strongest Nature, arising from Profit and Gain. The *American* manufacturer, by the Cheapness of his Iron, the Profit of manufacturing it at home, and by saving the many Expenses, Disappointments and Damages, that must necessarily attend exporting this Bar-Iron to *England*, and importing the manufactured Goods back again to *America* will have an Advantage of £45 per Cent."[3]

It was apparent, irrespective of the inability of the

[1] See Report of the Inspector General of Customs for February 7, 1760, Hist. Soc. of Penna. Transcripts.

[2] P.R.O. T. 64. 274. New England's contribution to these totals for these years was insignificant with 21 tons of pig iron in 1750, 9 tons in 1751, and 40 tons in 1752.

[3] *Ibid.*, pp. 12-13.

Mother Country to enforce the Act of 1750, that little check had been placed upon iron manufacturing in the Plantations.[1] That the government was anxious with respect to this development and was seeking every available means of checking it is indicated by the instructions given to Colonel Hopson, who was sent to Nova Scotia in 1752 to take the place of Governor Cornwallis. He was desired not to give any encouragement to the working of the collieries in that Province "which might prevent the clearing of Land and is not consistent with the ... policy observed by this country in relation to its colonies, as the use of Coals in America would furnish the people with the means of carrying on a variety of manufactures, the raw materials of which we now receive from them and afterwards return manufactured."[2]

The Statute of 1750, it was charged by English critics, was given its peculiar reading in the interests of the ironmasters as against the manufacturers of iron. "This law," complained a writer, "is of no service to the manufacturer who lives above ten miles from London. Pig iron must go into the hands of the Iron-Masters to be made into Bars which give them an opportunity of setting their own price upon American as well as English bar-iron, and the Swedish Iron, called Orgroon, is monopolized."[3] In 1757 the Bristol Merchant Venturers, in light of the disappointing results of the act, again petitioned Parlia-

[1] This point is developed in a recent excellent study by A. C. Bining, *British Regulation of the Colonial Iron Industry*, Chap. V.

[2] Board of Trade *Journal, 1749-1753*, p. 302.

[3] See *Reasons for Allowing the Importation of Bar-Iron from America* (without date), Penn Papers Relating to Iron. Orgroon was the popular name for Oregrund iron.

ment to admit freely the importation of bar iron.[1] This time they were successful,[2] with the result that the amount of this quality of iron exported from the colonies mounted from 69 tons received in that year to 1,059 tons in 1764.[3] However, the quantity was quite insufficient with the result that in 1765 the London and Birmingham manufacturers memorialized the Board of Trade in favor of a bounty on all American iron imported with ten shillings a ton for pig iron and forty shillings a ton for bar iron with a duty of ten shillings per ton on bar iron imported from Sweden, Russia, and Spain; they were joined in memorials from Wolverhampton and Walsall. Sheffield, however, opposed the duty on Swedish iron, "where it is imagined more steel is made than in the whole Kingdom besides." Its position was that American iron could not be made into anything that deserves the name of steel.[4]

It may in conclusion be said that the Iron Act did not prohibit—nor was it so worded as to prohibit— the production of American iron, or its manufacture into hardware. While it was hoped that through the inducements held out by means of free importation into Great Britain, American pig iron and bar iron would be sent over rather than fabricated in the colonies or turned into steel, there was a recognition of the utter unfairness of compelling mill owners operating before the act to destroy their property,

[1] "Merchants Hall Book of Charters" (1757), p. 339.
[2] 30 Geo. II, c. 16.
[3] G. L. Beer, Commercial Policy of England Toward the American Colonies, p. 87. By 4 George III, c. 15, iron was placed on the enumerated list.
[4] C.O. 323: 18. No bounty was granted on iron.

even with compensation. Therefore, the statute tended rather to favor those American ironmasters and steel producers already in business. In the words of a contemporary, "it is most certainly true that by prohibiting the future erection of Slitting Mills, etc., those who had such erected before the Act took place, will enjoy a sort of Monopoly. This was seen very clearly at the time of passing the Act. . . . "[1]

The attempts on the part of the Mother Country to regulate the production and sale of colonial iron in the middle of the eighteenth century serve to make clear that it was no easy task to shape by legislation, even with the best of motives, those complex economic forces within the Empire in the direction of realizing the ideals of imperial self-sufficiency and a planned economy which would supplement rather than destroy old, established interests within it, with consequent economic and social dislocations. Economic sectionalism, in fact, based upon particular sectional interests, served to defeat every effort put forth in this direction. However, it is certainly to the credit of Great Britain that she sought so to plan.

[1] R. Charles of Leicesterfields in England to Thomas Lawrence of Pennsylvania, Feb. 10, 1750, *Penna. Magazine of History and Biography*, VII, 232-233.

CHAPTER IX

HUDSON BAY BEAVER

EVER SINCE the twenty-second year of the reign of Charles II, when the Governor and Company of Adventurers of England trading into Hudson Bay was incorporated and granted the lands in the region of Hudson Bay with the sole trade and commerce to it, England has succeeded in exploiting the far northern fur trade in America.[1] The Bay is a rather forbidding region with very low temperatures in winter. In the eighteenth century it was quite cut off from communication with the Mother Country for a period of about nine months in the year on account of the blocking of Hudson Strait with impenetrable ice floes and icebergs. Although the Company had been in existence as a corporation for eighty years, there was little enough in 1750 to show in the way of development and improvements within the limits of the grant. The latter, outside of a scattered Indian population and the wild life upon which it preyed, was in the main a vast solitude. Probably not more than one hundred and twenty Englishmen, all employees of the Company, were living within its confines along the fringes of the great Bay at the various trading posts. Eight of these posts were located near the western shores between fifty-one degrees and fifty-nine degrees north latitude on important rivers that emptied their waters into the Bay. There were

[1] This excepts the brief period of French control to be mentioned.

233

THE NORTHERN PLANTATIONS

Moose Fort and Brunswick House on the Moose River, Albany Fort and Henley House on the Albany, York Fort on the Hayes, a branch of the Nelson, together with a small fort at Flamborough Head and another at Split Lake,[1] and lastly the most northern post, Prince of Wales, an unfinished stone fort on the Churchill,[2] where some forty-five of the Company's servants were dwelling. On the eastern shore of the Bay were Eastmain House on the Slude and Fort Richmond to the north.[3] Brunswick House on the Moose, the southernmost of these posts, and Henley House, situated one hundred and twenty miles up the Albany, were especially designed to offset the pressure of the French upon the Indians to the south and southwest of the Bay. York Factory, built of timber in the form of a square with four small bastions, seems to have been by far the most important trading center possessed by the Company,[4] and yet in 1750 only thirty-six men were there, including servants and factors, hardly enough to man the nineteen cannon—twelve, nine, and six pounders—which, with a double palisade, constituted the formal defense. The Company, of course, realized that the chief protection of its possessions lay in their isolation and in the

[1] R. E. Ponkerton, *Hudson's Bay Company*, p. 86.
[2] In the year 1734 this stone fort was erected in place of the old wooden structure. Beckles Willson calls it one of the strongest forts on the Continent, *The Great Company*, p. 18.
[3] *Ibid.*, p. 19.
[4] "This is looked upon to be in all Respect the most valuable of the *Hudson's-Bay* Company's Settlements because the most considerable part of their Trade is carried on here, where it is computed they deal for between forty and fifty thousand rich furs annually!" Henry Ellis, *A Voyage to Hudson's Bay* (London, 1748), p. 212; see also H. A. Innis, *The Fur Trade in Canada*, p. 143.

234

very great difficulties involved in any hostile movement against the Bay.[1]

In order to prosecute its fur-trading activities, the Company customarily sent out each year from England four ships which entered Hudson Bay about the middle of July and left, as a rule, about the first of October. These sturdy vessels with powerfully reinforced hulls built for this hazardous work were from 120 to 190 tons' burden and on the outward voyage were loaded with stores for the various needs of the posts, together with articles of trade, and returned with fur and other objects of value.[2] In the Company's report for the fiscal year 1747-1748, it is stated that the ships brought back over 52,000 beaver skins, over 8,000 marten, about 1,500 otter, some 1,200 wild cat, together with lesser quantities of bear, fox, wolverine, wolf, elk, deer, and other pelts and such articles as "bed feathers," whale fins, and goose quills to a total value of £30,160.5.11.[3] The cost of carrying on this trade in 1748 was placed at £17,-

[1] In 1690 the French captured Fort Severn and later Fort Nelson. Their hold on a part of the Bay was continued without much interruption until after the Treaty of Utrecht.

[2] For figures on the cost of maintaining the forts see Innis, op. cit., p. 135. Innis stresses the efforts made by the Company to reduce the amount of supplies, especially food supplies, annually required from England by rendering the various posts more self-sufficient.

[3] See No. X of the Appendix to the "Report from the Committee appointed to enquire into the State and conditions of the countries adjoining the Hudson Bay and the Trade carried on there together with an Appendix," 1749, in Reports from Committees of the House of Commons Reprinted by Order of the House, Vol. II, Miscellaneous Subjects, 1738-1765 (London, 1803). See also the Shelburne Papers, 112: 72-74, for tables showing the imports and exports to and from Hudson Bay. For this same period the imports from the Bay are valued at £12,-

352.4.10 to which was also added the value of the trading goods amounting to £3,453.2.7 and consisting principally of guns, powder, shot, knives, and blankets.

The Company regulations governing the trade with the natives were very strict. Not more than two men at a post were entrusted with this responsibility, and all others were forbidden to have any intercourse with the Indians. The latter, arriving at the posts from up the rivers in their birch-bark canoes in parties generally numbering about thirty, carried their pelts to the Company store. There they remained outside, since all transactions apparently took place at a window or hole in the supply house. As a measure of security in connection with this trade large numbers of Indians were never allowed within the palisades enclosing the post.[1] Moreover, great caution was exercised, it would appear, in supplying the Indians with strong drink. Richard White, a company factor before 1749, testified in the parliamentary investigation of that year that he had known eleven canoes to leave Fort Albany at one time for want of a present of a bottle of brandy.[2]

The influence of the presence of the French to the south, particularly to the north and west of Lake

392.14 and exports to, at £3,651.11.8. The differences in these figures lie perhaps in the appraised value of these furs at the time of importation and their value when released for sale from the Company's warehouses. See also Shelburne Papers, Vol. 102, for "A Sketch of the Trade to and from England to Hudson's Bay."

[1] Examination of Joseph Robson. "Report from the Committee on Hudson Bay, 1749." *Reports from Committees of the House of Commons, 1738-1765.*

[2] Examination of Richard White, *ibid.*

Superior, is evidenced by the fact that the Indians who came to the Moose and Albany rivers to trade could get a blanket for six beaver skins whereas at York Fort farther removed from French competition, the trader demanded seven; at the former a beaver skin entitled the Indian to eight knives and to only four at the latter.[1] This fur trade, it should be pointed out, was mostly with natives such as the Crees and the Assiniboines who lived at a distance from the Bay and acted as the middlemen for the Far West Indians. The Company's agents, however, did not travel to their abodes to prosecute this trade, although Henry Kelsey, it is true, between the years 1690 and 1692 traversed over five hundred miles of wilderness country and reached the Indians of the Plains and was followed over sixty years later by Anthony Hendry who in 1754 entered the country of the Blackfeet.[2] According to the trader, Joseph La France, some Indians dwelling to the Far West actually took two years to reach the Company factories, moving along leisurely, inactive during the heat of the day and hunting for food along the way.[3] The regions subject, therefore, to the Company's exploitation must have been very great indeed. However, trade was not continuous. At the Prince of Wales factory on the Churchill, for example, the Indians

[1] See H. A. Innis, op. cit., pp. 145-148 for a careful anaylsis of this.

[2] For Kelsey's "Journal" see the Kelsey Papers (1929); the Journal of Hendry has been edited by L. J. Burpee (Royal Soc. of Canada Proc. and Trans., third series, I); see his Search for the Western Sea.

[3] Examination of Joseph La France, "Report from the Committee on Hudson Bay" (1749), in Reports from Committees of the House of Commons, 1738-1765.

would arrive in July in their birch-bark canoes and in three weeks' time would be leaving while the river could still be safely navigated; after Christmas, however, some would return on the ice.

It does not appear that the Company made any efforts to civilize or Christianize the savages. Indeed it had very little contact with them outside of trade. While it is true that a few elderly Indians lived about the forts, they were seldom employed, except on occasions to secure fresh meat. Neither did the Company put forth any effort to establish interior posts and settlements. The very limits of its wilderness possessions were by no means determined. According to a memorial which was laid before the Board of Trade in 1750,[1] it claimed that the boundaries of the grant under the charter were the farthest northern extent of lands down to Cape Perdrix[2] on the Labrador Coast, located in the latitude of fifty-nine and one-half degrees, and from that point to Lake Miscosinke (Mistassini) southeast of Hudson Bay and thence to the forty-ninth degree of north latitude and along that meridian westward—certainly an empire! Indeed, had these limits been acknowledged by the French they would have been stripped of most of the regions from which they were drawing their wealth in furs.

After all, it was perhaps not so vitally important that the boundaries of the Company's grant should be precisely established so long as France made no further hostile thrust in the direction of the factories about the Bay such as the invasion that took place

[1] C.O. 323, for the memorial of Oct. 3, 1750.
[2] It reads: " ... at an Island called Grimington's Island otherwise Cape Perdrix. ... "

in the latter part of the seventeenth century. The enterprise was not for colonization but for trade and profits to the Company members. In 1749 the capital stock amounting to £103,950[1] was distributed among 103 people, including the minor heirs or administrators of the estates of deceased who had been stockholders to the number of twenty-six, and it is of interest to note that the only one among them who seems to have occupied a station in public life of some importance was Mark Thurston, Accountant-General of the Court of Chancery.[2] A great change from the days when the Company met at the lodgings of Prince Rupert in Whitehall!

The headquarters of the Company, where the annual General Court was held, were located in Fenchurch Street and were known either as Hudson's Bay House or Beaver House. This former structure has been recently described as "a very elegant, brick building adorned with pilasters and architraves... the vast repository of the Northern furs of America ...lodged here till they are sold and exported to various parts of the world, even to the distant China."[3]

In the disposal of the skins it was customary to offer them for sale at open auction at Beaver House.[4]

---

[1] In 1676 the stock was £10,500; in 1690 it was trebled to £31,500 and in 1720 it was trebled to £94,500. See Appendix XVIII of the "Report from the Committee on Hudson Bay" (1749), from *Reports from Committees of the House of Commons, 1738-1765*

[2] See Appendix VIII, *ibid.*

[3] Report of the Governor to the General Court of the Hudson's Bay Company held June 26, 1928, Ottawa *Journal*, July 8, 1928.

[4] This had been required by law. Should all the furs not be

At these auctions the Bay beaver brought during the years 1747-1748 an average price of seven shillings and six pence a pound, marten six shillings and eight pence, otter nine shillings, seven pence and a farthing. These furs were easily the finest brought out of America, superior as a rule to the peltries secured from the Great Lakes region, and among prospective buyers there was the keenest competition.[1]

The Bay beaver had at first been used largely for the making of muffs and the lining of garments; then the hatters began to employ this fur and it is asserted that by the year 1701 they had become the most opulent and extensive traders within the Kingdom, employing over twenty thousand people in the making of beaver hats alone.[2] However, from 1701 to 1711 the French were in military control of much of Hudson Bay and used this opportunity to encourage the production of beaver hats at home. For the English manufacturers were cut off from any adequate supply of skins as a result of the prohibition of the export of these from France. So energetic were the French hatters that they succeeded ultimately, according to a memorial of their English rivals, in monopolizing the hat trade of Spain, Portugal, Italy, Germany, Sweden, and Denmark.[3] The loss of these

disposed of at auction the price of the remainder, if disposed of at private sale, was determined by the last auction price.

[1] H. A. Innis, *op. cit.*, pp. 1-2.

[2] Hatters' Memorial of March 12, 1764. Chatham Manuscripts, P.R.O.

[3] *Ibid.* "And the French are so tender of this Branch of Trade and so sensible of the Advantages that arise from the manufacture of these American commodities, that no one can reëxport Beaver from France unmanufactured, under the severest penalties. When these Goods are manufactured, they exceed the

markets had a demoralizing effect upon the English manufacturers. In fact, one who travelled through France in 1727 was surprised to find large numbers of English hatters who had been forced to leave England on account of the stagnation there of this handicraft.[1] What added to the discouragement of the English felt-makers was the rise of hat manufacturing in the colonies. In both the provinces of Massachusetts Bay and New York there was considerable activity along this line. Not only were beaver hats sold in the local markets in competition with the English hats but it was reported that these were exported to Spain, Portugal, and the West Indies. Faced, it seemed, with ruin, the British hatters in 1731 petitioned Parliament for relief. In an effort to save the situation, that body passed the Act of 1732.[2] For it was felt that a colonial industry must not be permitted to destroy a well-established and important industry of the Mother Country—something that no colonizing power in the eighteenth century would have permitted, it goes without saying.

The statute in question sought to regulate the American beaver-hat industry. It not only limited the number of apprentices that might be employed by American plantation hat-makers to two but pro-

value upon importation in some Cases, ten fold, and they have greatly improved this Branch of Trade and Supply most Parts of Europe and Spanish America with Hats." *The Present State of the British and French Trade to Africa and America* (1745), p. 8.

[1] *Ibid.* For an extended account of this industry see J. H. Hawkins, *History of the Worshipful Company of Feltmakers of London.* The method of making a beaver hat, "the highest achievement of the hatter," is described on pages 16 to 19.

[2] 5 Geo. II, c. 22.

hibited the export of their manufactures outside of the colony where these were produced. The measure, however, while certainly having the effect of discouraging the expansion of American beaver-hat manufacturing, did not result in restoring the one-time prosperity to this important branch of British industry.[1] The great foreign markets were irretrievably lost. It was estimated in 1764 that the French drew the equivalent of £3,000,000 into France through the sale of their hats. For they continued, it appears, to secure the bulk of the Hudson Bay beaver on account both of their ability to outbid the English manufacturers by reason of liberal drawback provisions under the English customs arrangements for

[1] "It appeared before a committee of the House of Commons last Thursday night, that there had been near 200,000 beaver skins exported from hence to France the very last year, and proved by several hat-makers that before the last war they could employ but 20 men but that during that interruption caused by the war of exporting of beaver to France they had augmented their number to 500, but since the peace, their trade had so diminished that they can scarcely now employ 40 men & that a great number were perishing for want of employment and that they the masters had heard there were several agents here to engage them to go to France." Hatters' Memorial of March 12, 1764, Chatham Manuscripts, P.R.O.

According to the hat-makers and hat-vendors a beaver skin when imported paid a duty of 7 3/20d.—5/8d.; when reëxported there was a drawback upon this duty of 4 6/20d.—13/16d. They sought to have the drawbacks on reëxportation discontinued and in place an export duty levied upon all beaver skins and unmanufactured beaver wool. *Acts of the Privy Council, Col., 1745-1766*, pp. 650-651. That the English hat industry was in a declining state cannot be questioned in light of the custom-house figures for the exportation of hats for three-year periods, that is for 1735-1737, 1750-1753, and 1759-1762. During the first period the number was 371,014; during the second, 335,644, and during the third, 94,602. *Ibid.*, 651-652.

the exportation of these skins[1] and the lower wages paid to workers. Moreover, the truth is that the French produced a finer beaver hat than their English rivals. For example, during the war of the Austrian Succession a French ship bound for the Spanish West Indies with white beaver hats fell into the hands of the English who sold a quantity of these in the London market. The hats were considered so superior to anything that the British manufacturers could produce that it was declared by one writer that "they were much beyond what they could have imagin'd."[2] This was the situation in 1750.[3]

From what has been stated it can be seen that the Hudson's Bay Company was at this period in an enviable position. It was asserted by Joseph Robson, who, it should be pointed out, was a critic of the Company although a former employee, that the

[1] 8 Geo. I, c. 15.
The beaver fur considered most desirable for hat-making was *castor gras d'hiver*, that is, the fur of the beaver taken in winter. *Castor sec* was the parchment beaver. H. A. Innis, *op. cit.*, pp. 2, 10-11. This was also largely monopolized by foreigners as the following item makes clear:
"We hear that at the Publick Sale of the Hudson Bay Company on Thursday last, the Parchment Beaver was wholly bought up for exportation at an advanced Price of seventy-five per Cent, which together with the Advance on the sale of that Company November last, has more than doubled the Price of that Commodity, and rendered it impossible for the manufacturer in England to purchase, whereby several poor families dependent thereon are rendered incapable of getting a livlihood." *Aris's Birmingham Gazette*, March 18, 1751.
[2] *The Present State of the British and French Trade to Africa and America* (1745), p. 8.
[3] The bill of 1759 "for regulating the Company of Feltmakers, of London" refers to the fact that "the said Company or Fellowship is of late Years much diminished and decayed." J. H. Hawkins, *History of the Feltmakers of London*, p. 157.

Company could export a quart of English spirits at six pence, mix it with one-third water and then exchange it for a beaver skin weighing a pound and a half, for which they could get at auction nine shillings and a penny, making a 2700 per cent profit.[1] It was calculated that the Company secured about two hundred and sixteen per cent profit upon the annual stock in trade after all expenses had been deducted and about seven and two-thirds per cent profit upon their nominal capital of $103,950.[2]

In light of this situation it is not to be wondered at that there were those who sought to break through the monopoly and to secure for themselves some of the benefits of this lucrative trade. In 1749 the combined overseas trading interests of Bristol and Liverpool directed an assault against these exclusive rights, feeling doubtless that as they had succeeded in breaking through the monopoly of the great Royal African Company they might hope for the same success in connection with that of the Hudson's Bay. A petition to Parliament was prepared by a committee from the two merchant groups, requesting "that the trade of Hudson Bay may be free and open." A body of the ablest Bristol merchants was thereupon sent to London to support it.[3] This attack was doubtless connected with the well-known attempt of the Irishman,

[1] Joseph Robson, *An Account of Six Years' Residence in Hudson's Bay* (London, 1752), pp. 49-51.

[2] *Ibid.*, Buckles Willson estimates that even in dull times there was a profit of forty per cent on the actual paid-up capital. *The Great Company, 1667-1871*, p. 9.

[3] "The Book of Proceedings of the Bristol Merchant Venturers, 1745-1752," under dates of April 1 and 25, 1749, Merchant Venturers' Hall, Bristol.

Arthur Dobbs, with a group of associates, to undermine the Hudson's Bay Company charter during the
period under consideration.

In 1745 Parliament, to stimulate an interest in the
discovery of the Northwest Passage through Hudson
Strait, had passed an act offering a reward of £20,000
to the owner of the vessel that should discover this
passage.[1] As a result, Dobbs and his associates sent
out an expedition which wintered in Hudson Bay
and the members of which were kept from perishing
by the Company servants at York Fort and incidentally provided with so much strong drink as to destroy
the morale of the group.[2] While no passage was
found, some information was gained which was considered of value, and the Dobbs group thereupon
formulated a plan to secure a grant of land adjoining
Hudson Bay.[3] The two avowed objectives that they
had in mind were, first, the establishment of a permanent base whence exploration by land and sea
could be carried on for the discovery of the Passage;
second, the settlement and improvement of the lands
"in all the countries on that northern continent by
making alliances with and civilizing the natives and
incorporating with them"—surely not an unambi-
tious task! They drew a picture of a great agricultural development with herds of cattle and various
growing crops in a region still held to be unfavorable

[1] 18 Geo. II, c. 17.
[2] Henry Ellis, *A Voyage to Hudson's Bay by the Dobbs Galley
and California in the years 1746 and 1747 for Discovering a
Northwest Passage* (Dublin, 1749).
[3] For some years Dobbs had been interested in the lands of this
region. See his *Account of the Countries Adjoining Hudson Bay*
(London, 1744).

for such exploitation. But the impression is created
that what they had in mind, among other things, was
to secure land grants that would have the effect of
cutting the Hudson's Bay Company off from its
great sources of wealth—the western Indian trade.
Early in 1748, in the furtherance of this plan, the
Dobbs group petitioned the Privy Council for the
necessary concessions to allow them to carry out their
avowed aims; the petition was referred to the Attorney and Solicitor-General, who reported unfavor-
ably upon it.[1] The issue then found its way into
Parliament and led to the appointment of a committee to investigate the activities of the Hudson's
Bay Company in light of charges made against this
organization. It was not difficult for the parties opposing the Company's monopoly to find witnesses
willing to testify as former servants and employees
of the latter that it had taken no serious steps to
bring about the discovery of the Northwest Passage,
which it had agreed to do at the time of the granting
of its charter.[2] These also complained that it had
not been friendly to the colonization by Englishmen
of the region adjacent to the Bay and charged that its
prices as fixed for company goods were so exorbitant as to discourage the Indians from trading. In this
connection it was stated on oath that the local governor at Churchill was accustomed to charge twice

[1] Henry Ellis, A Voyage to Hudson's Bay by the Dobbs Galley
and California in the years 1746 and 1747 for Discovering a
Northwest Passage (Dublin, 1749).
[2] For an account of the various vessels sent out from the posts
for the work of discovery during the period between the years
1719 and 1737, some eight in all, see George Bryce, The Remarkable History of the Hudson's Bay Company, p. 72.

the amount fixed by the Company standard and to require far more marten skins for a gun than did the French, which led the Indians of the interior to prefer to sell the lighter and more valuable skins to the French and to bring to the Bay as a rule only those beaver and other skins which the French traders far removed from any post could not handle in canoes that had to be carried across the portages.

The Company, however, was too powerfully entrenched to be reached. It weathered this and many succeeding storms. In 1750, so assured was it of its position, that it had no hesitancy in memorializing the government to secure a settlement with France not only for damages amounting to some £100,000 it had sustained by French attacks on its posts before the treaty of Utrecht but also for the final determination of the boundaries between New France and Hudson Bay, complaining in this connection that the French had established themselves in forts to the west of the Bay—clearly within its territory.[1]

As to the French rivalry, it may be pointed out in conclusion that by the middle of the century there had been established in the neighborhood of Lake Winnipeg, Fort Dauphin on Lac des Prairies, Fort Bourbon on what is now Cedar Lake, and Fort Poskioac at the juncture of the Carrot and Saskatchewan, as well as Fort Maurepas at the mouth of the Winnipeg and Fort La Reine on the Assiniboine.[2]

[1] See Memorial of the Governor and Company of Adventurers of England Trading into Hudson's Bay, Oct. 3, 1750. C.O. 5: 6, p. 323.

[2] The two last-named posts, it appears, were not occupied in 1750 as the result of wars between the Sioux and the Assiniboines

Further, in 1748 Le Chevalier de la Vérendrye had established a temporary post at the forks of the Saskatchewan which gave way in 1753 to Fort St. Louis and Fort à la Corne, and in 1751 still another temporary post was established on a branch of the south fork of the Saskatchewan within sight of the Rocky Mountains.[1] These posts sought to monopolize the trade of the upper Churchill, of Lakes Cumberland and Winnipegosis, and of the Saskatchewan, Assiniboine, and Red rivers. That this was not accomplished was due to the fact that they were far removed from Montreal. To reach them involved portaging and other difficulties. This meant that goods given and received in the course of trade had to be adapted to the exigencies of this situation. For canoes could not be overloaded either in going or returning. Therefore, only the lighter, less bulky trading goods could be conveyed to the posts, and only the lighter pelts could be accepted for transfer to Montreal. Therefore, as Professor Innis has made clear, this meant that even the Indians in contact with French traders, who desired to secure such articles as guns, ammunition, kettles, iron tools, and tobacco and to trade their heavier furs and skins, were perforce led to descend either the Nelson or the Churchill to resort to the Hudson Bay posts.[2]

which, according to Pierre de la Vérendrye, brought about the ruin of La Reine and the burning of Maurepas. For a discussion of this see H. A. Innis, *op. cit.*, pp. 96-97.

[1] *Op. cit.*, p. 97.
[2] *Ibid.*, pp. 98-99.

CHAPTER X

BANKERS AND SACKMEN. THE PROVINCE OF AVALON

WE HAVE now passed in review the colonial establishments in North America and the West Indies. There yet remains for consideration the overseas activities of the British in the region of the great Island of Newfoundland.

For almost two hundred and fifty years, Englishmen had resorted to "the Banks" for the catching of cod; there also had come hardy Breton and Norman fishermen, Basques, and Portuguese. In 1750 the catching and curing of these fish was one of the world's great staple industries and was largely in the hands of the French and English. The Island of Newfoundland, somewhat larger than Ireland, did not, in spite of important resources, attract permanent settlers for the first century after its discovery, although it is true that some of the fishermen wintered there in small groups; and then came attempts at colonization—such as that made by Gilbert and his associates in 1583 and by the Newfoundland Company in 1611 —even before Sir George Calvert's effort to settle at Ferryland and Sir William Vaughan's, at Trepassey in the third decade of the seventeenth century.[1]

[1] See R. G. Lounsbury, *The British Fishery at Newfoundland, 1634-1763*, for a recent and illuminating account of British activities in the region of Newfoundland. The standard work on

Nevertheless, the importance of the Island was realized and, as a consequence, in the duelling between
France and England in the seventeenth and eighteenth
centuries Newfoundland became a principal prize. By
the treaty of Utrecht the former assigned her territorial claims to it while reserving the right to resort
to the coasts from Cape Bonavista, on the eastern
shore, northward to the farthest point and then
southward along the western shore to Cape Riche,
which included the peninsula of Petit Nord—a con-
cession that, taken together with her continued control of the Island of Cape Breton, placed her St. Malo
and Cape Breton fishermen for all practical purposes
in control of the most favorable parts of Newfoundland for the exploitation of the fisheries. In the words
of Captain Griffith Williams, who was in the Island
in the middle of the century, "This was the Fishery
we had then [after the Treaty of Utrecht] cause to
lament the loss of; and, indeed, so we have to this
Day; the Fish in those Parts being in greater Abundance, and the Fishery carried on at Half the Expense,
the Weather being much better for curing, because
the Fogs don't go any farther Northward than the
great Bank of Newfoundland. . . . "[1] It was, as a

Newfoundland is D. W. Prouse's *History of Newfoundland;*
even more important because more scholarly is J. D. Rogers'
Historical Geography of Newfoundland.

[1] *An Account of the Island of Newfoundland with the Nature
of its Trade* (London, 1765), p. 13. Captain T. Cole, who made
proposals to the government in 1761 for excluding the French
from the fisheries also emphasized the above points in declaring
that the French were permitted to get their fish to the markets
sooner than was possible for the English and to carry it in better
condition, "Because the South Part of this Coast where our
People fish, is always covered with Fogs, and mizzling Rains,

consequence, generally conceded that, notwithstanding the very great activity of the English off the
Banks and in the inlets of the Island, the French had
by far the best part of the cod trade. Other reasons
than the above can be assigned for this superiority:
French cod was more highly esteemed, as it was better
cured;[1] it reached the world markets before the English commodity, as the Cape Breton fishermen could
begin operations before the close of winter, and it
sold at a low price. Indeed, according to Captain
Cole writing in 1761, "The French ... so far succeeded in that most valuable Branch of Trade, as to
get the Preference in most of the *European* markets
—which makes a difference to this nation of upward
of £2,000,000 per annum." This was, he affirmed, the
situation before the outbreak of hostilities, in connection with the Seven Years' War.[2]

In 1750 the Avalon Peninsula was the center of the
English activity. There was St. John's which in 1746,
according to Captain James Douglas, contained a
population of 263 English Protestants fit to bear
arms and 311 Irish Catholics who were considered
neither fit for this function nor for liberty of conscience.[3] This town was not only the port of chief

which keep the Fish so long in drying, that the Maggots breed
in them, and render them of less Value at the *European* Markets."
Ibid., p. 27.
  [1] C.O. 5: 200, p. 589. "The benefit of pure salt is apparent in
the cod, as well as in the herring," declared a writer in 1749,
"those the Dutch cure are clear and white: those the English cure
are brown and dirty. So it is in Newfoundland, where the
French fish are much better coloured, and most agreeably tasted."
Wealth of Great Britain in the Ocean (1749), p. 54.
  [2] Captain Cole's "State of the Fisheries," in Griffith Williams,
Account of the Island of Newfoundland, p. 28.
  [3] C.O. 5: 200, p. 596.

resort for the merchantmen, known as "sack-ships," destined to load for Portugal, Spain, and Italy, but also for the vessels of the "Bankers," or "West Countrymen," fishermen from the West of England ports, who soon after their arrival each spring dispersed along the shores of the Island from Bonavista to Placentia bays—south of these regions where the French were privileged to dry their catch—to begin the season's operations.[1] There, also, on the Peninsula was Placentia, where was stationed the most important body of troops detached to guard the Island, and Ferryland, Carbonear, and Trinity, where, likewise, small garrisons were maintained in the middle of the century.[2]

Various estimates of the population living permanently on the Island can be found. It appears that by the middle of the eighteenth century considerably more than seven thousand people were settled within the Peninsula. Indeed, in 1753 it was affirmed in a statement to the Crown that, exclusive of those coming for the fisheries, there were, at the least estimation, twelve or thirteen thousand, including men, women, and children,[3] while the numbers coming in

[1] Among the ports deeply interested in the cod fisheries in the middle of the century were Bideford, Bristol, Dartmouth, Exeter, Poole, Teignmouth, and Topsham. Falmouth, Fowey, Plymouth, Southampton, Truro, and Weymouth also earlier took an important part in these fisheries.

[2] Board of Trade *Journal, 1749-1753*, p. 37.

[3] See the "Case of the Right Honorable Frederick, Lord Baltimore, relating to the Province of Avalon in America" (1753), p. 4. Calvert Papers, Maryland Historical Society. In 1765 the Board of Trade stated that from the best accounts the number of inhabitants was not less than fifteen thousand, including men, women, and children. See its representation of April 29, 1765, *Papers Relating to Newfoundland* (1793), p. 5.

for the fishing season were placed at 15,420 operating some 1,676 ships and shallops.[1] The permanent inhabitants from all accounts were by-boatmen, merchants with New England connections,[2] tavern keepers, those employed by the Bankers during the season at the fish-stages, those engaged in trapping beaver, otter, and other fur-bearing creatures about the streams and the great swamps of the still little known interior, together with those who near the seashore were making a beginning of cultivating the land. Most of the habitations on the Island were humble; cattle, sheep, and horses were few in number and the hardy dwellers were obliged to depend upon water transportation largely, although a breed of powerful dogs was already commonly employed to do the work of hauling sledges loaded with wood and other necessities.

From early in October to the middle of May little activity was evidenced on the Island. Everything wore a deserted aspect: the long lines of empty fish-

[1] See "Case of Lord Baltimore," p. 3.

[2] By the early part of the century it appears that the Boston merchants were playing a dominant rôle in the life of Newfoundland as the result of the importation of various commodities and the establishment of stores in the fishing communities. These stores were accustomed, with the close of the fishing season and the departure of the ships in the fall, to sell rum and provisions at exorbitant prices but on credit. By this means the inhabitants ran into debt and were compelled to sacrifice the next season's catch. C. P. Nettels, *The Money Supply of the American Colonies before 1720*, p. 77. The fish turned over to the New Englanders, if prime, was as a rule sold in turn to the English sack-ships for money or bills; if refuse fish, it was carried to the West Indies. This had long been the settled practice on the part of those who came from North America to trade. For example, see the testimony of Captain Norris to the Board of Trade, Nov. 3, 1698, quoted in *ibid.*, p. 78.

staging and cook houses along the shores of the bays, the villages but partly inhabited and many of the taverns closed. In truth, most of the inhabitants not occupied in trapping and in building boats and getting materials from the woods for staging, and so forth,[1] all but hibernated between the departure of the sack-ships, the West Countrymen, and the New Englanders in the fall and their return in the spring. One may well imagine with what resignation they waited during the months of gloom, fog, and snow and—with the passing away of winter and with it of the field ice and icebergs—with what anticipations must they have looked for the first appearance of the ships from the home ports! For these brought news from the outside world, rum, and countless other supplies, buyers of pelts, train oil, and other raw products that had been accumulated for sale, and also, perchance, friends who, to make their way to Newfoundland, had joined the fishing ships. For the masters of the latter were required to enlist each year numbers of green men who only too frequently deserted the ships before the return voyage and thus recruited the number of the permanent inhabitants.

In contrast with the apathy of winter were the scenes of animation during the height of the fishing season: the movement out of the bays in the early morning hours of hundreds of shallops propelled by oars aided by lugsails; the feverish activity of thousands of men at the fish-stages on the beaches, especially in case of rain when the great piles of fish must be turned with backs uppermost to be kept

---

[1] Captain Griffith Williams, *An Account of the Island of Newfoundland* (1765), p. 10.

from spoiling and then re-turned with the coming of
the sun; the swarming of hard-drinking sailors, fishermen, traders, and trappers in the taverns after the
labors of the day, with all the wild life that was associated at that and at every period with towns on the
fringes of civilization.

By 1750 the methods employed by the English in
the catching and curing of cod had been systema-
tized. The ships of the West Countrymen, instead of
remaining on the Banks until a cargo was secured,[1] as
a rule were anchored in the bays, and the main activities were carried on in the "by-boats" or shallops
which generally did not go more than two leagues
from land, where the hardy fishermen cast their lines
and returned every evening to the shore,[2] bringing
the catch, which was thrown upon a platform. There
the fish were dressed in a flash with a double-edged
knife by the "cut-throat," handed to the "carver"
who, with a great single-edged knife, split them and
passed them to the "salter." But with this the process
of curing had just begun. After some days in the
salt, the fish were washed and laid out to dry on long
but narrow fish-stages and flakes extending for some

[1] This had been an earlier practice of the Portuguese, the
Basques, and the Bretons who engaged in the "wet" fishery. The
English who preferred to dry the fish found the problem of
caring for the catch on board ship was too great. "Many have
been the times," declared Captain Griffith Williams, "when the
Masters of Vessels have left the Banks with a fine loading of
Fish; and, ... upon opening their Hatches found their Cargo
turned to Maggotts," *Account of the Island of Newfoundland*
(1765), p. 12. Yet some West Countrymen in the eighteenth
century did resort to the Banks for their fish. R. G. Lounsbury,
The British Fishery at Newfoundland, pp. 310-311.

[2] Capt. John Knight to George Brydges Rodney, from Placentia, Aug. 7, 1749, Rodney Papers, Vol. 6, P.R.O.

distance from shallow water back into the land; were thereafter piled and aired and then piled in ever larger heaps and sweated, and were at last ready for shipment—a process covering some weeks and demanding great watchfulness and experience to secure the best results.[1] This was known as inshore fishing.

The cod thus caught and cured at the end of the season was carried by the sack-ships either to southern Europe or to the West Indies. The first-quality fish was disposed of in the seaports of Spain, Portugal, and Italy; the inferior grades were carried to the sugar islands. The ships that came from England to load for southern Europe were apt to bring commodities to the American continental colonies. After these were discharged they sailed to Newfoundland for fish and then southward. The colonial sack-ships brought American continental and West India commodities to Newfoundland, which were exchanged usually for the inferior grades of fish, called "Jamaica" fish. This was thereupon carried to the West Indies and sold to the merchants and planters as slave provisions; with the proceeds of the sale, West India products, especially sugar and molasses, were secured to be carried home.

As to the value of the fisheries, no accurate statement can be made. Figures for the period under consideration show the most striking divergence. Surveyor-General Robert Dinwiddie in the early '40s estimated that Newfoundland secured annually 800,-000 quintals of cod. The value of this with the oil, he figured at £400,000.[2] Captain Griffith Williams es-

[1] D. Fenning, A New System of Geography (1765), II, 631.
[2] See Abercrombie's "Examinations," Shelburne Papers, 47: p. 29.

timated that the true value of the cod alone before the outbreak of the Seven Years' War was not less than £1,032,000, with fish selling at an average price of 20s. per quintal, certainly a high figure.[1]

However, even the cod fisheries do not represent the full value of Newfoundland to the Mother Country in financial returns. Along the coast were taken great numbers of whales, seals, and porpoises which together yielded thousands of barrels of train oil annually; in the forests were bear, deer, moose, foxes and wolves, sought by trappers; while the streams and swamps yielded beaver and otter; lastly, for many years a flourishing salmon fishery had been carried on by merchants of Pool, Southampton, Weymouth, and Lyme in the fresh waters between Cape Bonavista and

[1] See his *An Account of the Island of Newfoundland* (1765), pp. 1-6. Williams, who had engaged in the fisheries in the '50s, had the utmost contempt for the figures sent from time to time by the governors on the state of this industry. He declared that the information secured was from merchants at each of the harbors who were accustomed to fill out the forms at random. To test one report from Harbour Grace as to the total catch along Conception Bay with a shoreline of at least seventy miles, Williams visited every cove and creek where boats were kept. Upon the basis of this information he was impelled to estimate that between the years 1745 and 1752 the annual catch was 1,032,000 quintals. On the other hand, according to the *Traveller's Magazine*, of March, 1749, the catch was but some two hundred thousand quintals, the value of which was £120,000. In 1741, according to Captain Smith, the catch equalled 366,600 quintals which at 10s. 6d. per quintal amounted to £192,465. "Newfoundland's Establishment and Output" (1741), by Captain Smith. Chatham Papers, Transcripts in the Canadian Archives from volumes 74-94, p. 157. Williams estimated the amount of the oil produced from the fish livers annually at this period at 5,160 tons. The total fish and train oil annually secured was calculated in 1753 to be 36,655 tons. "Case of Lord Baltimore" (1753), p. 3.

St. John's.[1] Frederick, Lord Baltimore, in 1754 estimated the total returns from the Island, including
profits from freight charges, at the conservative figure
of £470,547.[2]

Since most of the fish yield, as has been made clear,
was taken southward by the sack-ships, only a small
quantity of cod was transported to England. Indeed,
the direct commerce between the two islands was
unimpressive in light of the total wealth abstracted by
fishermen and trappers. For example, in 1752 Newfoundland sent raw materials valued at only £41,-
459.4.7 to England, and, of this total, £29,666 covered
the chief item, train oil; while she imported from the
Mother Country commodities amounting to but £46,-
995.2.11, the chief item of which was woolen goods.[3]

The decline in the cod fisheries was a source of great
uneasiness to the British government. In fact, since
the early part of the eighteenth century, if not before,
the English dried cod had apparently lost favor in the
markets, and the governors were called upon to correct this situation, if possible.[4] When Rodney was

[1] See *Atlas Maritimus et Commercialis*. London, 1728, p. 325;
C.O. 5: 200, p. 593.
[2] See "Case of Lord Baltimore" (1753), p. 4.
[3] See the Shelburne Papers, Vols. 102, pp. 12-13 and 122, p.
12. (Canadian Archives Transcripts). London enjoyed only a
small percentage of this direct commerce, receiving in 1751
commodities valued at £3,589.9.4 and shipping directly those
valued at £2,603.7.2.
[4] The Board of Trade in its representation of 1718 referred to
reports from British consuls and merchants residing in Spain,
Portugal, and Italy that the fish brought to these markets from
Newfoundland "for some years past, has been for the most Part
so ill cured, that the consumption thereof is greatly abated, and
that the Trade is in Danger of being thereby lost." "Copy of a
Representation of the Lords Commissioners for Trade and Plan-

commissioned governor in 1749, the sixty-first article of his instructions stressed the vital importance of preventing the sack-ships, between the commanders of which there was great rivalry to reach the markets first, from sailing with fish until it had been properly cured; for by the sale of badly cured fish, it was stated, the consumption had been so lessened that there was fear lest that trade would be quite lost to the nation;[1] further, he was to see that the admirals of the harbors were strictly enjoined to take the greatest care that in curing the cod not only should good salt be used but a sufficient quantity of the same, "that the credit thereof may be again recovered and that it may be well received and esteemed in the several places to which it is carried for sale."[2]

Another great object of solicitude on the part of the government and people of England was continually evidenced: that there should be no development of activity by those established on the Island or in North America which would deprive either the English merchants of a profitable, if limited, market for woolens and other such commodities or the English fishing towns of the western coast of their ancient interest in the cod fisheries—leading thereby to a decline in British manufacturing and in shipping. For the Banks of Newfoundland in the eighteenth

tations to His Majesty relating to the Newfoundland Trade and Fishery." Dec. 19, 1718. *Papers Relating to Newfoundland* (1793), p. 2. Commodore Lee in his report for the year 1736 stressed strongly this point.

[1] C.O. 5: 200, p. 596.

This injunction was also embodied in earlier instructions. It certainly was pertinent to the situation in the middle of the century.

[2] *Ibid.*

century, as in the seventeenth, were regarded as a great school for seamanship. Each governor was instructed to see that every fifth man was a fresh or green man both in the fisheries and on the ships coming to the Island, as was laid down in the regulations passed under King William.[1] The national sentiment behind these regulations is well expressed by one writing in the middle of the eighteenth century who declared with reference to the wealth derived from the fisheries, "all this sum is actually got by our labour, and, therefore, is of much more service to the nation by breeding up useful seamen than if so much was to be dug out of the mine, with a thousandths part of the labour."[2]

The desire to foster British seamanship and the home mercantile marine had led to efforts in the seventeenth century to discourage permanent settlement; and when this came, to break it up, but without success.[3] It was feared with good reason toward the latter part of the seventeenth century that just as the New England fisheries had been earlier engrossed by the people living in the plantations so would the

[1] See "An Act to Encourage the Trade to Newfoundland," 10 and 11 William III, c. 25. This requirement was previously embodied in the so-called New Charter issued Jan. 27, 1675-76. The provisions of this patent are summarized in the representation of the Board of Trade of Dec. 19, 1718. *Papers Relating to Newfoundland* (1793), pp. 8-9. See also *Acts of the Privy Council, Col., 1613-1680*, Par. 915 for the order in council of 1671 providing for the employment of new or green men.

[2] *Traveller's Magazine*, March, 1749.

[3] For a full account of this see R. G. Lounsbury, *The British Fishery at Newfoundland*, Chap. III-IV; also G. L. Beer, *The Old Colonial System*, Part I, Vol. II, Chap. X.

Newfoundland fisheries if due care were not taken.[1]
It was, therefore, provided that neither the inhabitants nor any others should take possession of, or in
any way injure, the beaches, stages, cook-rooms, flakes,
and other conveniences for the carrying on of the
fisheries that were left behind when the ships returned
home in the fall; it was also laid down that the admirals of the harbors should be limited to those from
the Mother Country arriving earliest each spring in
their fishing ships, to whom there fell the authority
of allocating the conveniences mentioned to those
who came from Great Britain to fish.[2] Also, to prevent the New England ships which resorted to these
waters from bringing in commodities prohibited by
the Navigation Act of the fifteenth year of the reign
of Charles II and from carrying away seamen, mechanics, and workmen, thus defeating one of the

[1] According to the Board of Trade, in 1677 there were 109
fishing ships, 4,475 seamen and 892 fishing boats belonging to
these ships. In that same year it was estimated that 152
"planters" were settled on the Island who employed 1,355
servants and 337 boats. In 1682 the number of fishing ships
coming from England dropped to 32, the number of seamen to
1,012 and the number of fishing boats to 183, while the inhabitants operated 299 ships and 304 fishing boats. As the result of
the Act of 1698, "An Act to encourage the Trade to Newfoundland," the fishermen from the Mother Country were again attracted to the Banks with the result that by 1716 they employed 86 fishing ships, 319 fishing ship boats and 184 by-boats,
although the settled inhabitants had 408 boats. Representation
of the Board of Dec. 19, 1718. *Papers Relating to Newfoundland* (1793), pp. 9-16.

[2] 10 and 11 William III, c. 25. The so-called Western Charter
of Feb. 10, 1633-34 provides that every ship that first enters
the harbor shall be admiral. The provisions of this charter as
well as those of the charter of 1675-76 are given in the representations of the Board of Trade of Dec. 19, 1718. *Papers Relating to Newfoundland* (1793), pp. 3-4, 8-9.

prime purposes of its enactment, each succeeding governor was expected to watch these ships.[1] This act had strictly limited the number of articles that could be transported to the colonies and plantations without being laden at some one of the ports of the Mother Country. Indeed, so suspicious was the home government of the activities of the New England ships that the governors were instructed to oblige all these vessels which might happen to be there to leave Newfoundland at the time they were ready to sail for England in the fall of the year.[2]

In light of the vast economic importance of Newfoundland to Great Britain it is perhaps surprising that its government in the middle of the eighteenth century was, at most times, rather a figment of the imagination.[3] It is true that, after almost a century of agitation, Captain Henry Osborne was sent to the Island in 1728 as the first governor under a formal crown commission, and that there followed a series of appointments, each one holding office, frequently hardly longer than the period of the annual voyage. With this office after 1731 went also that of commodore of the convoy.[4] For example, we have the ap-

[1] The Board of Trade asserted in 1718 that in 1716, according to the testimony of Captain Passenger who was the commander in chief of the convoy, thirteen hundred men were carried off by New England vessels, *ibid.*, p. 18.

[2] For an interesting discussion of the importance of the New England trade to Newfoundland see Ralph G. Lounsbury's "Yankee Trade at Newfoundland," *The New England Quarterly*, III, 607-626.

[3] For the government in 1730 see P.R.O., Nova Scotia State Papers, Correspondence, Vol. XIX (Canadian Archives Transcripts.)

[4] During the War of the Austrian Succession between 1746 and 1748 no governor was sent to the Island.

pointment of Admiral Charles Watson in 1748 to succeed Captain Richard Edwards; thereupon George Brydges Rodney in 1749 displaced Watson, and Francis William Drake in 1750 displaced Rodney. Drake, however, was recommissioned the following year.[1]

An examination of Rodney's instructions of May 2, 1749, which follow closely earlier instructions, will indicate that much was expected of the Newfoundland governor.[2] Those guilty of capital offenses were to be sent to England with witnesses and other sufficient proof of their crimes;[3] the Placentia garrison was not to be permitted to concern itself with the fishery; no engrossment of commodities was to be allowed to the prejudice of the Island's chief activity; and the provisions of the navigation acts and the act of the reign of William III for the encouragement of the fisheries were to be strictly enforced. Further, all inhabitants but Papists were to be guaranteed freedom of conscience, although laws governing blasphemy and immorality were to be vigorously enforced by the justices of the peace. Again, steps were to be taken to prevent not only the throwing of ballast into the harbors and the destruction of stages, cook-

[1] For these appointments see C.O. 5: 20, p. 21.

[2] C.O. 5: 200 (Canadian Archives Transcripts). R. G. Lounsbury op. cit., p. 296, note 34.

[3] The "Western Charter" of 1633-34 provided that one killing another on the Island should be brought to England that the Earl Marshal might take cognizance of the case. This order of the Privy Council also regulated the disposition of ballast, protected the conveniences used in fishing and the trees growing on the Island, forbade the selling of intoxicating beverages and tobacco, and gave authority over a harbor to the first shipmaster arriving in the spring. *Papers Relating to Newfoundland* (1793), pp. 3-4.

rooms, and flakes used in the fisheries, but also the appropriation on the part of the admirals of the harbors of more of the beaches and flakes than were necessary for their own use. Further, those inhabitants of the Island who had engrossed any of these conveniences since the year 1685 to the prejudice of the fishing ships were to be compelled to relinquish them; while masters of vessels, by-boat keepers, and inhabitants were to be compelled to employ such numbers of green or new men as the law required.

Not only was the governor to follow out the above injunctions, but he was to protect the woods from destruction, except for the necessary repairs of houses, ships, and stages. He was also to make investigations and to report whether or not manufacturers from the plantations or from foreign countries were being brought into the Island; whether the inhabitants had enclosed land and erected buildings close to the shores; whether the flakes for drying the fish extended from the beach up into the land, rather than along the shore so as to hinder others from building these; and whether the old laudable custom was followed of allowing ship companies a share of the total catch for the season rather than wages. Further, he was to determine the strength of the Irish Catholics on the Island,[1] the methods employed by the New England merchants in carrying on their Newfoundland trade, and the manner of conducting the taverns on the Island so as to judge whether or not poor seamen were

[1] In addition to the instructions given to the earlier governors appears one to Governor Charles Watson in 1748 directing him to give an account of Irish Roman Catholics in the towns of Newfoundland. *Acts of the Privy Council, Col., 1745-1766,* p. 777.

tempted or permitted to go so deeply into debt as to be forced to remain behind as servants or even to betake themselves to New England. In this connection he was to study the practices of the New England traders to discover if the latter still continued to entice away from the Island handicraftsmen, seamen, and fishermen and he even was to compel them to enter into obligations before returning not to engage in this practice. Finally, he was to watch over the movements of the French who, under the thirteenth and fourteenth clauses of the Treaty of Utrecht, were privileged, as has been made clear, to seek the shores of the Island within the prescribed area for the purpose solely of erecting temporary huts for the fishing season and stages for the drying of fish, but not for the purposes of settlement or for exploiting the resources of the Island.

In spite of the multiplicity of duties assigned to the governor, it appears that he performed very few of these, at least effectively.[1] That this was the case is not surprising, in light of the fact that he was generally absent from his post between nine and ten months of the year. Moreover, in the carrying-out of his instructions he was obliged to rely upon subordinate officials and there was constant friction between the justices of the peace and harbor admirals, representing respectively the traditionally hostile interests of inhabitants and Bankers. The justices of the peace,

---

[1] For example, the commanding officers at Placentia asserted in letters to the Duke of Bedford that many inconveniences had arisen "from his Majesty's Ships not having visited that Harbour for several years." These letters were placed before the Board of Trade at its meeting of April 14, 1748. Board of Trade *Journal, 1741-1749*, p. 279.

appointed by him from among the permanent residents, were expected to be "Men of Property and good Character." Nevertheless, as a rule they were weak, and their authority was not infrequently quite ignored even by the inhabitants, although it is true that some of them were accused in 1749 of great irregularities and oppressions. The same thing can be said of the harbor admirals. Generally, however, the latter appear to have grossly neglected their official duties, so absorbed were they in their fishing activities during the limited period they were present in the waters of the Island.

The problem of maintaining order in Newfoundland was made especially difficult on account of the presence of many unruly characters who had been attracted to the fisheries. It appears from a report made by Rodney to the Admiralty in 1749 that by far the greater part of the inhabitants of Newfoundland were Irish Catholics who were hostile to the King's authority. For, among more than three hundred of them living in St. John's, there apparently were only six who would take the oath of allegiance when tendered to them.[1] According to the same governor the great purpose of the Newfoundland fisheries was being defeated because of the "Notorious Practices of the Fishing Ships . . . of bringing nothing but Irish Papists. . . . I think it my duty," he declared, "to acquaint your lordships that numbers of the merchants of this place agree with me that the Trade of Newfoundland, as it is at present carried on, is far from being a nursery for British seamen. The great

[1] Rodney to John Cleveland, September, 1749, Rodney Papers, (P.R.O.), Vol. 6.

numbers of Papists employed in it being notoriously
disaffected to his Majesty and the present happy
establishment."[1]

There can be but little doubt as to the turbulent
nature of the population. Even the commanding officers at Placentia in writing home stressed the failure
of justice at that place.[2] A description of conditions
at this period has survived which is probably not far
from the truth, and which shows how little there
actually was in the way of an effective exertion of
governmental authority.

"That as few of the Fishing Admirals from the
nature of their Employ'ts can act during their short
Occasional Residence in Newfoundland in the
Adm'^{tion} of Justice ... the Country is for the Space
of 9 or 10 months in the year Destitute of any form of
Governm^t, the Military Authority & that of a few
Justices of the Peace only Excepted & which is Exercised in so Imperfect & Unsatisfactory a manner as
to Answer no wholesome End or purpose & during
this Long Interval of Anarchy & Confusion the common Method of Recovering Debts & Adjusting many
other Disputes is by the strongest Hand, the Creditors
Using no other Ceremony with their Supposed D$^{rs.}$
than by Calling a Suff'^{t}. Number of People to their
Assistance and with open force Carrying off from the
D$^{rs.}$ Plan$^{tn.}$ a Suff^t. quantity of Fish to pay the pretended Debt; nor is it less frequent for the Admiralty
Judge, though without the least Authority, being
Invested only with his Admiralty Com̃'ion to Issue
his Warr$^{ts.}$" to Attach the Persons of his Ma$^{tys.}$ Subjects on Land upon a bare Surmise or Complaint
without any Oath made to the Pretended Debt &

[1] *Ibid.*
[2] Board of Trade *Journal, 1741-1749*, p. 279.

even to Seize their Goods & Effects in the first Instance & afterwards to Compell the Paym^{t} of such pretended Debts and even Impose & levy such Fines upon his Ma$^{tys.}$ Subjects as he thinks proper."[1]

One thing that hindered the maintenance of law and order on the Island was the requirement that those accused of serious offenses be sent to England for trial. This presented so many inconveniences and was so repugnant to the sentiments of the inhabitants that governors were reluctant to carry out the instruction. The year following his appointment, Rodney represented to the Duke of Bedford, Secretary of State for the Southern Department, the difficulties confronting him by reason of his lack of authority to appoint persons who were competent to take cognizance of capital crimes.[2] The question of increasing the powers of the Governor to this extent was submitted to both the Attorney and Solicitor-General, with the result that Francis Drake in 1750 was empowered to appoint commissioners of oyer and terminer for the trial of capital offenses on the spot, treason excepted, with, however, the proviso that no one should be executed until the pleasure of His Majesty were known.[3] The following year this pro-

---

[1] For this report see the "Case of Lord Baltimore" (1753), p. 4.

[2] Board of Trade *Journal, 1749-1753*, p. 50; also C.O. 195: 8, pp. 179-181 and *Acts of the Privy Council, Col., 1745-1766*, Par. 74.

[3] For Drake's Instructions on this point for the year 1750, see the Order of Council of June 4, 1751, C.O. 5: Vol. 21. *Acts of the Privy Council, Col., 1745-1766*, pp. 117-119, 777-778.

In an opinion delivered March 27, 1750, Attorney-General Ryder took the position that a power to take cognizance of capital crimes in Newfoundland could not be granted by instruction

viso was omitted in the new commission he received. It was therefore at last possible for the commissioner to order the execution of criminals, but with the important limitation that no officer of a ship-of-war or of any British trading ship should be deprived of life and limb by any sentence of such court, but should be reprieved upon conviction, until the pleasure of the King were known.[1]

Slight and salutary as was the provision made to prevent anarchy, it appears that there were those who became alarmed at the tendency to erect a stable government for the inhabitants of Newfoundland— something that the cod-fishing ports of England had consistently opposed for a century and a half. For example, a memorial drawn up by the merchants of Dartmouth trading to Newfoundland and presented to the Board of Trade in 1752 expressed the hope that the form of government already established would subsist without any alterations.[2] However, from this period one may date the beginnings of a somewhat more effective political control of the Island. Yet the amenities of civilized life appeared but slowly. The Board of Trade, in a representation to His Majesty of April 29, 1765, stressed the fact that the population, then consisting of about fifteen thousand souls, mostly Roman Catholic Irish, were still living in the most savage state, giving themselves

---

but must be inserted in the governor's commission under the great seal. See "Edward Northey's Legal Opinions" (Ms.), Library of Congress Accessions.

[1] *Acts of the Privy Council, Col.*, 1745-1766, p. 778.
[2] Board of Trade *Journal*, 1749-1753, p. 374.

over to every species of debauchery, violence, and wickedness.[1]

With all the turbulence of its coast-dwelling population and in spite of its rather forbidding climate and the decline in the value of the English cod fisheries, Newfoundland was, it need not be further emphasized, an extraordinarily valuable British possession in the middle of the eighteenth century. Therefore, it is not a matter of surprise that at this period the great importance of the Island should attract the attention of the heir to the Baltimore family interests; for among these interests were the claims to the Peninsula of Avalon established in 1623 by Sir George Calvert, later the first Lord Baltimore. As a result, in the early '50s a serious attempt was made on the part of young Frederick, the sixth and the last Lord Baltimore, upon attaining his majority, to secure recognition of the so-called family rights. The

[1] For this representation see *Papers Relating to Newfoundland* (1793), p. 5. Captain Griffith Williams declared that after the withdrawal of the troops following the Peace of Aix-la-Chapelle, the traders and inhabitants were left to shift for themselves, without troops to support the magistrates in the execution of justice. "At this Time great Numbers of *Irish Roman Catholics* were in the Island as servants; but no sooner (had the troops) been sent away, than they became the most outrageous Set of People that ever lived: Robberies were committed almost every Day in one Place or other, the Magistrats insulted in the executions of their Office, and the Chief Justice murdered; many hundred of West of *England* People were afraid of going over, many of the *Newfoundland* men left the Island, and the *Roman Catholics* transported themselves by Hundreds from Ireland: so that at the Time the *French* took the country, [1762] the *Irish* were above six Times the number of the *West County* and *Newfoundlers*. In short, they were in Possession of above three-quarters of the fish rooms and Harbours of the Island, who consequently received the French with open Arms." *Account of the Island of Newfoundland* (1765), pp. 9-10.

episode is of such importance in making clear the implications of the earlier proprietorial grants in connection with the later imperial system as to justify a somewhat detailed consideration.

In the year 1753 Baltimore presented an ably drawn petition to the Crown[1] setting forth the facts that his ancestor, Sir George Calvert, principal Secretary of State to James I, having at his own great expense purchased a large tract of barren, uncultivated land in Newfoundland and, having made great preparations for settling an English colony there, was granted letters patent, dated April 7, 1623.[2] This patent confirmed to him and his heirs those lands, from fifty to sixty miles in depth lying south of a line extending westward from Petit Harbour to the Bay of Placentia, a distance of upwards of sixty miles, together with all the islands within ten leagues of the eastern shore, to be held *in capite* by knight's service. The sole obligation of the Calverts in return was to render a white horse as often as they should come into the said province, together with a fifth part of all gold and silver ore found there. According to this instrument, they were to have power, with the consent of the majority of the freeholders of the Island, not only to make laws that would be binding upon all persons within the limits of the Province, whether resident there or sailing to or from the said Province, and to

---

[1] For reference to the Committee on July 19, 1753 of the petition of Frederick, Lord Baltimore, see *Acts of the Privy Council, Col.*, 1745-1766, p. 223.

[2] C.O. 7: 2, nos. 20, 23. On the background of this see *The Cambridge History of the British Empire*, VI, *Canada and Newfoundland*, pp. 127-128; R. G. Lounsbury, *The British Fishery at New Foundland*, pp. 37-47.

enforce the same by fine, imprisonment, or any other punishment, even to life and limb, but also to appoint ministers, officers, judges, justices, and other magistrates; they might also in emergencies make ordinances for the regulation of the people and establish ports for the loading and unloading of ships, conferring upon these such rights and privileges as they should think proper, provided that they reserved to all English subjects the liberty of fishing in the sea and in the ports and creeks of the Province and of salting and drying the fish on the shore as had been customary; finally, they might enjoy all subsidies, customs, and impositions payable for the lading and unlading of goods in their Province.

In turning to the history of the relations of the Baltimore family to Avalon, the name given to this grant, it may be noted that soon after the receipt of the charter, steps were taken to plant a settlement within it. Sir George first of all provided for the construction of a house and a fort at a place that he called Ferryland. Subsequently, resigning his post with the King, he departed in 1627 to inspect his possession, and, returning the year following, again left for the Island, this time with his family. During the French war he assisted in its defense[1] and, upon his final departure, committed Avalon to the care of a deputy, Captain William Hill. After his death in 1632, Cecil, his heir, in a somewhat vague fashion continued its possession and settlement, with Hill still acting as governor until 1638. In 1651 it appears that he sent to it another deputy to manage his in-

[1] *Op. cit.*, p. 48.

terest, who for some years lived in the lord proprietary's house and who was succeeded successively by John Littlebury and Walter Sikes.[1] This precaution for maintaining title did not, however, prevent the Marquis of Hamilton and others, under cover of a grant from the Crown in 1637,[2] of finding means to dispossess him, not only of his mansion house at Ferryland, but of other rights, continuing in possession of Avalon by force during the period of the Great Rebellion until the Restoration.[3] In 1660, upon petition, King Charles referred the dispute to the Lord Chief Baron of the Exchequer, Sir Orlando Bridgeman, and others, for the purpose of reporting the true state of the Province. These commissioners, after some deliberation, certified that they conceived the patent given to Sir George Calvert was still in force and therefore was not voided by any subsequent grant. As a result, on the twentieth of March the King ordered the possession of Avalon to be reconfirmed to Baltimore; he also enjoined Sir Lewis Kirke, who had a military force on the Island, and all others, not to give him the least interference in the possession

[1] "Case of Lord Baltimore" (1753), p. 1.

[2] The patent of 1637 granted proprietary rights over Newfoundland. For the background of the grant to the Marquis of Hamilton, the Earl of Pembroke, the Earl of Holland, and Sir David Kirke see *Acts of the Privy Council, Col., 1618-1680*, pp. 214-220.

[3] During the commonwealth Baltimore attempted to recover his possession, but without success. See L. D. Scisco, "Calvert's Proceedings against Kirke," *Canadian Historical Review*, VIII, 132-136. At the time that the patent to all of Newfoundland was being pressed by Hamilton and his associates the King had agreed never to issue a *quo warranto* against the Baltimore grant of Avalon. R. G. Lounsbury, *op. cit.*, p. 79.

of the same.[1] The latter thereupon, in 1661, not only appointed as governor for the Province, Robert Swanley, which was approved by His Majesty by royal proclamation, but also soon afterwards sent out Captain Pease to take over Avalon, with Captain John Raynor as deputy governor. Although Baltimore's representatives apparently made little headway in establishing control, it seems that in 1668 he commissioned as his deputy William Hutton; again, in 1674, Swanley was reappointed for a second term, after which there is no evidence that other commissions were given. In fact, the death of Cecil in 1676 ended the active interest of the Baltimore family in Avalon until the middle of the eighteenth century.

In 1699, Parliament at last intervened in the affairs of the Island in the "Act to Encourage the Trade of Newfoundland,"[2] granting thereby to all resorting to the Island, free trade and fishing, with the right of curing fish on shore and of cutting wood for building stages. This statute took no notice of the Baltimore grant nor was the family consulted upon the occasion of its passage. Lord Cecil had been succeeded by his son, Lord Charles; the latter surviving until 1715 was followed by Lord Benedict who also passing away the same year left his son, Charles, as heir. Therefore, upon his death in 1751 Avalon legally had descended to Frederick; so, at least, affirmed the petition referred to above.

To make clear why it was that the Baltimore family had not continuously prosecuted their claims, the petition of 1753 stressed the point that, as Catholics,

[1] "Case of Lord Baltimore" (1753), p. 2.
[2] 10 and 11 William III, c. 25.

they had come under suspicion during the Revolution. Even the government of the Province of Maryland, which, with full proprietorial rights was patented to Lord Cecil about ten years after the grant of the Province of Avalon to the family, was taken into the hands of the Crown where it remained till 1720, when Charles, who had been educated in the persuasion of the Church of England and had attained the age of twenty-one, was allowed to resume it. The family, it was claimed, suffered much distress by the temporary loss of these powers in Maryland, especially since the profits received from that Province while it remained in the hands of the Crown were inconsiderable. Therefore, it had been impossible, at least so it was alleged, to prosecute the further settlement of Avalon. Moreover, in the course of the war of the Spanish Succession, the whole Island came under the subjection of France and was retained until the Peace of Utrecht.

Frederick now sought permission of the Crown "to settle an established and regulated form of government" for Avalon with its numerous population. Pursuant to the several powers and the authority vested in his ancestor by the patent of 1623, he offered in his petition to appoint as a permanent resident governor John Broadstreet, Esq., described as a gentleman of great ability who was well acquainted with the circumstances of the Province, having been for several years past entrusted by His Majesty with the administration of its affairs. He at this time made clear that in suing for his rights he did this without any intention of overturning or infringing upon the regulations already made by the Act of King William.[1]

This petition was referred by His Majesty in Council to the Lords of the Committee of Council for Plantation Affairs, who sent it to the Board of Trade by whom it was referred, as a matter of "great importance," to the Attorney and Solicitor-General on November 20, 1753.[2] It involved, of course, practically the entire portion of Newfoundland that had been settled and to any degree developed, and included most of the English fishing villages.

While the petition was being considered by these two eminent counsellors, an elaborate series of objections and answers was prepared by Baltimore's legal advisers, which, among other points, urged that by no act either of the courts by writ of *scire facias* or that of *quo warranto*, or of the legislature, had the validity of the patent ever been called into question. As to the statute of the year 1699 for encouraging the fisheries, neither the grant nor the proprietor's rights were once mentioned; the object of the law, it was contended, had to do with the entire Island, while the Province of Avalon was but a district, so that the act would still be satisfied while allowing the heir to the patent the enjoyment of the same. This, it was argued, was possible, since under the law in question no new constitution or civil government was prescribed for it—as the statute provided only temporary regulations for the fisheries which had, indeed, been expressly reserved to all English subjects in the patent

[1] "Case of Lord Baltimore," (1753), p. 7.
[2] D. Ryder and W. Murray to the Board of Trade, April 5, 1754. Calvert Papers, Maryland Historical Society.

of 1623. In this connection it was further urged that the Crown up to the present had never assumed the exercise of any of the regalities or powers given to the Baltimore family by the charter other than the limited privileges prescribed by the act which, with reference to the fisheries, even in 1699, were ancient usages.

To meet the objection that there were no traces of the Baltimore family to be found in Newfoundland for sixty or seventy years and that every grant of land in America carried an implied condition of cultivation and improvement within a reasonable time and that the patentee's neglect to pursue and to accomplish these ends had always been considered as a desertion and forfeiture of his patent, it was urged that this was a grant of seigniory, an *imperium in imperio,* a type of grant very distinct from a mere grant of the soil and such as had never been set aside for a nonexercise of the powers of government; so that should the Crown resume the soil it was apprehended that the dominion must still remain in the patentee. And as to the right over the soil it was believed that no instance could be found of a grant being set aside for noncultivation where the original grantee had cultivated and improved, which, in the case of Avalon, had been the case. For the first two of the patentees had gone over in person with their families, had built houses and cultivated the country and, for over fifty years subsequent to the grant, had continued in possession of these improvements through legally appointed agents. In light of all this, should not the religious disabilities and low estate of the family from the Revolution to the late Lord's

277

restoration to Maryland about 1720 be received in extenuation of a supposed neglect in prosecuting this charter? Further, was it not a matter of moment that the Crown had established this grant to be good in an issue with a subsequent grantee? Should, therefore, the officers of the state be now admitted to question the royal determination? For, if it were once good, pray when had it first become vitiated? Surely, not at the time when the Act of King William was passed, for the family had not long left the country. While it was true that, were the patentee to appoint a governor, he must receive the royal approbation; suppose, however, that he himself were to go over in person to exercise the power of his grant on the spot as did his ancestors, was there any restraint upon him? Who then, it was asked, could restrain him from immediately erecting courts of judicature, granting lands, and so forth, and upon what foundation and by what means?

These objections and answers were submitted to the distinguished jurist, Sir Robert Henley, soon to be appointed attorney-general in place of Ryder. Henley on March 25, 1754 submitted his opinion, which offered cold comfort to Baltimore. He declared "that it will be very difficult for my Ld Baltimore to maintain the Effect of this Grant, which upon all the Circumstances of the Case appears to me to be obtained on an untrue Suggestion & is therefore void as against the Crown. It appears by the Recital of the Grant," he went on to state, "that Sir George suggested that he was about to transport a Colony thither, to which End most of the Provisions & authorities of the Letters patent are adapted, & I take it Such sort of a Suggestion in $L^{d's}$ patent amounts to a Condition, which not being performed the $L^{d's}$ patent became void, & tho the Grant was confirmed in 1660 (if the Act stated would amount to a Confirmation) yet the End & Condition of the Grant, not having been complied with I think that Confirmation would have no Effect."[1]

In spite of discouragement, Baltimore with counsel appeared before the Solicitor and Attorney-General in support of the petitions. On April 5 the latter sent to the Board their opinion as to the merits of the case. Their position, following Henley's line of argument, was that, in spite of the determination of the year 1660, there was no evidence of any actual possession of the Province claimed or of the exercise of any powers of government there by the Baltimore family, but on the contrary it seemed probable that at least from the year 1638 they had been out of possession and that from the year 1669 there had been many proceedings which appeared inconsistent with the right now set up. Therefore, they were of opinion that it was inadvisable for His Majesty to comply with the said petition.[2]

The decision of the Crown against the Baltimore claims need not cause great surprise. Yet, to the student of today there seems something irreconcilable in the utter ignoring of these in light of the recognition in the eighteenth century of the proprietorial rights of Sir Robert Heath. Heath's patent dating from

[1] This is among the Calvert Papers, Maryland Historical Society, pp. 8-9.
[2] D. Ryder and W. Murray to the Board of Trade, April 5, 1754. Calvert Papers.

the year 1629 was for the region south of Virginia, lying between the thirty-first and thirty-sixth parallels of north latitude. Although his "plans fell stillborn among colonial ventures,"[1] and the same region was granted in 1663 to the Carolina proprietors, nevertheless Daniel Coxe, who had come into possession of the Heath claims, was accorded one hundred thousand acres of land in provincial New York as indemnification and full satisfaction.

There were, it is clear, numerous weighty considerations of public policy that dictated the finding of a decision adverse to the claims of Frederick. He was already a beneficiary, in the possession of one of the most valuable provinces in America as the result of the generosity of the Crown to his ancestors; it must have been felt by the King's advisers in 1754 that Maryland had in a sense been given by Charles I as an equivalent, and more than an equivalent, for Avalon—although it is true there was no formal act of surrender when Sir George Calvert came to the conviction that the latter place was unsuited for the carrying out of his plans for a proprietary and "numerous colony" and, as a result, sought out new lands within the bounds of Virginia. Again, both the spirit of the age and the genius of government in the middle of the eighteenth century were in opposition to the conception of vast proprietorial possessions carrying with them the exercise of governmental powers, something that Lord Baltimore sought for in demanding Avalon. The Board of Trade, then led by the powerful Halifax, had had a record of consistent hos-

[1] C. M. Andrews, *Colonial Self-Government*, p. 130.

tility to both proprietorial and corporate colonial charters and, far from aiding in the restoration of those that had lapsed, was ever seeking the means to recall the few which out of the many of the seventeenth century had survived. Further, with respect to Newfoundland it must have been apprehended that a recognition of the proprietorial rights of Frederick to Avalon would lead to the greatest confusion. Under this old patent Baltimore could have levied port duties on merchandise and made other exactions; he could have collected quit-rents on the lands of Avalon; he could have required satisfaction of shipmasters and fishermen for any unusual waste of his woods; he could have established a permanent government, appointed officials, summoned a legislature, and made laws—all of which activities held out the possibilities of infinite embarrassment and discouragement to those who came each year to the Banks and to the coves of the Island to fish. For a settled government would almost inevitably mean that the permanent inhabitants would control the law-making processes, and therefore would at last be placed in a position of superiority with respect to their rivals, the West Countrymen—something that certainly would have at this juncture aroused the English fishing towns and would in nowise have appealed to the Crown. Lastly, and more weighty than all other considerations, there was the fear that, should a settled form of government be introduced into the Island, there was every likelihood that the population that had already attached itself to the Island would absorb the great Newfoundland fisheries as those of New England had been absorbed by the men who settled in Massachusetts Bay; this, statesmen were convinced, would mean the decline of English maritime power and the decay of numerous English seaports.

CHAPTER XI

IN THE preceding volumes various local and sectional aspects of the old British Empire have been emphasized. It now seems desirable, before concluding this study, to suggest certain broad characteristics of the Empire in the middle of the eighteenth century.

First of all, the Empire evidenced a remarkable degree of both vitality and what may be called dynamic energy. Indeed these characteristics were so pronounced with respect not only to the governmental units embraced within it but to the individuals dwelling therein as to render unattainable the closest sort of coördination and articulation of imperial policy by the central authority. One need only cite by way of illustration the conduct of Indian relations. In contrast to the highly centralized and unified system developed by the French monarchy in North America, various British governors in 1750 were actively promoting policies that in some cases were mutually antagonistic and resulted in great confusion, in order to favor the particular interests of aggressive Indian traders from their own colonies respectively. The Guinea trade was also in confusion, owing to this same inability of government to check the activities of individuals, although this had been achieved by the French King in the support of the French company in that region. In fact, the Royal

283

African Company found itself by 1750 in possession
of a ruinous privilege as the result of ever increasing
encroachments of British free traders upon its operations. The same thing may be said regarding the
South Sea Company which had come to realize even
before war was declared against Spain in 1739 that
its trading monopoly was quite unprofitable, largely
on account of the impossibility of curbing the rest-
less operations of private venturers in the region of
the Spanish Main.

Again, the liberal political institutions of England,
established for the expression of the national will, had
been allowed to spread into all of those dependencies
prepared to receive them. As a result, there existed
throughout the Empire a political sense and awareness
quite beyond anything to be found in any of the
other contemporaneous imperialistic systems. This
usually was manifested in terms of an intense localism
or particularism which was not slow to challenge
whatever did not accord with the popular conceptions within these dependencies of personal freedom
and political liberties held to be the birthright of all
Britons. The exaltation of these conceptions, in fact,
created some of the most insistent problems faced by
the Empire and led not only to innumerable clashes
between provincial governors and the legislatures
over questions such as those involved in the binding
force of royal or proprietorial commissions and instructions but finally to that *impasse* between Parliament and the American colonies as to the assumed
competence of the former to exercise supreme legislative authority over all embodied within the Empire. A reconcilement between the conflicting claims

of the central and local authorities as to the exact limits within which the former was free to act for the good of the Empire was never reached.[1]

Further, the eighteenth-century Empire stood for a large measure of religious toleration. By the middle of that century the bitter antagonism between Roman Catholicism and Protestantism, and between various sects embraced within the latter had largely passed away, and only where, as a rule, serious political implications seemed to be involved in permitting complete freedom of action to some religious group were attempts made to apply the restraints imposed by law. As a consequence, while Roman Catholics could not purchase land or vote in Ireland, they were permitted to do both on the Island of St. Christopher where their strength was not feared. If the nonjuring Anglicans of Scotland were debarred from preaching by reason of their sympathy with the Stuart cause, they were free to hold forth in England. Unlike the French and Spanish empires in which but one religion was established and in which the rights of non-Catholics were either nonexistent or extremely shadowy, the British Empire embraced three churches established by law: the Anglican, the Presbyterian, and the Congregational. Further, the application of the principle of religious toleration had gone so far in some colonies that no church among the Christian groups was given a privileged position. This was true of Rhode Island, Pennsylvania, and the Lower Counties on the Delaware; in the case of the royal provinces of New York and New Jersey, while attempts were made by means of royal instruction to establish the

[1] See *ante,* pp. 140-141, on this issue before 1750.

Anglican communion, in practice this was done in neither of them. If one thing above others characterized the Empire from the religious aspect in 1750 it was the welcome extended to various Protestant groups of continental Europe that could not live happily or in security at home. Even Catholics, in spite of the movement of many of them from Ireland to the Continent after the battle of the Boyne, generally preferred to submit to the sort of religious supervision imposed by Protestants within various parts of the Empire than to accept expatriation in favor of a home in a foreign Catholic land. There was something indeed in the atmosphere of the old British Empire that seemed not only to call forth in most men individual initiative and resourcefulness and an ardent spirit of personal independence but also confidence in the future. This doubtless helps to explain why thousands of dissatisfied people, alien in speech and in habits of thought, felt the lure of the British plantations so strongly that they were eager not only to break all ties of kin and fatherland but to endure great temporary hardships to find shelter within them.

In the middle of the eighteenth century, moreover, the old British Empire differed in numerous fundamental ways from the empires of ancient and classical days. In no respect, however, was this dissimilarity more strikingly evidenced than in the absence of design on the part of the Government to exploit the people of the dependencies for the benefit of those living at the seat of power. This was true even with respect to the conquered Kingdom of Ireland, with the exception of the maintenance of the pension list,

the burden of which fell upon the wealthier groups.[1]
Contrary to popular understanding, the British mercantile system as embodied in various acts of Parliament was evolved not to levy tribute upon the colonies but to provide a system of protection along
imperial lines for all those great interests that were
sources of material wealth and power. In its actual
operation, while it produced inconveniences and even
grave injustices as in the case of the Irish woolen industry, the same is likely to be true of any conceiv-
able set of restrictions of national or imperial scope.
Indeed, it may not unfairly be compared to modern
systems of state interference with the liberty of the
subject in matters involving industry and trade, accepting the differences involved in the nature of the
regulations respectively. In each case, individuals or
groups within the state are forbidden to follow out
lines of action that, while highly beneficial to those
locally or personally concerned, are considered inim-
ical to the larger national objectives. It seems clear
in analyzing the restraints of the old British system
that for every demand made upon the dependencies
an attempt was made to provide a reciprocal return
of benefits either direct or indirect. If Irishmen could
not freely send their woolens abroad they were
encouraged by subsidies to export their linens; if foreign ships were forbidden to carry colonial commodities, colonial ships enjoyed that privilege; if Virginia tobacco could not be sold directly to European
buyers, at least its sale in Great Britain was protected

[1]Taxation burdens, for example, were very much heavier per
capita in Great Britain than in Ireland or in the North American
colonies.

both by laws prohibiting its growth in that kingdom and by very high import duties on the product of foreign countries. In fact, no rule of statecraft was followed more imperatively in the eighteenth century than the maxim that the welfare of England itself depended upon the welfare of the Empire. That this maxim had borne fruit is abundantly evidenced. Almost everywhere throughout the Empire in the middle of the century—in spite of the disturbing type of foreign competition that the English were obliged to face and to which reference will be made—conditions were such as to permit men of ambition, business capacity, and foresight to prosper, and industrious communities to enjoy a standard of living that was the envy of almost every foreign observer. In this connection it must be emphasized that the wretchedness of large numbers of Irishmen and Scottish Highlanders was the result largely of factors other than those relating to the lack of opportunity for useful and profitable activity.

In the eyes of contemporaries, one chief justification for the maintenance of the mercantile system, with its complicated and frequently embarrassing restrictions, was the widespread conviction that the Empire was facing a rival that bade fair, unless great care were exercised, to undermine the foundations of its material strength and leave it a great sprawling congeries of communities, weak and defenseless. For France was not only the first military power of the world—a power that had already largely encircled the British colonies in North America with a chain of inland forts and had also so entrenched itself in both the East and West Indies as to threaten to supplant the British—but was actually stripping her rival of leadership in many important fields of industry, thereby depriving it of its old markets. This was taking place by means of a coördination of effort on the part of the French perhaps only possible to the same degree under an absolutism. With this was combined a superior technical precision and artistry which, taken together with a lower standard of living on the part of the French worker and consequently a lower wage scale, seemed to give the French industrialist a fatal advantage. With deep concern the British witnessed what appeared to be the growing superiority of the French in the Newfoundland cod fisheries, in the production and sale of sugar, molasses, indigo, ginger and other commodities that came out of the West Indies. With dismay they likewise witnessed the apparent decline in England of their important manufactures of North American furs into hats and other useful articles with the consequent rise of such manufactures in France. They feared, also, that in addition to being surpassed in the production of innumerable articles of luxury, they would lose to their rivals—should restrictions to trade be removed —the greatest of their national industries: the weaving of wool.

Therefore it is not surprising that among all groups of British statesmen there was practical unanimity regarding the vital necessity of retaining a system which they conceived not only made possible the degree of prosperity existent throughout the Empire, but guaranteed the integrity of the first line of defense: British naval power. Also, by means of the maintenance of favorable balances of trade through the operation of this system they felt that the Mother Country could be assured the possession of those essentials to any prolonged resistance in case of war, especially war for the Empire: that is, an abundant supply of the precious metals and foreign credit.

One factor involved in the interrelations within the Empire itself that continuously influenced policy with respect to the plantations was that of the necessity of protecting the long-established but somewhat inelastic economic system of England from injury on the part of those colonies where conditions were especially favorable for the building-up of competitive industries. Had there existed a much greater mobility of labor and capital, the consequences of competition from this source might have been faced with a certain resignation if not entire equanimity, at least on the part of the Government. But this mobility did not exist. It is important to bear in mind that whenever any important industry in the Kingdom languished — the iron industry as an example — the inevitable result was not only widespread unemployment but the pauperization of many of those dependent upon it for a livelihood. This in turn brought a train of evils not the least of which was the encouragement of men to take up lawless pursuits. Moreover, should unemployment prevail on a large scale, the burdens of the rates in the parishes affected, always sufficiently heavy, were thereby increased sometimes to proportions almost unendurable to the harassed English taxpayer. It is therefore perfectly explicable why Parliament from not unworthy motives was led on occasions to legislate adversely to the development either in Ireland or in the New World colonies of particular types of industries, or to the exportation abroad of the products of these. To Irishmen and colonials, however, laws such as that against the exportation of wool or woolens were simply the outcome of cynical and selfish policies pursued with success by those in England immediately interested in these industries and consequently desirous of strangling an incipient Irish or American competition. Certainly to many Virginians the monopolization of Great Britain of the tobacco trade was little more than a shrewd way of enriching the British tobacco merchants and helping to fill the royal exchequer. However, to the Government, the maintenance of this restriction on trade was doubtless justified as a guarantee that the markets of the colonies concerned in the growth and exportation of this commodity would not pass to some other commercial power after the manner of many colonial markets a century earlier when, before the Act of 1651, the enterprising Dutch traders were busy driving the merchant marine away from even English colonial seaports.

Another factor that affected British imperial policy was the development during the first half of the eighteenth century of a sharp divergence of interest between the West Indian possessions and those of the continent of North America. This came with the growth of a destructive type of competition between the French sugar islands and their British neighbors. The former—with their slave supply provided cheaply by means of royal subsidization; in the possession of lands of marvelous fertility in Santo Domingo, Martinique, and Guadeloupe which were

not, as in the case of those in the British Leeward
Islands and Barbados, showing signs of exhaustion;
freed also from various burdens that their rivals were
compelled to assume—were not only able to take away
from the latter many of their most important European sugar markets but also the profitable molasses
market in the British North American plantations.
With respect to the latter the situation was such as to
make it unlikely that this could be recovered by the
British sugar planters except through restrictive legislation. For the French government, while anxious to
encourage the production and sale of sugar on the
part of its West India planters, was determined to
keep their molasses and rum from injuring the market
for French brandy, and therefore forbade its importation into France. As a result, molasses, a necessary by-product in the manufacture of sugar, became
almost an embarrassment rather than an asset to the
French planters until an outlet for it was found in
North America. No price that the British planters
could afford to set, loaded as they were with various
charges, could possibly meet the counter offers of
their French rivals. The distillers of North America,
as a result, naturally purchased in the lowest market
and incidentally enormously expanded their own
activities and those of the French.

Out of this situation came inevitably an issue that
faced the British government in the fourth decade of
the century. Should it listen to the pleas of the
distressed and overburdened sugar colonies to elimi-
nate the French planters from the American market,
or should it favor the counter pleas of the American
traders for a continuance of the right to barter

freely with the foreign West India Islands? The decision was made in favor of the protection of an old and vastly important industry against a newer and, all in all, less important. At this point it is necessary to refer to a presumption on the part of many students that the existence of a powerful sugar lobby, and especially the influence of sugar planters with seats in Parliament, sufficiently explain the decision of government, as embodied in the famous law of 1733, placing high import duties upon foreign-produced sugar, molasses, and rum carried to the Continental Colonies. The indefensible nature of the law has in the past been also a presumption on the part of many historians, especially American. It is, however, hard to see how the British Government could have done less for the British sugar islands in light of the fact that the most important factor in the rise of competition in the French islands was the very great burdens that Parliament had placed upon British-produced sugar as a result of the wars for the Empire. This policy naturally affected its price in the world markets and offered an opportunity which the French planters were not slow in seizing. Indeed the wealth of the British West Indies had in more ways than one helped to support the imperial system elsewhere.[1]

In tracing the development of this growing political and economic sectionalism within the Empire it is to be noticed that after the Sugar Act of 1733 had manifestly failed of its objective by reason of wide-

[1] The crushing weight of taxation in Barbados and Jamaica may also be contrasted to the absence of taxation in New Jersey and Pennsylvania in 1750.

spread evasion, an effort was made in the middle of the century on the part of the sugar-planter interests to secure the enactment of a statute that would prohibit all commerce between the American plantations and the French islands. This proved abortive, for the Government was not unmindful of the great importance that America attached to this intercourse. Consequently, the vast illegal trade continued to flourish. In other words, the problem of reconciling conflicting economic interests within the Empire presented extraordinary difficulties, and no attempted solution could hope to leave all parties satisfied.

The government of the Empire, while characterized by a spirit of compromise in dealing with conflicting group interests, as is illustrated above, was at the same time based upon well-established principles. There was a certain consistency, also a certain continuity, manifested in the management of imperial affairs throughout the first half of the eighteenth century. For example, all the royal colonies were organized and maintained upon a fairly uniform basis. Though differences in the machinery of local government were to be found among them, these differences were unimportant in light of great similarities. Not only were the various governors' commissions frequently all but identical, but their instructions, especially those prepared for them at the time the commissions were sealed, manifested as much uniformity as changing circumstances and diversity of conditions would admit.[1] Indeed, the very inelasticity of these was open to criticism. One comment, however, should be made with respect to this criticism:

[1] L. A. Labaree, *Royal Instructions to British Colonial Governors, 1670-1776*, I, Intro. viii.

not only the commission of a royal governor but also his instructions largely determined the character of the constitution of the province over the affairs of which he presided. While frequent alterations in the terms of the instructions so as to provide for contingencies arising within a colony might have great advantages, disadvantages would not be lacking. In fact, the experience of the British people with constitutional arrangements has pointed to the desirability of infrequent change and a certain quality of permanency in the basic arrangements for provincial government.

It must not be assumed, however, that the instructions prepared for the governors were not most carefully scrutinized at this period and that where deviations from those of their predecessors seemed desirable these were not made in light of prevailing conditions. For example, when William Henry Lyttelton was appointed Governor of South Carolina in 1755 in place of James Glen, the Board of Trade omitted nine articles that had a place in the instructions of the latter "as having become useless and improper." Three other articles having to do with appeals were likewise omitted as the result of an order in council, and were replaced by an article in conformity with this. Alterations were also made in the older instructions relating to the revision of laws and the granting of lands. Finally, certain instructions were added, such "as have been given from time to time to the Governors of other Colonys, conceiving the same to be equally well adapted to the Circumstances of this Province, and have made such alterations in those

Articles which have been usually given to all the Governors as have been lately approved of by His Majesty in the Instructions to the Governors of New York, the Leeward Islands, Jamaica, and North Carolina."[1]

One feature of the imperial administration that made for desirable continuity in colonial government, to which reference has been made in the preceding paragraph, was the constant attention bestowed by the Board of Trade upon imperial affairs. This important advisory body, established by letters patent at the end of the seventeenth century, by the middle of the eighteenth had accumulated a degree of knowledge and had come to possess an expertness in dealing with those matters coming before it that made its work of vital importance to the government and doubtless saved the King's ministers frequent costly errors in colonial administration. The Board was in reality the liaison or contact branch of the central government with the colonies. To this body the Privy Council or its committees of the whole or the departments of state referred most of the important questions involving either the plantations or the trade of the Empire. In dealing with these questions, the Board not only had the advantage of possessing in its archives important accumulations of letters and printed documents, such as periodic reports on the state of the colonies, governors' correspondence, and copies of colonial laws, but was able, as a rule, to call before it not only the official London representatives of the colonies concerned, but groups of interested individuals in private life frequently holding opposing points of view. With the various sources of infor-

[1] *Acts of the Privy Council, Col., 1745-1766,* pp. 276-278.

mation thus available, it was able, with the aid of its own legal adviser or of the Attorney and Solicitor-General, to prepare its answers to these questions. The answers, customarily in the form of recommendations technically known as "representations," were generally drafted not only in a spirit of unusual detachment and impartiality, but frequently in light of experience in handling similar questions, and in harmony, in so far as was possible under the circumstances, with precedent and established principles. In addition to finding the proper solutions to various problems, this body also drew up, by request, royal commissions, instructions, and similar authorizations for the exercise of powers within the colonies. Its responsibility for imperial policy was therefore very great, even during those periods when it was apparently least active. That it usually showed its competence in meeting this responsibility can hardly be denied by any student who has had the patience to examine with care the records of its activities.

In considering the relations between the Privy Council and the Board of Trade at this period a final point may be stressed. While it is true that the representations of the latter were usually accepted by the Lords of the Committee and favorably reported to the Council, at times this was not so. For example, in 1753 the Lords Commissioners represented for disallowance twelve acts passed by the Jamaica general assembly in 1751-52. The Committee, soon after receiving this representation, gave a copy of it to the agent of the Island, John Sharpe, who later in the year petitioned His Majesty to be heard in support of the acts. As a result of additional light being thrown upon the circumstances leading to this legislation it was finally determined early in the following year to disallow but seven of the measures. Of the remaining five, two were confirmed, and three running for the term of but a year were permitted to run their course, although they were considered to be so objectionable as to lead to an additional instruction to the Governor not to approve in the future any similar acts.[1]

One of the greatest objectives of the Crown was to make the Empire economically self-contained. The ambitious project was greatly advanced by the constant application of the Board of Trade to further it. By the middle of the eighteenth century this had in great measure been realized except in the case of articles of luxury and a very few essential basic commodities which were wholly or partly drawn from the Continent of Europe, the islands adjacent thereto, the foreign West Indies, and the Far East beyond India. For Parliament had effectively supplemented the efforts of the Crown. In the case of many commodities it had given special encouragement to bring about the production of these, be it in the Mother Country, in Ireland, or in the colonies. This was either in the form of bounties, as in the case of British sailcloth, Irish linen, or colonial ship timber, naval stores, indigo, and potash, or, of discriminating tariffs or other legislation in favor of colonial products as in the case of tobacco, sugar, and rum. As a result, English wool, coal, iron, and corn, Irish

[1] *Acts of the Privy Council, Col., 1745-1766,* pp. 215-223. For other instances covering the period from 1721 to 1739 see *ibid.,* Unbound Papers, p. 630.

flax and live stock, supplemented by a variety of other local products, supported the chief industries of the British Isles. From British waters, Newfoundland, and the Gulf of Maine came a surplus of fish; from Hudson Bay and from the back-country to the west of the English settlements in North America, large quantities of furs and skins; from New England, ship timber and ships; from the middle colonies, articles of food and iron; from the Chesapeake Bay region, tobacco and iron, and from North Carolina, naval stores. South Carolina grew rice and some indigo; Georgia was busy experimenting with the production of raw silk; Honduras Bay furnished logwood, the British West Indies, sugar and an inadequate amount of molasses; the West African Coast, slaves, gold, and ivory, and finally, the East India posts, a variety of desirable articles of consumption.

In concluding this survey, it may be affirmed that from the point of view of the development and dissemination of liberal political conceptions and institutions and the successful establishment of varied forms of individual enterprise in an attempt to realize not only favorable conditions of life for a widespread population but an ideal of imperial self-sufficiency the old British Empire in 1750 was undoubtedly the most imposing politico-economic structure that the world had ever known. It is therefore probable that the distinguished Pennsylvanian, John Bartram, reflected the attitude of most well-informed colonials when, in viewing the growth of the Empire in North America at this period, he declared prophetically, with a certain patriotic pride and fervor:

"England already possesses an uninterrupted line of well-peopled provinces on the coast successively begun within less than 150 years. She sees them every year augmented by an accession of subjects excited by the desire of living under governments and laws formed on the most excellent model upon earth. In vain do we look for an equal prosperity among the plantations of other European Nations, because every power has transplanted its constitution with its people. This surprising increase of people is a foundation that will bear a mighty superstructure, . . . "[1]

[1] *Observations on the Inhabitants, Climate, etc. made by Mr. John Bartram in his Travels from Pennsylvania,* etc. (London 1751), pp. iii and iv.

MAPS

INDEX

INDEX

A

Abeel, the Rev. John H., notes on New York by, 121.

Abercrombie [Abercromby], James, London agent for Virginia and North Carolina, the "Examination" of, 9.

Abridgment of . . . Indian Affairs . . . from the year 1678 to the Year 1751, by Peter Wraxall, 130.

Academy of Philadelphia, 187.

Acadia. *See* Nova Scotia.

Account of Six Years' Residence in Hudson's Bay, An (1752), by Joseph Robson, 244.

Account of the Island of Newfoundland with the Nature of its Trade, An (1765), by Griffith Williams, 250.

"Account of the Several Provinces in North America" (1756), 52.

Acts and Laws of Connecticut (1750), 81.

Adams, John, Massachusetts Bay statesman, on the advantages of New England, 38-39.

Adams, Samuel, later revolutionary agitator, at Harvard, 26.

Adjournment, the Assembly of Pennsylvania and the power of, 194.

Admirals of harbors, the powers of, limited in Newfoundland, 264.

Adultery, the capital law of 1650 against, in Connecticut, 94, 95.

Affirmation, the right of, accorded in Pennsylvania, 174.

Africa, supplies of slaves, gold and ivory from, 299.

Agent, the London, of New Hampshire, 47; of Rhode Island, 73-74; of Connecticut, 101-107; of New York, 128; of New Jersey, 142; of the East New Jersey Proprietors, 142-143; of the Pennsylvania Proprietors, 222.

Agricultural products, of Massachusetts Bay, 15; of New Hampshire, 40, 52; of Rhode Island, 57; of Connecticut, 76; of New York, 119; of New Jersey, 134; of Pennsylvania, 183.

Aix-la-Chapelle, the Peace of, and Louisbourg, 34.

Albany, a great fur-trading center, 124; a description of, 124-125; avarice of the traders at, 126; a resort for Indians preying upon the New England settlements, 126.

Albany County, New York, and land riots, 114.

Albany, Fort, a Hudson's Bay Company post, 234.

Alexander, James, an East New Jersey Proprietor, the private concessions of, 149.

Alexanders, the, among the New York aristocracy, 116.

Alexander, William, New York merchant, 113.

Aliens, Parliament forbids the sale of lands to, 192.

Allen, Samuel, Governor of New Hampshire and Proprietor, furnishes white-pine masts, 44.

America, and the fisheries, 17; and the white-pine belt, 40; and the issue of bills of credit, 137; and the manufacture and exportation of iron, 229, 231; the exportable surplus of commodities of, 298.

Ames' Almanack (1756), 52.

Anabaptists. *See* Mennonites.

Anarchy, in the affairs of New Jersey, 148; in Newfoundland, 267.

Anchors, the manufacture of, in Rhode Island, 217.

Ancram ironworks, in New York, 122.

Andros, Sir Edmund, Governor-General of the Dominion of New England, 29; the cautious land policy of, as Governor of New York, 100.

Angel, Nathan, a leading Rhode Island merchant, 60.

Anglicanism, in Massachusetts Bay, 23; in New Hampshire, 52-53; in Rhode Island, 55-56; in Connecticut, 81-82, 99; in Pennsylvania, 162, 163, 173, 177-178; in New York, 121, 285; in New Jersey, 285.

Anglo-French Commission of 1750, the, tasks assigned to, 35.

Annapolis Royal, Nova Scotia, menaced by the French in King George's War, 34.

Appointment, the power of, exercised by the New York Assembly, 128; by the Pennsylvania Assembly, 194.

Apprentices, the number of, employed by American hatters, restricted, 241-242.

Aris's Birmingham Gazette, 211.

Aristocratic tendencies, in Massachusetts Bay, 5; in New Hampshire, 53; in Rhode Island, 58; in Connecticut, 83; in New York, 116; in New Jersey, 159; in Pennsylvania, 188.

Arminius, the doctrines of, in New England, 24.

Arms, to be possessed by all Connecticut householders, 91.

Armstrong, Charles, Surveyor-General of the King's Woods, 42.

Arnold, Benedict, of New Haven, Connecticut, popular military leader, 92.

Arson, the crime of, in the Connecticut code of 1750, 96; in Pennsylvania, 181.

INDEX

Ashfield, Lewis Morris, appointed to the New Jersey Council, 161.

Ashurst, Sir Henry, London Agent for Massachusetts Bay, appointed for Connecticut, 102; the effective work of, 102-103.

Asiento trade, the, difficulty of controlling, 284.

Assemblies, the American colonial, Attorney-General Richard Bradley, on the aims of, 128; friction between, and governors, 284.

Assembly, the colonial, of Massachusetts Bay, composition and powers of, 30; attitude toward Governor Shirley, 35; denounces the disloyalty of the inhabitants of Nova Scotia, 37; expresses loyalty to the Crown, 37; votes, to support the claims of those moving into Livingston Manor, 114; of New Hampshire, opposes the garrisoning of Fort Dummer, 48-49; opposes the seating of deputies from the unprivileged towns, 49-50; of Rhode Island, the issue of bills of credit by, 70-71; dominated by inflationists, 73; opposes the regulation of colonial paper money by Parliament, 74; of Connecticut, the powers of, 75; of New York, and the land law of 1699, 110; and opposition to the Governor, 127-130; censured by the Board of Trade, 132; the appeal of, to settle the New York-New Jersey boundary dispute, 157; of New Jersey, meets alternately at Perth Amboy and at Burlington, 147-148; the hostility of, to the early governors, 158; the relations of, with Governor Morris, 158-159; with Governor Belcher, 160-161; of Pennsylvania, acts to limit the number of people on board an immigrant ship, 168; the distribution of members of, 177-178; and the extension of British criminal law to the Province, 181; the aggressiveness of, and power of, 194-195; indulged by the Crown and Proprietors, 197; the claims of, to exemption from all royal and proprietorial instructions, 197-198.

Assiniboines, the, and the Hudson's Bay Company trade, 237; hostility between the Sioux and, 247-248.

Assistants, the governor's, of Massachusetts Bay, 30; the election of, in Rhode Island, 69; in Connecticut, 84.

Atkinson, Theodore, member of the New Hampshire Assembly, 45; Chief Justice of the Supreme Court, 53.

Atlas Maritimus et Commercialis (1728), 258.

Avalon Peninsula, Newfoundland, a description of, in 1750, 251-252; a revival of the Baltimore claims to, 270-282.

Avery, Dr. Benjamin, Chairman of the Committee of English Dissenters, refuses the Connecticut London agency, 105.

Axes, the manufacture and exportation of, by the ironmasters of Massachusetts Bay, 217.

Axtell, William, on the English dependence upon Swedish iron, 220.

Ayrault, Daniel, a leading Rhode Island merchant, 60.

Ayrault, David, a Rhode Island merchant, the interest of in slaving, 67.

Ayrault, Stephen, a leading Rhode Island merchant, 60.

B

Bachelor house, the keeping of, punished by the Connecticut code of 1650, 95; and the Connecticut code of 1784, 100.

Badge of shame, a, and the Upland code, 179-180.

Balance of trade, the, between England and Massachusetts Bay, 9, 10; the importance of a favorable, to Great Britain, 289-290.

Ballast, the disposal of, regulated in Newfoundland, 263.

Ballot, the, in Connecticut, 84; in Pennsylvania, 177.

Baltimore, Benedict Calvert, 4th Baron, 274.

Baltimore, Cecil Calvert, 2nd Baron, sends deputies to Avalon, 272-274.

Baltimore, Charles Calvert, 3rd Baron, 274.

Baltimore, Charles Calvert, 5th Baron, 274.

Baltimore, Frederick Calvert, 6th Baron, the petition of, for the recognition of his rights to Avalon, 270, 275-279; the reasons for the failure of the petition of, 280-282.

Baltimore, George Calvert, 1st Baron, the attempt of, to settle at Ferryland, 249, 270, 272; a patent to, for lands in Newfoundland, 271; powers conferred upon, 271-272; the death of, 272; the patent to, declared in force, 273.

Baltimore family, the, poverty of, after the English Revolution, 275.

Banister, John, Newcastle ironmaster of the Crowley Works, the testimony of, respecting the iron industry in New England, 217.

Banister, Captain Thomas, on the value of Massachusetts Bay exports in 1715, 15; author of the "Essay on the Trade of New England," 15.

"Bankers." *See* West Countrymen.

Banking, in Boston, 8; the Rhode Island government and, 70-74; the New Jersey government and, 136-146; the Pennsylvania government and, 190-191.

Banks of Newfoundland, the, fishing interests upon, 249.

"Banks," the history of the Rhode Island, 70-74.

Baptists, the, and the Massachusetts Bay Establishment, 23; the strength of, in Boston, 23; the leading denomination in Rhode Island, 55-56; the persecution of, in Connecticut, 57; support Quakers for office in Rhode Island, 57; and the local ecclesiastical society in Connecticut, 81-82; the progress of, in eastern Connecticut, 99; fewness of, in Pennsylvania, 163; in the Pennsylvania Assembly, 178.

Barbados, signs of exhaustion of, 292; taxation in, 294.

Barberry, the, and the growing of wheat in Massachusetts Bay, 15; the eradication of, and the Connecticut towns, 90.

Barclays, the, among the New York aristocracy, 116.

Bar iron, the process employed in 1750 in the production of, 209; a shortage of, in England, 209; a decrease in the amount of, produced in England, 212; the total amount of, consumed in England, 213; the effect of the breaking off of relations between England and Sweden on the price of, 213; of America, the importation free of duties of, into the port of London, 227; the amount of, shipped from America to England, 227-228, 231.

Barnstable County, Massachusetts, the number of towns within, 19.

Barrington, New Hampshire, the fortified post of, 49.

Basel, Switzerland, an edict against the Moravian Brethren by the City of, 165.

Basque fishermen, and the Grand Banks of Newfoundland, 249; and the "wet" cod fishery, 255.

Bayards, the, among the New York aristocracy, 116.

Bear Skins, brought out of Hudson Bay in 1749, 235.

Beaver, and Newfoundland, 253.

Beaver hats, the manufacture of, in New York and the Act of 1732, 123; the making of, 240; the French take up the manufacture of, 240; the English hatters lose their markets for, to the French, 240-241; the making of, in the colonies restricted, 241; great wealth drawn to France through the sale of, 242-243; the decline of the English manufacture of, 242-243; the high quality of the French, 243.

Beaver House, London, a description of, 239.

Beaver skins, the number of, brought out of Hudson Bay in 1748, 235; the use of, in industry, 240; import and export duties on, 242.

Beawes, Windham, applies for Massachusetts Bay lands for London merchants, 19.

Bed feathers, brought out of Hudson Bay in 1748, 235.

Beekman's Patent, New York, 108; the creation of, 111.

Beekmans, the, among the New York aristocracy, 116.

Belcher, Jonathan, Governor of Massachusetts Bay and New Hampshire, instructed respecting import duties on negroes and felons, 31; the opposition of Shirley to, 33; on the growing scarcity of white-pine trees, 44; on the boundaries of New Hampshire, 46-47; seeks to unite his two governments, 47; represents Connecticut in London, 104; on the absence of taxation in New Jersey, 136; becomes Governor of New Jersey, 160; favors the New Jersey bills of credit bill of 1748, 142; the policies of, designed to win the support of the House of Representatives, 160; opposed by the Council, 160; censured by the Board of Trade, 161.

Bellomont, Richard Coote, Earl of, Governor of New York, Massachusetts Bay, and New Hampshire, on the high quality of New England codfish, 17; the cautious land policy in New York under, 110.

Bellows, the use of, in the iron-furnace, 207.

Bennington, the creation of the town of, by Governor Wentworth, 112.

Bergen County, New Jersey, Dutch settlements in, 147; the spread of land riots to, 151.

Berkeley, George, Bishop of Cloyne, on the sectaries of Rhode Island, 55; the sojourn of, at Newport, Rhode Island, 68.

Berkeley, Lord John, an original proprietor of New Jersey, 152.

Berks County, Pennsylvania, the creation of, and the racial complexion of, 173-174; the representation of, in the Assembly, 177.

Berkshire County, Massachusetts, the number of towns within, 19.

Bernard, Francis, Governor of New Jersey, permitted to assent under conditions to the issue of bills of credit, 146.

Bestiality, the capital law of 1650 against, in Connecticut, 94-95; and the Connecticut code of 1784, 100.

Bethlehem, Pennsylvania, the founding of, by the Moravian Brethren, 165.

Bibles, Connecticut selectmen to see that homes were furnished with, 98.

Bideford, England, the interest of, in the cod fisheries, 252.

Billiards, the playing at, forbidden in Connecticut, 98.

Bills of credit, of Massachusetts Bay, the redemption of, in 1749, 11-12; of other New England colonies, not to circulate, in Massachusetts Bay, 13, 72-73; a petition to the Crown by Boston merchants against the circulation of New England, 13; the history of, in Rhode Island to 1750, 70-74; the distribution of, to the towns to loan out, 70-71; the depreciation of, 71-73; not to circulate in Connecticut, 72-73; Parliament restricts the issue of, in New England, 74; the low value of, in Rhode Island, in 1753 and 1762, 74; the disastrous effects upon Rhode Island trade of depreciated, 74; the cautious use of, in New Jersey, 136; the early attitude of the Crown toward, 137; colonies not involved by 1715 in the issue of, 137; the instruction of 1720 regarding, 138; the hostility of the Privy Council in 1731 toward, 138; the high standing of the New Jersey, 142-143; arguments by Paris against the further issue of, 143; the House of Representatives petitions the King for the right to issue further, 144; royal instructions of 1753 respecting, 144-145; bills of 1755 and 1757 for, meet with royal disapproval, 145; instructions of the Governor relative to, modified, 146; of New York and Pennsylvania, the Governors, violate the royal instruction regarding, 145; the loan of, in Pennsylvania, 191.

Birmingham, the iron industry about, 205; the iron manufacturers of, desire a bounty on American iron, 231.

Blasphemy, the capital law of 1650 against, in Connecticut, 94-95; and the Connecticut code of 1784, 100; laws against, to be enforced in Newfoundland, 263.

Bloomeries, in Pennsylvania, 183.

Bluchers, the, among the New York aristocracy, 116.

Board of Trade, the, requests an account of bills of credit issued in Rhode Island, 72; censures the New York Assembly, 132; the attitude of, toward colonial bills of credit, 138-146; recommends disallowance of the New Jersey bills of credit act of 1748, 143-144; the report of, respecting the New Jersey petition of 1753, 144-145; reprimands Governor Belcher of New Jersey for recommending unfit men for the Council, 161; the representation of, against the Pennsylvania convict transports law, 196; and continuity in colonial government, 295-296; the chief activities of, 296-297; the "representations" of, 297-298.

Boars, the hiring of, by the Connecticut towns, 90.

"Body of Libertys," the, of Massachusetts Bay, 94.

Bole, William, Philadelphia merchant, on the lack of demand in Pennsylvania for English-made ironware, 218.

Bolingbroke, Henry St. John, 1st Viscount, influences the Connecticut agent, Dummer, 103.

Bontin, M., master of the *Jupiter*, and the Jamaica vice-admiralty court, 62-63.

"Book of Proceedings of the Bristol Merchant Venturers, 1745-1752," 244.

Boring of the tongue, the, and the Duke of York laws, 179.

Boston Gazette, the, founded by William Booker, 27.

Boston, its greatness as a commercial center, 4; as a cultural center, 5; its homes, 5-6; its shipping, 6; compared to that of New York, 6; the decline in shipbuilding at, 6-7; the evasion of the customs by merchants of, 9; the entrepôt for a vast territory, 11; trade stagnation in 1750 in, 11, 14; the merchants of, petition against New England bills of credit, 13; religious groups in, 23; the representation of, in the Assembly, 30; commercial and social relations of, with Connecticut, 76, 78; compared to Philadelphia, 186; the interest of the merchants of, in Newfoundland trade, 253.

Boston News-Letter, the, issued by John Campbel, 27.

Boston Weekly Post, the, issued by Thomas Fleet, 27.

Boundary dispute, the, of Massachusetts Bay and New Hampshire, 47-48; of New Hampshire and New York, 51-52, 112; of New York and Massachusetts Bay, 113-114; of New York and New Jersey, 154-157.

Bounties, on ship timber, 43; a demand for, on American iron, 231; the giving of, by Parliament to promote economic self-containment, 298.

Bowls, the playing at, forbidden, in Connecticut, 98.

Bowsprits, a bounty on American, by Parliament, 43, 219.

Boyne, the battle of the, and Irish emigration, 286.

Bradley, Richard, New York Attorney-General, on the aims of the colonial assemblies, 128.

Branders, of horses and other animals in Connecticut, 89; of flour, and of beef and pork, and the Pennsylvania Assembly, 194.

Branding, in Connecticut, of Deacon Drake, 80; and the Connecticut code of 1650, 94; and the Duke of York laws, 179; and the New Castle code, 180.

Brands, town, in Connecticut, for horses, 89.

Bread, the export of, by New York, 123; by Pennsylvania, 183.

Brenton, Jahleel, Surveyor-General of His Majesty's Woods, 42.

Breton fishermen and the Grand Banks of Newfoundland, 249; and the "wet" cod fishery, 255.

Brick, the use of, in Boston, 5; in Philadelphia, 187; the superior quality of Pennsylvania, 187.

Bridgeman, Sir Orlando, Chief Baron of the Exchequer, and other commissioners decide on the dispute over Avalon, 273.

INDEX

319

INDEX

Castor gras d'hiver, and the making of hats, 243.

Castor sec, and the making of parchment, 243; the monopolization by foreigners of the Hudson Bay, 243.

Castration, punishment by, in Connecticut, 96; punishment by, in the New Castle code, 180.

Catechisms, Connecticut selectmen to see that homes were furnished with, 98.

Catherwood, John, 133.

Cattle, the scarcity of, in Newfoundland, 253.

Cedar Lake, the French trading post of Fort Bourbon on, 247.

Cedar Wood, the use of, in Pennsylvania, 187.

Certificated goods, the importation into Pennsylvania of, 184-185.

Chandler, Joshua, New Haven deputy, the conservative leanings of, 85.

Charcoal, an essential in the smelting of iron ore in 1750, 208, 209.

Charles, R., of Leicesterfield, England, on the Iron Act of 1750, 232.

Charles, Robert, Secretary to Sir Peter Warren, employed as London agent by the New York Assembly, 128.

Charming Polly, the, Rhode Island merchant ship to the West Indies, 60.

Charter, the, of Massachusetts Bay, of 1691, an analysis of, 29-31; the explanatory, of 1725, 30; of Rhode Island, analyzed, 69; of Connecticut, and the Congregational Establishment, 100; the preservation of, 101.

Checkley family, the, of Newport, Rhode Island, 68.

Cheesecook [Cheesecock] Patent, New York, 109; the creation of, 111.

Chesapeake Bay, and exports of tobacco and iron, 299.

Chester County, Pennsylvania, religious elements within, 173-174; the representation of, 177-178.

Chester, New Hampshire, the fortified post of, 49; deputies from, summoned to the Assembly by Wentworth, the dispute over seating of, 49-50.

Chester, Pennsylvania. *See* Upland.

Chests of drawers, the manufacture and export of, by the people of New Hampshire, 52.

Children, the death penalty for smiting parents by, in Connecticut, 94; in Duke of York code, 179.

Church communion, the, in Connecticut, 79-80.

Churches, in Boston, 23; in Rhode Island, 56; in Connecticut, 79-82; in New York City, 121; in Albany, 124; in New Jersey, 147; in Philadelphia, 187.

Church services, the punishment by the Connecticut code of 1650 for staying away from, 95.

Clarke, George, Governor of New York, the financial policies of, and the Assembly, 127-128.

Classes, social, in Pennsylvania, 189-190.

Claverack, New York, riotous procedure at, 114.

Clee Hill iron, and the making of gun barrels, 206.

Clergy, the Massachusetts Bay, in the seventeenth and eighteenth centuries, 20-28; in Pennsylvania, in 1750, 162-163.

Clerk, the town, in Connecticut, the election of, and duties of, 89.

Clinton, George, Governor of New York, and the New Hampshire boundary dispute, 51, 112-113; issues a proclamation to arrest Massachusetts Bay rioters, 114; son of the Earl of Lincoln, comes to New York with expectations, 127; the character of, and early relations with de Lancey, 127; gives his confidence to Colden, 129; the relations of, with the Assembly, 127-133.

Coal, the lack of, in Pennsylvania in 1750, 184; an essential in the production of iron in 1750, 207; the use of, in turning pig iron into bar iron, 209; iron manufacturing in Worcestershire, the result of deposits of, 209; the importance of, to England, 298.

Cod, the methods of catching and curing, in Newfoundland, 254-256.

Cod fisheries, the, nations participating in, 249; the French enjoy the advantage in, 250-251; the value of, to England, 256-257.

Code, the, of Connecticut of 1650, 94; of 1750, 95-99; of 1784, 100; of the Duke of York, 178; of Pennsylvania, 178-182; of Massachusetts Bay, 179; of New Haven Colony, 179.

Codfish, the quality of Massachusetts Bay, 17; commands a high price in Portugal, 17; French cured, preferred in the European markets, 251; the value of, to France, 251; the poor quality of, carried by the British to southern markets from Newfoundland, 258.

Coke, the use of, in England before 1750, 208.

Colden, Cadwallader, Surveyor-General of New York, on the vague terms of land grants, 111; characterized, 129; the support of Clinton and opposition to the Assembly by, 129-133.

"Cold short" iron ore, the location of, and use of, in England, 251.

Cole, Captain T., seeks to exclude the French from the cod fisheries, 250; author of *State of the Fisheries* (1761), 251.

College, Harvard, 28; Yale, 28; King's, 78; Princeton, 147; The "Log," 147; of Philadelphia, 176, 187.

Collenson, Peter, 136.

Collieries, instructions against the opening of, in Nova Scotia, 230.

INDEX

Collins, Francis, furnishes New England white-pine masts, 44.

Colony, the corporate, of Massachusetts Bay, under the charter of 1691, 2-38; of Rhode Island, under the charter of 1663, 55-74; of Connecticut, under the charter of 1662, 75-102.

Colony, the proprietary, of Pennsylvania, 162-203; of the Lower Counties on the Delaware, 192, 285.

Colony, the royal, of New Hampshire, 40-54; of New York, 108-132; of New Jersey, 134-161.

Commerce, of Massachusetts Bay, 7, 9, 15-16; of New Hampshire, 52; of Rhode Island, 59; with the West Indies, 60-68; with Africa, 65-67; of Connecticut, 76; of New York, 121-122; of New Jersey, 135; of Pennsylvania, 185-186.

Commissioners of oyer and terminer, the appointment of, for Newfoundland, 268.

Commissions, the governors', the similarity of, in royal colonies, 294.

Commission, the New Hampshire-Massachusetts Bay boundary, supports New Hampshire claims, 47; the New York-New Jersey boundary, vindicates the New Jersey claims, 157.

Communion, the church, in Massachusetts Bay, 22-24; in Connecticut, 79-81.

Conception Bay, Newfoundland, cod fisheries on, 257.

Concord, New Hampshire. See Penacook, 20-21.

Congregational Church, the, in Massachusetts Bay, in 1650 and 1750, 21-26; fellowship within, 21-22; the halfway covenant of, 22; and the Great Awakening, 24-26; Old Light and New Light congregations within, 26; in New Hampshire, 52-53; in Connecticut, 79-82; at the end of the eighteenth century, 100; the end of the Establishment in 1818, 100; gives way to the Presbyterian, in East New Jersey, 147; in New England, 285.

Connecticut Courant, the, 99.

Connecticut Gazette, the, the first newspaper in the colony, 99.

Connecticut Journal, the, 81.

Connecticut, the value of imports and exports of, 10; Boston merchants petition the Crown against the bills of credit of, 13; the persecution of Baptists within, 57; the leading towns of, 75-76; the shipping of, 77; characteristics of, as a corporate colony, in 1750, 75; the government of, 75; the population of, 76; the economy of, 76; the exports of, 76; the commercial relations of, 76; industries in, 77; Puritanism and, 79; local government in, 79-93; the land policy of, 86; the code of 1750 of, compared with those of 1650 and 1784, 93-100; the preservation by, of the charter and with it the Congregational Establishment, 100; the activities of the London agents of, in the eighteenth century, 101-107; the low rate of taxation in, 107; the thrifty government of, 107; an appeal to the government of, by the rioters of Hunterdon County, New Jersey, for annexation, 153; has eyes on northern Pennsylvania, 153; an appeal of New York settlers to the government of, for lands west of the Hudson, 156.

Connecticut River, the, an abundance of white pine on the upper, 44; report on the lands of the upper, 50; divides Connecticut into economic and social sections, 77.

Considerations on the Bill now Depending before the Honourable House of Commons for Encouraging the Importation of Pig and Bar Iron from America (1749), 225.

Conspiracy against the Colony, the capital law against, in the Connecticut code of 1750, 96.

Constables, the town, of Connecticut, the election of, and duties of, 89; to suppress vice and enforce the law of the Sabbath, 98.

Contemptuous behavior, the punishment for, in the Connecticut code of 1650, 95.

Continuation of the History of the Province of Massachusetts Bay (1798-1803), by G. R. Minot, 9.

Contacook [Contoocook], New Hampshire, the fortified post of, 49.

Convict transports, Massachusetts Bay laws imposing import duties on, disallowed, 31; the issue over the Pennsylvania law placing an import duty on, 195-196.

Cook-rooms, for the cod fisheries, protected in Newfoundland, 263.

Coppices, the distribution of, in England and Wales, 206; the problem of the preservation of, in England, 210-211.

Cornbury, Edward Hyde, Viscount (later becomes the 3rd Earl of Clarendon), Governor of New York and New Jersey, extravagant land grants of, in New York, 110-111; the New York Assembly under, seeks financial control, 128; the opposition of Lewis Morris to, 158.

Cornell, Gideon, Newport merchant, owner of the *Jupiter,* 62-64; wins appeal from the vice-admiralty court of Jamaica, 63.

Corner, John, London merchant, seeks Massachusetts Bay lands, 19.

Corn, the dependence of Massachusetts Bay upon imported, 15; the export of, by Rhode Island, 57; a leading Pennsylvania crop, 183; the importance of, to England, 298.

Cortlandt Manor, New York, 108; the creation of, 111.

Cosby, William, Governor of New York, financial policies of, and the Assembly, 127.

321

INDEX

De Lanceys, the, among the New York aristocracy, 116; and the Canada trade, 130; the interest of, in the Minisink Patent, 155.

Delaware Company, the, organization of, 156; an Indian grant secured by, 156.

Delaware, the Lower Counties on the, a surviving proprietary, 192; possessed no religious establishment, 285.

Denial of the true God, and the death penalty in New York, 179.

Denmark, an edict against the Moravian Brethren by the King of, 165; the loss of the market of, by English hatters in favor of the French, 240.

Deputies, the reluctance of towns in Massachusetts Bay to send, 30; the refusal to seat, in the New Hampshire Assembly from the unprivileged towns, 49; the election of, in Rhode Island, 69; in Connecticut, 83; in Pennsylvania, 177; the religious complexion of the, in the Pennsylvania Assembly, 177-178.

Deputy governor, the election of, in Rhode Island, 69; in Connecticut, 84.

Desks, the manufacture and export of, by the people of New Hampshire, 52.

Dice, the use of, forbidden in Connecticut, 98.

Dinwiddie, Robert, Surveyor-General of the Customs of the southern ports of the continent of America (later Deputy Governor of Virginia), estimates the value of the British colonial trade, 9-10; and of the Newfoundland fisheries, 256.

Disallowance, the royal, of Massachusetts Bay legislation, 31; of Connecticut legislation, 107; of Jersey legislation, 143-144; of Pennsylvania legislation, 195-196.

Dissolution, the Governor and the, of the Massachusetts Bay Assembly, 32; the Assembly of Pennsylvania and the power of, 194.

Distilleries, in Massachusetts Bay in 1750, 15; the number of, in Newport, Rhode Island, 64; in New York, 123; North American, profit by the French West India molasses, 292.

Dobbs, Arthur (later Governor of North Carolina), the plan of, to overthrow the Hudson's Bay Company monopoly, 245; an expedition sent out by, to find the Northwest Passage, 245; author of *Account of the Countries Adjoining Hudson Bay* (1744), 245.

Dogs, the use of, in Newfoundland, 253.

Dominica, West Indies, and Rhode Island trade, 60.

Dominion of New England, the, 29.

Dongan, Thomas, Governor of New York, and the New Jersey boundary, 154.

Douglas, Captain James, on the state of St. John's, Newfoundland, 251.

Douglass, William, on the Ulster Scots as indentured servants in America, 172; author of, *A Summary, Historical and Political . . . of the Present State of the British Settlements in North America* (1755), 7.

Dracut, New Hampshire, the dispute over the seating of deputies of, 49-50.

Drake, Deacon Nathaniel, of Windsor, Connecticut, the branding of, 80.

Drake, Francis William, appointed Governor of Newfoundland, 263.

Dress, in Pennsylvania, 188-189.

Drinking at night, the punishment for, in the Connecticut code of 1650, 95; and the Connecticut code of 1784, 100.

Drunkenness, the penalty for, in Connecticut, 95.

Dudley Castle, the decay of iron-works about, 208.

Dudley, England, unemployment and poor-rates at, 214.

Dudley Furnace, the, and the smelting of iron with coal, 207-208.

Dudley, Massachusetts Bay, fined for neglect to send deputies, 30.

Duke of York laws, the, origin of, and description of, 178.

Dukes County, Massachusetts Bay, the number of towns within, 19.

Dummer, Dr. Jeremiah, London agent for Connecticut and Massachusetts Bay, falls under Bolingbroke's influence, dismissed from his Connecticut post, 103.

Dummer, Fort, New Hampshire, the dispute over the garrisoning of, 48-50; New Hampshire troops occupy, 50.

Dunbar, David, Surveyor-General of His Majesty's Woods, 42; sells his post to Benning Wentworth, 45.

Dunkards. *See* Dunkers.

Dunkers, the, in Pennsylvania, 162; support the Quakers in office, 175.

Durkee, John, of Bean Hill, Connecticut, popular military leader, 92.

Durlach, the unhappy lot in Pennsylvania of immigrants from, 166-167.

Dutchess County, New York, and land riots, 114-115.

Dutch patroons, the, of New York, 108.

Dutch Reformed Church, the, in New York City, 121; in Albany, 124.

Dutch, the success of the, in the curing of cod, 251.

Dutch West India Company, the, 109.

Duties, the failure to pay, on sugar and molasses, brought to Massachusetts Bay, 9; to Rhode Island, 63-64; on iron, 212, 227; on beaver skins, 242.

E

Ears, the loss of, and the Pennsylvania code, 181.

East Haddam, Connecticut, 76.

East Haven, Connecticut, iron production at, 77.

East India, goods from, to Massachusetts Bay, 9.

East India posts, the, and articles of consumption, 299.

Eastmain House, a Hudson's Bay Company post, 234.

East New Jersey, characterized, 147.

Ecclesiastical society, the, in Connecticut, 81-82.

Economic sectionalism, and the British Empire, 291-294.

Economic self-containment, and the British Empire, 298-299.

Education, in New England, 28; in New York, 78; in reading for all in Connecticut, 97; in New Jersey, 147; in Philadelphia, 187.

Edwards, the Rev. Jonathan, pastor at Northampton, Massachusetts Bay, and the Great Awakening, 24-26; the repudiation of, by his congregation, 26.

Edwards, Captain Richard, Governor of Newfoundland, 263.

Elections, in Massachusetts Bay, 30; in Rhode Island, 69; in Connecticut, 84; in Pennsylvania, 177.

Elizabethtown, New Jersey, the New England background of, 147; the East New Jersey proprietors and the lands of, 152.

Elk skins, brought out of Hudson Bay in 1748, 235.

Ellery family, the, of Newport, Rhode Island, 68.

Ellis, Henry, on the imports of York Fort on Hudson Bay, 234; the experiences of, and associates in attempting to discover the Northwest Passage, 245; author of *A Voyage to Hudson's Bay by the Dobbs Galley and California in the Years 1746 and 1747 for Discovering a Northwest Passage* (1749), 245.

Emigrant ships, arrangements for German emigrants on board, 167-168.

England, the cost of shipbuilding in, 7; the shortage of ship timber in, 41-42; the iron industry in, 205-213; a great decrease in the amount of iron produced in, 224; the high level of taxes in, 225; the decline of hat-making within, 241-242; the spread of the liberal institutions of, 284; the people of, dependent upon the welfare of the Empire, 288.

Englishmen, as indentured servants, in Pennsylvania, 171.

Engrossment of commodities, the, instructions of Newfoundland governors against, 263.

Entail of lands, the, in Massachusetts Bay, the repeal of a law involving, 31.

Episcopalians. *See* Anglicans.

Essex County, Massachusetts Bay, the number of towns within, 19.

Essex County, New Jersey, land rioters of, 150, 151.

Establishments, religious, within the Empire, 285.

Evangelicals, the strength of the, in Pennsylvania, 162.

Evans, Lewis, Pennsylvania surveyor and map-maker, on the economical habits of the Pennsylvania Germans, 171; on the defects of the provincial government, 182; on the lack of durability of ships built in Pennsylvania, 184; on the difficult position of the Pennsylvania governors, 193; a description of the Pennsylvania land system by, 201-202; on the Iron Act of 1750, 228.

Ewing Mansion, Boston, 6.

Excise masters, the town, in Connecticut, the election of, and duties of, 90.

Excise, the, in Pennsylvania, amounts raised by, 191; the collectors of, appointed by the Pennsylvania Assembly, 194.

Exeter, England, the interest of, in the cod fisheries, 252.

Exports, the, of Great Britain to the colonies, 9-10; of Massachusetts Bay, 15-17; of New Hampshire, 52; of Rhode Island, 58; of Connecticut, the value of, 76; of New York, 123; of New Jersey, the value of, 135; of Pennsylvania, 183; of Hudson Bay, 235; of Newfoundland, the value of, 256-258.

F

Fairfield, Connecticut, the rating of, for taxation, 76.

Falmouth, England, early interest of, in the cod fisheries, 252.

False testifying, a capital offense in the Connecticut code of 1650, 94; and the Connecticut code of 1784, 100.

False witnessing, and the death penalty in New York, 179.

Fane, Francis, legal adviser of the Board of Trade, comments upon the Connecticut law respecting freemen, 83; reports against the Pennsylvania convict law of 1742, 195.

Faneuil, Peter, the activities of, 6, 17.

Farmers, public aid to, in Rhode Island, 70-75; in New Jersey, 136; in Pennsylvania, 190.

Farming, and the northern plantations, 1; in Massachusetts Bay, and wheat-raising, 15; in New Hampshire, 52; in Rhode Island, 57; in Connecticut, 76; in New York, on the manors, 119; in New Jersey, 134; in Pennsylvania, 182-183.

Farmington, Connecticut, the rating of, for taxation, 76.

Farms, as distinguished from plantations, characteristic of the northern colonies, 3; of Rhode Island, the size of, 58; of Pennsylvania, the average size of, 183; the products of, 183.

Felonies, capital, in Connecticut, in 1750, 95; in Pennsylvania, 181.

INDEX

Felons, laws imposing import duties on, in Massachusetts Bay, disallowed, 31; the Pennsylvania law of 1742 imposing duties on, reported for repeal, 195-196.

Fence viewers, in Connecticut, 86; the election of, and the duties of, 89.

Ferguson, Captain, Rhode Island slaver, 66.

Fermor, Juliana, daughter of the Earl of Pomfret, marries Thomas Penn, 202.

Ferryland, Newfoundland, a garrison stationed at, 252; the building of a mansion at, by George Calvert, 272; the occupation of, by Hamilton and associates, 273.

Finance, public, in Massachusetts Bay, 11-13; in New Hampshire, 48, 51; in Rhode Island, 70-74; in Connecticut, 107; in New York, 127; in New Jersey, 136-146; in Pennsylvania, 190-192, 194.

Fines, the paying of, by Massachusetts Bay towns, 30; the punishment by, in Connecticut, 94.

Firelocks, to be possessed by all Connecticut householders, 91.

Fish, 17, 18, 249, 255, 257, 299.

Fisheries, the, and the northern colonies, 4; and Massachusetts Bay, 17-18; and Newfoundland and Grand Banks, 249-261.

Fish-stages, 253, 254, 261.

Fitch, Thomas, of Norwalk, Connecticut, refuses the London agency, 104-105; as Deputy Governor of Connecticut acts as legal adviser of the Elizabethtown, New Jersey, rioters, 153.

Flakes, for the cod fisheries, protected in Newfoundland, 264.

Flamborough Head, a Hudson's Bay Company post at, 234.

Flax, exported by Connecticut, 76; the growing of, in New York, 123; the importance of, to Ireland, 298.

Fletcher, Benjamin, Governor of New York, commissioned to command the Connecticut militia, 102; extravagant land grants by, 110.

Flour, the production of, in the colonies, 4; a great reputation once enjoyed by New York, 123; the sale of unmerchantable, 123; the exportation of large quantities of Pennsylvania, 183.

Food, surpluses, of the southern colonies, 15; of Massachusetts Bay, 16; of Rhode Island, 57; of Connecticut, 76; of New York, 123; of New Jersey, 135; of Pennsylvania, 183; of Newfoundland, 256; of the Middle Colonies, 299.

Fordham Manor, New York, 108.

Forest of Dean, the, qualities of the iron of, 206; the advantages of, for iron production, 209.

Forfeiture of goods, the, and the Upland code, 179. See Felonies.

Forges, a lack of, in Rhode Island, reported in 1750, 67; in Connecticut, 77; in Pennsylvania, 184; the

number of, in England, 206; the idleness of, in England, 214; the number of, in New England in 1733, 217; in the Middle Colonies, in 1750, 218.

Fort à la Corne, on the Saskatchewan, a French trading post, 248.

Fort Bourbon, Cedar Lake, a French trading post, 247.

Fort Dauphin, Lac des Prairies, a French trading post, 247.

Fort George, Goat Island, Narragansett Bay, fires upon His Majesty's cutter St. John, 64.

Fort La Reine, on the Assiniboine, a French trading post, 247.

Fort Maurepas, on the Winnipeg, a French trading post, 247.

Fort Paskoyac [Poskoyac or Poskioac], on the Saskatchewan, a French trading post, 247.

Fort Richmond, a Hudson's Bay Company post, 234.

Fort St. Louis, on the Saskatchewan, a French trading post, 248.

Fowey, England, the early interest of, in the cod fisheries, 252.

Fox skins, brought out of Hudson Bay in 1748, 235.

"Frame," the Pennsylvania, of 1701, and the eighteenth-century provincial government, 193.

France, the Court of, encourages the illicit trading of Rhode Island with the French West Indies, 61; the military power of, 288; the encircling movement of, in North America, 288; the coördination of the efforts of the population of, 288-289; the advantages of, over Great Britain, 289.

Franchise, the, in Massachusetts Bay, 30; in Rhode Island, 56-57, 69-70; in Connecticut, 75, 83-85; in New York, 116; in Pennsylvania, 177.

Franklin, Benjamin, editor of the Pennsylvania Gazette, the experiments of, with electricity, 188.

Franklin, James, editor of the New England Courant, attacks the clergy, 26.

Freedom, personal, in Rhode Island, 60-64; in Massachusetts Bay and New York, 113; in New Jersey, 149-153; in Pennsylvania, 162-163; ideas of, and imperial unity, 284.

Freemasons, in Pennsylvania, 162.

Freemen, in Rhode Island, the qualifications for, 56-57, 69; the meetings of, at Newport, 69; in Connecticut, the qualifications for, and responsibilities of, 82-83; the proportion of population enjoying rights of, 83; the conservative leanings of, 85.

Freethinkers, in Pennsylvania, 162.

French sugar islands, the, advantages enjoyed by, 291.

French, the, capture Canso, 33-34; the return of Louisbourg to, 34; negotiations with, 35; trade relations with, 15-16, 60-61; competi-

INDEX

Great Awakening, the, and Jonathan Edwards, 24-26; and New England Congregationalism, 25-26, 80-81; the influence of, upon New Hampshire, 53; upon Rhode Island, 56; upon Connecticut, 80.

Great Britain, the value of commodities shipped from, to the colonies, 9-10; the merchants of, secure ships built at Philadelphia, 181; the extension of the criminal laws of, to Pennsylvania, 181. *See* England.

Great Nine Partners' Patent, the, in New York, 108; the creation of, 111.

Green men, and the Newfoundland fisheries, 260; the employment of, on the Island of Newfoundland, 264.

Greenwich, Rhode Island, the share of the "banks" allotted to, 70-71.

Greyhound, the, carries Virginia iron to Bristol, 215.

Grimington's Island, Labrador, and the boundary of the Hudson's Bay Company territory, 238.

Guadeloupe, the fertility of, 291.

Guinea trade, the, and Massachusetts Bay, 9; and Rhode Island, 65-68; the difficulty of controlling, 283.

H

Halfway covenant, the, and the Congregational Church of New England, 22.

Halter, the wearing of a, and adultery in Connecticut, 96.

Hamilton, James Hamilton, 3rd Marquis of, later 1st Duke of, proprietary rights over Newfoundland granted to, and associates, 273; dispossesses Lord Baltimore of Avalon, 273.

Hamilton, James, Lieutenant Governor of Pennsylvania, on the freedom of the people from taxation, 192; resigns his post by reason of disputes with the Assembly, 203.

Hamlet, Captain, Rhode Island slaver, at Anamaboe, 66.

Hammond, Captain, Rhode Island slaver, at Anamaboe, 66.

Hampshire County, Massachusetts Bay, the number of towns within, 19.

Hancock, Thomas, Boston merchant, the activities of, 8; illegal traffic by, 8.

Handicrafts, in the northern colonies, 4.

Hanover, a proclamation against the Moravian Brethren by the Elector of, 165.

Harbor admirals, the friction in Newfoundland between the justices of the peace and, 265; the neglect of duties by, 266.

Harbors, the jurisdiction over, in Newfoundland, 263.

Hardenburgh Patent, the, New York, 109; the creation of, 111.

Hard money, adopted as a basis by Massachusetts Bay in 1749, 11-13. *See* Specie.

Hardware, the widespread distribution of Birmingham, in 1747, 205; the curtailment of England's great export trade in, 213, 214; the exportation of New England, 217; the excellent quality of American, 218.

Harrisons, the, among the New York aristocracy, 116.

Hartford, Connecticut, a joint capital, 75; the population of, 76; the rating of, for taxation, 76.

Harvard College, the growing liberalism of, in the eighteenth century, 28.

Hatters, English, and French competition, 239-241; American, and the Hat Act of 1732, 241-242.

Haveland, Captain, brings Germans to Pennsylvania, 164.

Haverhill, Massachusetts Bay, families from, settle at Penacook, 20-21.

Haverhill, New Hampshire, the dispute, over seating deputies of, 49-50.

Haywards, in Connecticut, 86; the election of, and duties of, 89.

Health Officer, the, appointment of, by the Pennsylvania Assembly, 194.

Heathcotes, the, among the New York aristocracy, 116.

Heath, Sir Robert, the patent of, to Carolina, 279-280.

Heilbronn, Württemberg, the journey from, to America by German emigrants described, 167.

Hemp, premiums on American-made, 218.

Hempstead, New York, the adoption of the Duke of York laws at, 178-179.

Hendry, Anthony, the journey of, into the country of the Blackfeet, 237.

Henley House, a Hudson's Bay Company post, 234.

Henley, Sir Robert (later Attorney-General), the opinion of, adverse to the claims of Baltimore, 278-279.

Heretics, a Connecticut act for suppressing, disallowed by the Privy Council, 107.

"Herrnhuter" Brethren. *See* Moravian Brethren.

Hill, Captain William, placed in charge of Avalon by Baltimore, 272.

Hill, Lieutenant, of His Majesty's cutter *St. John,* in charge of the custom-house, fired upon in Narragansett Bay, 64.

Hill, Thomas, a circular letter by, on the iron act, 217.

Hispaniola, the shipping of Spanish dollars from Boston to, 14; Rhode Island trade relations with, and the court of France, 61.

Hogs, regulations regarding, and the Connecticut town meetings, 90.

Holland, Henry Rich, 1st Earl of,

327

proprietary rights over Newfoundland granted to, and associates, 273.

Holland, money secured from, and sugar carried to, by Rhode Island merchants, 67-68.

Homes, in Boston, 5-6; in New York, 121; in Albany, 124; in Philadelphia, 185-187.

Honduras Bay, logwood from, 7, 299.

Honeyman family, the, of Newport, Rhode Island, 68.

Hopkins, Stephen, a leading Rhode Island merchant (later Governor of Rhode Island), 60.

Hopson, Colonel, Governor of Nova Scotia, instructions to, against the opening of collieries, 230.

Horseneck, Essex County, New Jersey, the dispute over the lands of, 149.

Horses, exported from Connecticut, 76; used in tillage in Pennsylvania, 171; the fewness of, in Newfoundland, 253.

Hospitality, of the people of Pennsylvania, 183.

House frames, the exportation of, from New Hampshire, 52.

House of Commons, the, of Great Britain, resolutions of, in 1740 respecting colonial bills of credit, 139; a committee of, considers petitions from English ironmasters, 221-222.

House of Representatives, the, of Massachusetts Bay, 30, 37; of New Jersey, and the bills of credit bill of 1744, 140.

Hubbard, Thomas, Speaker of House of Representatives of Massachusetts Bay, 37.

Hudson Bay, a description of, in the eighteenth century, 233-234; trading posts in 1750 upon, 234; Indian groups resorting to, 237.

Hudson's Bay Company, the posts of the, and the New York fur trade, 124; the charter of, 233; the activities of, in 1750 and value of its exports and imports, 235; the Indian trade and the vast region exploited by, 236-238; the extent of territory claimed by, 238; the financial condition of, 239; auction sales by, 239-240; the great profits of, 244; attempts to overthrow the monopoly of, 243-246; the memorial of 1750 by, for the settlement of claims against the French, 247.

Hudson's Bay House, a description of, 239.

Huguenots, in New York City, 121.

Hume, Benjamin, Jamaica Receiver-General of Customs, seizes the *Jupiter*, in Jamaica waters, 63.

Hunterdon County, New Jersey, the spread of land riots to, 151.

Hunter, Robert, Governor of New York and New Jersey, the failure of the attempt by, to produce naval stores, 117; secures general appropriations for a five-year period, 127; the instructions of, as to equal import duties for the two provinces, 135.

Hutchinson, Thomas, the education of, 28.

Hutton, William, appointed Deputy Governor of Avalon, Newfoundland, 274.

I

Idolatry, the capital law of 1650 against, in Connecticut, 94, 95.

Immigration, into North America from Germany, 164-168; from Ireland, 172; into Newfoundland, 249, 260.

Immorality, laws governing, in Connecticut, 94, 100; in the Duke of York laws, 178; to be enforced by the governor in Newfoundland, 263.

Import duties, to be the same in New York and New Jersey, 135.

Imports, of Massachusetts Bay, in 1743, 7-8; the great value of, 9; of Pennsylvania, the Jersies, New York, Rhode Island, Connecticut, New Hampshire, and Nova Scotia, in 1743, 10; the unreliability of figures of, in the eighteenth century, 10; of Connecticut from Boston and New York, 76; into New York, the value of, compared to those of Antigua, 121-122; into Pennsylvania, the value of, in 1747, 184-185; of England, of iron from Sweden, Russia, and Spain, 210; of iron from the American plantations, 228; of furs from Hudson Bay, 235; of fish and other commodities from Newfoundland, 258; of Hudson Bay, from England, 235; of Newfoundland, from England, 258.

Imprisonment, in Connecticut, 94.

Income taxes, in Pennsylvania, 190-191.

Indentured servants, in Pennsylvania, 169-172.

Independent Advertiser, the, Boston news sheet, 27.

Independent Reflector, the, 117.

Indian deeds, secured by New Jersey squatters, 149-150.

Indian trade, the, of New York, 123-126; the profitable nature of, 123; adversely affected by competition, 124; Albany and Oswego and, 124-125; the value of, in 1749, 125; dishonest practices and, 126; strict regulation of, by the Hudson's Bay Company, 236; a description of, 236; brandy and, 236; the influence of the French competition upon, 237; the variation in prices offered in, 238; native groups involved in, 237; regions involved in, 237-238; the difficulty of coördinating, 283.

Indigo, the production of, promoted by bounties, 298; and South Carolina, 299.

Industry, in Massachusetts Bay, 6, 15, 216-217; in New Hampshire, 52; in Rhode Island, 67, 217; in Connecticut, 77, 217; in New York, 122, 124, 217-218; in Pennsylvania, 183, 185, 218; in New Jersey, 218; in England, 204-213, 218-232.

INDEX

Juries, the refusal of New Jersey, to convict rioters, 150.

Jupiter, the, the Rhode Island sloop, the vice-admiralty case involving, 62-64.

Justices of the peace, the election of, in Rhode Island, 69; the appointment of, in Connecticut, 92-93; the lack of qualification for, in Pennsylvania, 182; of Newfoundland, the duties of, 263; friction between the harbor admirals and, 265; the qualifications of, 266; weakness of, 267.

K

Kakiate Patent, the, New York, 109; the creation of, 111.

Kalm, Peter, a description of New York City by, 121; author of *Travels into North America* (1772), 121; on the New York fur trade, 126; a description of Philadelphia by, 185-187.

Keene, New Hampshire, troops of the Province occupy the post at, 50.

Kelsey, Henry, the journey of, to the Indians of the Plains, 237.

Kent, the County of, England, additional ironworks forbidden within, 208.

Key keepers, the town, in Connecticut, 89.

Kidnapping, the capital law of 1650 against, in Connecticut, 94-95; and the death penalty in New York, 179.

Killingsworth, Connecticut, steel production at, 77.

King George's War, Massachusetts Bay receives reimbursement for expenses incurred in, 11-12; the policy of neutrality in, pursued by the New York Assembly, 130; the Pennsylvania coast harassed by privateers during, 183.

King's attorney, the office of, in Connecticut, 93; in other colonies, 93.

King's College, New York, Dr. Samuel Johnson, the first president of, 78.

King's Province, Rhode Island, and the plantation system, 3.

Kingston, Rhode Island, and the plantation system, 58; a share in the "banks" allotted to, 70-71.

Kirke, Sir David, proprietary rights to Newfoundland granted to, and associates, 273.

Kirke, Sir Lewis, enjoined not to interfere with the Baltimore rights to Avalon, 273.

Knight, Captain John, on the methods employed in the Newfoundland cod fisheries in 1749, 255.

Knowles, Commodore Sir Charles, Governor of Jamaica, on the illicit trading of Rhode Island ships, 62.

L

Lac des Prairies, the French trading post of Fort Dauphin upon, 247.

La France, Joseph, a Hudson's Bay Company employee, reports on the Far West Indian trade, 237.

Lake Mistassini, and the boundary of the Hudson's Bay Company territory, 238.

Lake Winnipeg, French trading posts about, in 1750, 247.

Lamp black, the production of, in New York, 123.

Lancashire, petitions for relief by the ironmasters and ironmongers of, 218-219.

Lancaster County, Pennsylvania, the creation of, and racial complexion of, 173-174; the representation of, in the Assembly, 177.

Lancaster, England, the development of ironworks between Cumberland and, 211.

Land office, the, of Pennsylvania, 201.

Landowners, and the suffrage, in Massachusetts Bay, 30; in Rhode Island, 69; in Connecticut, 83; in Pennsylvania, 177; the dominant position of great, in New Hampshire, 51-52; in New York, 116; in New Jersey, 148.

Lands, the policy of Massachusetts Bay respecting, in the seventeenth and eighteenth centuries, 19-21; speculation in, 19; the policy of Wentworth regarding upper Connecticut, 51; the granting of, in Connecticut, 85-86; policies regarding, in New York and New England contrasted, 108; abuses in the granting of New York, 109-111; the improvement of New Jersey, aided from the provincial treasury, 136; policy regarding, in New Jersey, 148-149; the high price of, in Pennsylvania, 171; the improvement of, aided by the provincial government, 190; the sale of, to aliens, prohibited by Parliament, 192; the systematic disposition of, in Pennsylvania, 200-202; of England, the competition of three types of economy for, 210-211.

Land surveys, and New York lands, 110.

La Vérendrye, Pierre Gaultier de Varennes, Sieur de, the establishment of a post upon the Saskatchewan by, 248.

Law, Jonathan, Governor of Connecticut, refuses the London agency, 104.

Lawrence, Thomas, 232.

Lawrie, Gawen, Deputy Governor of East New Jersey, and the New York boundary, 154.

Laws. *See* Legislation.

Lebanon, Connecticut, 76.

Lechmere, Thomas and Anne, and the Winthrop estate appeal, 104.

Lee, Colonel Thomas, President of the Virginia Council, the report of, on the ironworks of Virginia, 216.

Lee, Commodore, on the poor quality of the Newfoundland cod carried to southern markets, 259.

Leeward Islands, the British, the governorship of, sought by Shirley, 36; signs of exhaustion of, 292.

330

INDEX

of New York, the control of, by
the Assembly, 128; of New Jersey,
urges the acceptance of the act of
1748 for printing bills of credit,
142; of the East New Jersey Proprietors, 142-143.
Londonderry, New Hampshire, the
fortified post of, 49.
London, the purchase of New England ships in, 7; the shipment of
Spanish dollars from Boston to,
14; the free importation into the
port of, of American bar iron,
227; the iron manufacturers of,
desire a bounty on American iron,
231; the slight interest of, in direct Newfoundland trade, 258.
Lopez, Aaron, a leading Rhode Island merchant, 60.
Lords of manors, the control over
tenants by New York, 116; multifarious activities of, 120.
Louisbourg, Cape Breton Island, the
expedition against, 11, 34.
Love and Unity, the, German emigrant ship, 168.
Lumbering, the importance of, in
New Hampshire, 40-47; in New
Jersey, 134.
Lutherans, of Pennsylvania, 162; in
the Pennsylvania Assembly, 178.
Lying in wait, the killing of a man
while, a capital offense by the
Duke of York code, 179.
Lyme, England, the interest of, in
the Newfoundland salmon fisheries,
257.
Lyttelton, William Henry, Governor
of South Carolina, the instruc-
tions of, 295.

M

Mackerel, Massachusetts Bay and
the catching of, 18.
Mackey, Robert, London merchant,
seeks Massachusetts Bay lands, 19.
Madeiras, the, and Massachusetts
Bay trade, 8.
Magistrates, of Pennsylvania, the
dismissal of, by Governor Thomas,
193. See Justices of the peace,
Local officials.
Maine, the Province of, absorbed by
Massachusetts Bay, 18, 29; the
Territory of, the number of towns
within, 19; Shirley makes treaties
with Indians living along the bor-
ders of, 34; an abundance of white
pine in, 44.
Malbone, Godfrey, a leading Rhode
Island merchant, 60.
Malt, the making of, with coke in
Staffordshire, 208.
Manors, of New York, 108; methods
of exploiting, 119-120.
"Man-stealers," the Dutch, and the
German emigrants, 166.
Manufactures, of New Hampshire,
52; of Rhode Island, 67; of Con-
necticut, 77; of New York, 122;
of Pennsylvania, 183-184; of Massachusetts Bay, 216-217.
Martinique, the fertility of, 291.

Marten skins, the number of, brought
out of Hudson Bay in 1748, 235.
Maryland, and the production of
flour and crude iron, 4; and the
purchase of English wrought iron,
222; the exportation of pig iron to
England from, 229.
Mason, Captain John, Deputy Governor of Connecticut, champions in
England the Mohegan Indian land
claims, 102-103.
Massachusetts Bay, the most dangerous rival of England in North
America in commerce and industry, 4; the heart of New England,
4; the shipping of, 6; shipbuilding
in, 6; commercial relations of,
with other regions, 8; the high
standards of living of the people
of, 9; balances due the Mother
Country from, 9; the export to
Spain and Portugal of codfish
from, 9; the triangular nature of
the commercial relations of, 9;
the value of goods shipped in 1743
to, 9; the value of the exports of,
10; receives reimbursement of expenses for the Louisbourg expedition, 11; the reorganization of the
public finances of, in 1749, 11-12;
the population of, 14; the occupations of the people of, 14-15; the
appropriation of the fisheries of
the Gulf of Maine and of Canso
by the people of, 17; the growing
interest of, in Newfoundland, 17;
the fine quality of codfish of, 17;
the number of ships of, engaged
in the fisheries, 17; the number of
towns within, 18-19; the people of,
press upon lands claimed by New
York, 19; the sea-to-sea claims of,
still preserved, 19; the traditional
policy of land grants modified by,
19; town settlement still characteristic of, 20-21; the Congregational Church of, 21-26; the Charter of 1691 and the Church Establishment of, 22-23; the witchcraft terror in, 23; the Great
Awakening and, 24-26; the press
and, 26-28; a semicorporate colony,
29; an analysis of the charter of,
29-31; powers of the General
Court of Assembly of, 30; the
franchise in, 30; the provincial
council of, 32; the governorship
of, 31-32; a commission to settle
the boundary between Rhode Island and, 33; the Assembly of, denounces the people of Nova Scotia
and expresses loyalty to the
Crown, 37; disputes with New
Hampshire over boundaries, 47-48;
and over the garrisoning of Fort
Dummer, 48-49; the religious
refugees of, settle in Rhode Island,
55; the interior of, dependent upon intercourse with Narragansett
Bay, 60; boundary dispute between
New York and, 113-115; the Privy
Council sends to the Governor of,
a peremptory instruction in 1737
respecting bills of credit, 139; the
iron industry within, 216-217;

332

INDEX

bounties offered by, on iron products, 217; the exportation of ironware from, 217; the making of beaver hats by, restricted, 241-242.

Masts, and the New England whitepine belt, 40-41; bounties on, granted by Parliament, 43, 219; secured from New Jersey, 184.

Mayhem, the crime of, in the Connecticut code of 1750, 96; a felony of death offense in Pennsylvania, 181.

McAulays, the, of New Haven, Connecticut, carry on commerce with Lisbon, 76.

Mennonites, the, in Pennsylvania, 162; support the Quakers in office, 175.

Mercantile system, the British, and the northern colonies, 2; and the Iron Act of 1750, 204-205; and the opening up of collieries in America, 230; and the act of 1732 regulating the American beaver-hat industry, 241; the purposes underlying, 287; compared to modern state interference, 287; compensation for restraints upon the colonies by, 287; the fruits of, 288; the justification for, 288; and France, 288-289; favored in England by all groups, 289-290; the attitude of Irish and colonials toward, 291.

Methuen, New Hampshire, the dispute over seating the deputies of, 49-50.

Middlesex County, Massachusetts Bay, the number of towns within, 19.

Middlesex County, New Jersey, the Scottish population of, 147; the spread of land riots to, 151.

Middletown, Connecticut, the population of, 75; the rating of, for taxation, 76.

Military officers, the election of, in Rhode Island, 69; and in Connecticut, 91-92.

Military service, exemptions from, in Connecticut, 91; in Pennsylvania, 190.

Militia, the, of Connecticut placed under the control of the governor of New York, 102. See Train bands.

Miller "Papers," the, 121.

Millom, Cumberland, England, the iron ore of, 207.

Minisink Patent, the, New York, 109; the extent of, and the interest of the de Lancey family in, 155.

Misprision of treason, a felony of death offense in Pennsylvania, 181.

Mittelberger, Gottlieb, German music master, on the liberties of Pennsylvania, 162-163; author of, *Journey to Pennsylvania in the Year 1750*, 162; a description of the journey to America on a British emigrant ship by, 168; on the good will manifested by people of Pennsylvania, 175-176; on the rich dress of the people of Pennsylvania, 188; on the women of Pennsylvania, 188-189.

Mohammedans, in Pennsylvania, 162.

Mohawk Valley, the Palatines in the, 117.

Mohegan Indians, the Connecticut controversy with the, over lands, carried before the Privy Council, 102-103.

Molasses, the sale of "Jamaica" fish to the West Indies to secure, 16; purchased of the French planters, 16; nonpayment of duties on, 16; the amount of, demanded by Rhode Island distillers, 64-65; why the British West Indies could not compete with the French, in the sale of, 292.

Money. *See* Bills of credit, Currency, Legal tender, Specie.

Monmouth County, New Jersey, the Scottish population of, 147.

Monmouth Purchase, the, 152.

Montgomery, John, Governor of New York, the financial policies of, and the Assembly, 127.

Moose Fort, a Hudson's Bay Company post, 234.

Moravian Brethren, in Pennsylvania, 162; the persecution of, in Europe, 165; a welcome to, in England, 166; the coming of, to Pennsylvania, 166; support the Quakers in office, in Pennsylvania, 175; in the Pennsylvania Assembly, 178.

Morrisania, the manor of, New York, 108; the creation of, 111; slavery upon, 119.

Morris County, New Jersey, the spread of land riots to, 151; the theft of timber from the Penn lands in, 151.

Morrises, the, among the New York aristocracy, 116.

Morris, Lewis, Governor of New Jersey, and the Assembly, 134; on the trade and shipping of New Jersey, 135; on the happy condition of the people of New Jersey, 136; refuses to sign the bill of 1744 for printing bills of credit, 140; the death of, 142; commissioned governor of New Jersey in 1738, 158; the qualifications of, 158-159; his quarrel with the Assembly, 159.

Morrison "Papers," the, 37.

Morris, Robert Hunter, an East New Jersey Proprietor, private concessions of, 149; opposes the appointment of William Morris to the Council, 160-161; Deputy Governor of Pennsylvania, on the freedom of the people from taxation, 192; on the great powers exercised by the Pennsylvania Assembly, 197.

Morris, William, of Hunterdon County, New Jersey, recommended by Belcher for a seat in the Council, 160-161.

Mortgages on land, in Rhode Island, 70-72; in New Jersey, 136; in Pennsylvania, amounts due on, 191.

Muffs, beaver skins and the making of, 240.

333

INDEX

New Hampshire, the value of the imports and exports of, 9-10; Boston merchants petition the Crown against the bills of credit of, 13; the separate existence of, threatened by Massachusetts Bay, 18; the chief source of the wealth of, 40; the lessening importance of, as a lumbering center by 1750, 44; the boundaries of before 1741, 46-47; a commission to settle the boundaries of, 47; the southern boundary of, established by order in Council, 47-48; and Fort Dummer, 48-49; the western lands of, granted upon a quit-rent basis, 51; the extent of the western claims of, 51; the boundary dispute between New York and, 51-52; the laying out of new townships within, on the upper Connecticut, 51; the aggressiveness of, 52; the population of, 52; economic activities of the people of, 52; religion in, 52-53; the influence of the Wentworth family in the affairs of, 53.

New Haven Colony, religion in, 79.

New Haven, Connecticut, a joint capital, 75; the population of, 75; the rating of, for taxation, 76; the commerce of, chiefly with New York, 78; a center of Anglican influences, 78.

New Jersey, the Province of, the value of the imports of, 10; the white-pine belt extends into, 40; the economic interests of, 134; the population of, 134; the exports of, 135; the commercial dependence of, upon New York and Pennsylvania, 135; advantageous living conditions within, 136; public financial burdens within, 136; the issue of paper money within, 137-147; the lack of solidarity of the population of, 147-148; sectionalism within, 148; the anarchic state of, in 1750, as the result of land riots, 148-154; the contest between New York and, over the boundary, 154-157; the struggle between the Governor and the Assembly of, 157-161; the importance of the iron industry within, 218; an attempt made to establish Anglicanism within, 285-286.

Newlanders, Dutch, and the German emigrants, 166.

New Light Congregationalists, and the Great Awakening, 26; in Connecticut, 80.

New London, Connecticut, the population of, 75; the rating of, for taxation, 76; and the treatment of Separatists, 80.

New London County, and iron production, 77.

New London Gazette, the, 99.

New Netherlands, the, vast land grants within, 109.

Newport, Rhode Island, the evasion of customs by the merchants of, 9; the Jewish merchants of, 57; the enterprise of people of, 59; the nonenforcement of the Sugar Act of 1733 at, 61; vies with New York as a commercial center, 66; the industries of, 67; a center of culture, 68; becomes involved in the struggle over financial policies of the Colony, 68-69; the citizens of, share in the public "banks," 70-71.

New Shoreham, Rhode Island, the citizens of, share in the "banks," 70-71.

Newspapers, the influence of, in Massachusetts Bay, 26-28; in Connecticut, 99-100; in New York, 152; in Pennsylvania, 175, 188.

New System of Geography, A (1765), by D. Fenning, 256.

New York, the City of, the shipping of Spanish dollars from Boston to, 14; the commercial relations of, with Connecticut, 77-78; the influence of the social ideals of, in western Connecticut, 78; the creation of King's College at, 78; the importance of, in 1750, 120-121; the defenses of, 120; the appearance of, 121; compared with Boston and Philadelphia, 121, 185-186; as a seaport, 121-122.

New York, the Province of, the evasion of customs by merchants of, 9; the value of imports and exports of, 10; the governorship of, sought by Shirley, 36; the dispute between New Hampshire and, over the eastern boundary, 51-52; aristocratic tendencies within, 108; the law of 1699 and exorbitant land grants within, 110, 111; the land claims of, threatened by those of New Hampshire, Massachusetts Bay, and New Jersey, 112; the slow development of, 117-118; the population of, 118-119; ironworks within, 122, 217, 218; the non-English-speaking elements within, 124, 147; a plan to maintain the neutrality of, in the French and English hostilities, 130; the Assembly of, censured by the Board of Trade, 132; the making of beaver hats by, restricted, 241-242; attempts made to establish Anglicanism within, 285-286.

New York Weekly Post-Boy, the, 152.

Nicolls, Richard, Governor of New York, and the Elizabeth and Monmouth purchases, 152.

Nomination, the system of, for colonial office, in Connecticut, 84.

Non-Christians and freemanship in Rhode Island, 56-57.

Nonjurors, the situation of the, in Scotland and in England contrasted, 285.

Normandy fishermen, and the Grand Banks of Newfoundland, 249.

Norris, Captain, the testimony of, respecting the New England trade with Newfoundland, 253.

North America, the fisheries of, 17-18; the white-pine forests of, 40; the furs of, 125, 235-237; the working of the iron of, 215-218.

335

INDEX

Northampton County, Pennsylvania, the creation of, and the racial complexity of, 173-174; the representation of, in the Assembly, 177; the amount raised by excise in, 191; the small amount of quitrents drawn from, in 1764, 200.

Northampton, Massachusetts Bay, the repudiation of Jonathan Edwards by, 26.

North Carolina, the commercial relations between, and Boston, 11.

Northern colonies, the, and farming, 3; and the development of handicrafts, 4; in the manufacture of rum and iron, 4; in shipbuilding, 4; in the fisheries, 4; arouse the apprehension of England, 4; do not fit into the mercantilistic theory of the rôle of colonies, 4; the French sugar islands take away the sugar markets in, from the British West Indies, 292. See New Hampshire, Massachusetts Bay, Rhode Island, Connecticut, New York, New Jersey, Pennsylvania, Delaware, the lower counties on the, Nova Scotia.

Northey, Sir Edward, Attorney-General, the opinion of, on the power of colonial legislatures, 197.

Northwest Passage, the, Parliament offers a reward for the discovery of, 245; the attempt on the part of Arthur Dobbs to find, 245.

Norwich, Connecticut, the population of, 75; the rating of, for taxation, 76.

Nottingham, New Hampshire, the fortified post of, 49.

Nova Scotia, the value of the imports and exports of, 9-10; and the Massachusetts Bay Charter of 1691, 29; the Treaty of Utrecht and, 29; menaced by the French in King George's War, 34; the conduct of the French-speaking inhabitants of, denounced by the Massachusetts Bay Assembly, 37; instructions against the working of collieries in, 230.

O

Oak, the, of Pennsylvania compared with that of New England, 184.

Oaths, the taking of, in Pennsylvania, 174; by Roman Catholics, favored by John Penn, 202; and Quakers, 203; required of all governors, 203.

Odiorne, Jotham, a member of the New Hampshire Provincial Council, 53-54.

Officeholding, in Connecticut, 81; compulsory features of, 90.

Ogden, David, recommended by the Board of Trade as a New Jersey Councillor, 161.

Old Light Congregationalists, the, and the Great Awakening, 26, 80.

Orange County, New York, great land patents within, 115.

Oregrund, Sweden, the high quality of the iron of, 221.

Orgroon iron. See Oregrund.

Osborne, Sir Danvers, instructions to, relating to exorbitant New York land grants, 109, 115-116; relating to a permanent revenue, 132; appointed Governor of New York, 133; the death of, 133.

Osborne, Captain Henry, Governor of Newfoundland, 262.

Oswego, New York, chief fur-trading post, 125.

Otter skins, the number of, brought out of Hudson Bay in 1748, 235.

Otter, the trapping of, in Newfoundland, 253.

P

Packers, the town, in Connecticut, the election of, and duties of, 89.

Packer, Thomas, High Sheriff in New Hampshire, 54.

Pagans, in Pennsylvania, 162.

Palatines, the, in New York, 117; leave for Pennsylvania, 117-118; unhappy lot in Pennsylvania of, 166-167.

Palmer, Anthony, President of the Council of Pennsylvania, dangers faced by the Province during the administration of, 193.

Palmer, Eliakim, London agent for Connecticut, 104.

Papers Relating to Newfoundland (1793), 252.

Papists. See Roman Catholics.

Paris, Ferdinand John, London agent for the East New Jersey Proprietors, opposes the approval of the bills of credit act of 1748, 142-143; proprietorial agent for Pennsylvania, and the papers on iron, 222; the comment of, upon the bill of 1738 for regulating the iron industry in America, 223-224.

Parkin, William, English ironmaster, on the small demand in America for English iron, 223.

Parliament, provides reimbursement to the New England colonies for the Cape Breton expedition, 34; and the protection of the North American white pine, 42; grants a bounty on American ship timber, 43; regulates the paper money of New England, 74; the denial of the constitutional right of, to regulate colonial currency by the New Jersey, New York, and Pennsylvania assemblies, 140-141; the encouragement of the production of iron in Ireland by the British, 210; regulates the American iron industry in 1750 and 1757, 228-231; restricts the colonial beaver-hat industry, 241; offers a reward for the discovery of the Northwest Passage, 245; the issue over the supreme regulatory authority of, 284-285; factors in the legislation of, adverse to particular colonial interests, 290-291; the fostering of industries within the Empire by, 298.

INDEX

Parmyter, Susanna, enjoys a monopoly for the manufacture of lamp black in New York, 123.

Particularism, within the Empire, 284.

Partridge, Richard, London agent for Rhode Island, Connecticut, and New Jersey, and the case of the Rhode Island sloop *Jupiter*, 63; opposes the regulation of colonial paper money, 74; while London agent for New Jersey and Rhode Island, assumes the Connecticut agency, 105; supports the New Jersey bills of credit act of 1748, 142-143.

Passenger, Captain, on the carrying of Newfoundland fishermen to New England, 262.

Patroonships, the, in New Netherlands, 109.

Patten, Matthew, of New Hampshire, the report of, on the lands of the upper Connecticut, 50.

Pawtucket Falls, and the New Hampshire boundary, 48.

Pease, Captain, sent by Baltimore to take over Avalon, 274.

Pelham Manor, New York, 108; the creation of, 111.

Pembroke, Philip Herbert, 4th Earl of, proprietary rights over Newfoundland granted to, and associates, 273.

Penacook [Concord, New Hampshire], the settlement of, by Massachusetts Bay people, 20-21; a fortified post, 49.

Penmure, Captain Richard, of the *Charming Polly*, trading voyage of, from Rhode Island to the West Indies, 60-61.

Penn "Collection of Papers Relating to Iron," the, 205.

Penn family, the, New Jersey lands of, stripped of timber, 151; and Pennsylvania, 198-203.

Penn, Hannah, wife of William Penn, the sons of, receive the Proprietary of Pennsylvania, 198.

Penn, John, receives one half of the proprietary, 198; his share goes to his brother Thomas upon his death, 198; characterized, 199; a "fighting Quaker," 202; favors the taking of oaths by Roman Catholics, 202.

Penn, Richard, joint-proprietor of Pennsylvania, 192; characterized, 199; the early repudiation of Quakerism by, 202.

Penn, Thomas, chief proprietor in 1750, 192; son of William Penn, 198; the share of, in Pennsylvania increased by the death of John Penn, 198; characterized, 199; the businesslike methods of, 199; revenues drawn from the proprietary by, 200, 202; the marriage of, 202; gives up Quakerism, 203; the unpopularity of, in Pennsylvania, 203.

Penn, William, his code of laws accepted at Upland, 179; the humane conceptions of, 180; issues his "Frame" of 1701, 193; the sons of, by Hannah Penn, 198; the will of, 198; suit brought by the descendants of the first wife of, 198; was more idealistic than his children, 199; lacks business methods, 199-200; dies a Quaker, 202.

Pennsylvania Gazette, the, edited by Benjamin Franklin, 188.

Pennsylvania Journal and Weekly Advertiser, the, 35.

Pennsylvania Journal, the, 13.

Pennsylvania, the Province of, the value of the imports and exports of, 9-10; the coming of the Palatines into, 117-118; the fur trade of, affects that of New York, 124; non-English-speaking elements in, 147; its many religious sects, 162; relative standing of various religious and racial groups within, 163; German immigration into, 164-171; Ulster Scottish immigration into, 172; the peopling of the frontiers of, 172; Quaker domination of the government of, until 1756, 172-177; the codes of laws of, 178-182; factors favoring, 182; the leading staples of, 183; exports from, and imports into, 184; the shipping of, 185; culture and social life within, 185-190; slavery within, 189-190; government finances and the people of, 190-192; as a proprietary, 192-203; Penn's charter for, 192; early experimentation with the government of, 193-194; law-making processes in, 194-197; the proprietors of, in 1750, 197-199; the attitude of the Penns toward, 199-202; the land system of, 201; the boundary dispute between Maryland and, 203; the importance of the iron industry within, 218; no religious establishment within, 285.

Pennsylvanische Berichte, the, edited by Christoph Saur, 175; the influence of, among the Pennsylvania Germans, 175.

Pension list, the, and the exploitation of the Irish, 286.

Pepperrell, William, commands the Louisbourg expedition, 34; knighted for his services, 34.

Persecution, within Massachusetts Bay in the seventeenth century, 55; the absence of, within Rhode Island, 57; of Baptists within Connecticut, 57; of Separatists, 80-81; of preachers, within Pennsylvania, 162-163.

Perth Amboy, New Jersey, as a free port, 135; a joint capital of New Jersey, 148; the release of prisoners in the jail of, by rioters, 151.

Peters, Richard, Secretary of the Province of Pennsylvania, on land monopolization in New York, 118; on the Pennsylvania magistrates, 182; compares New York with Philadelphia, 185-186.

"Petition of the Iron Merchants, Iron Masters and Iron Mongers to Parliament" (1736), 209.

337

INDEX

Potash, exported by Connecticut, 76; the production of, promoted by bounties, 298.

Pounds, the town, in Connecticut, 89.

Power, the use of water, in the production of iron, in 1750, 207.

Preachers, and the Great Awakening, 24-26; the trials of, in Pennsylvania, 162-163.

Premiums, granted by Parliament on American-produced ship timber, 43, 219, 298; a demand for, upon iron, 219; on naval stores and hemp, 219, 298; on indigo and potash, 298; on British sailcloth and Irish linen, 298.

Presbyterian Church, the, the dominant denomination in East New Jersey, 147; the Scottish Establishment of the, 285.

Presbyterians, the, strength of, in Rhode Island, 55-56; in New Jersey, 147; in Pennsylvania, 162; the distribution of, in Pennsylvania, 173.

Present State of the British and French Trade to Africa, The (1745), 243.

Pretender, the Old, James Edward Stuart, the attempt of, to gain the throne, and the Rhode Island law against Roman Catholics, 56.

Prince of Wales Fort, a Hudson's Bay Company post, 234.

Princeton College, and Presbyterianism, 147.

Principio ironworks, the, in Maryland, 216.

Privy Council, the, and Massachusetts Bay legislation before 1753, 31; the decision of, in the Massachusetts Bay-New Hampshire boundary dispute, 47; an appeal to the Lords of the Committee on Appeals of, in the case of the *Jupiter*, 63; the Mohegan Indians' appeal before, 102-103; the Connecticut intestacy law disallowed by, 107; the refusal of, to repeal the New York law of 1699 relating to exorbitant land grants, 111; a decision in favor of New York in the New York-New Hampshire boundary dispute by, 112; the sound-money position of, 146; the attitude of, toward colonial bills of credit, 137-146; refuses to approve the New York act for settling the New York-New Jersey boundary dispute, 157; the attitude of, toward the New Castle code, 180; an order of, repealing the convict transports law of Pennsylvania, 196; a petition to, for leave to settle lands west of Hudson Bay, 246; the regulations of the Newfoundland fisheries by, 263.

Probate districts, the, in Connecticut, 92.

Proclamation money, Massachusetts Bay currency and, 12-13; Rhode Island currency and, 71-72.

Proprietors, town, in Massachusetts Bay, 20; in Connecticut, the meet-ings of, 85, 86; the privileged position of, 86; of East New Jersey, 148-149; seek to settle the issue of the northern boundary, 155; the Pennsylvania, petition the Crown against calling into question old laws, 195-196; a description of the Pennsylvania, 198-199; the relations of, with their propriety, 199-203.

Proroguing the Assembly, the right of, in Massachusetts Bay, 32; in Pennsylvania, 134.

Protestants, of Northern Europe, the appeal of the Empire to, 286.

Providence, Rhode Island, the enterprise of the merchants of, 59-60; the small proportion of voters in, 70; the proportion of the "banks" awarded to, for loan, 70-71.

Prussia, an edict against the Moravian Brethren, by the King of, 165; why Württembergers were unwilling to go to, 175-176.

Public finance, in Massachusetts Bay, 11-15; in New Hampshire, 51; in Rhode Island, 70-74; in Connecticut, 101; in New York, 127-128; in New Jersey, 136-147, 159-160; in Pennsylvania, 190-192.

Public Occurrences, Both Foreign and Domestic, America's first news sheet, 27.

Puritanism, in Massachusetts Bay, 19, 21-26; in Connecticut, 79-82, 93-101.

Q

Quakers, the, in Massachusetts Bay, the exemptions secured by, 23; in Rhode Island, the strength of, 55-56; supported for office by Baptists, 57; in Connecticut, the local ecclesiastical society and, 81; in New York City, 121; in New Jersey, the predominance of, in West New Jersey, 147; the influence of, in the shaping of the public law, 178-179; in Pennsylvania, 162; the decline in the numerical strength of, 163; the dominance of, in the three old counties, 173-174; in the Assembly, 177-178; the resignation from the Assembly of, from Bucks and Chester counties in 1756, 178; and the punishment of crime, 178-182; the attitude of, toward slavery in 1749, 189-190.

Quebec Act, the, of 1774, 29.

Quit-rents, and New Hampshire, 51; lower on New Hampshire lands than on those of New York, 51; in New York, 109, 110; the low level of, 110; in New Jersey, 150; the collection of, in Pennsylvania, 200-202; the Baltimore claims to Avalon and the right to, 281.

Quoits, the playing at, forbidden in Connecticut, 98.

R

Radical elements in Connecticut, 85.

Randolph, Edward, Surveyor-General

INDEX

of His Majesty's Woods, 42; as
Surveyor-General of Customs, rec-
ommends the appointment of
crown attorney-generals in all the
colonies, 102.
Rape, the capital law of 1650 against,
in Connecticut, 94, 95; a capital
crime in Pennsylvania, 181.
Raynor, Captain John, appointed
Deputy Governor over Avalon, 274.
*Reasons Against the Importation of
Sow and Pig Iron from America
into Great Britain under the
Present low Duty*, 221.
*Reasons Against the Making and
Manufacturing of Barr Iron in
America*, 221.
*Reasons for Allowing the Importa-
tion of Bar-Iron from America*,
230.
*Reasons for Encouraging the Impor-
tations of Iron in Bars from his
Majesty's Plantations in America*,
213.
Rea, William, Monmouth ironmaster,
on the distribution of ironworks
and coppices in England and
Wales, 206.
Rebellion, the capital law of 1650
against, in Connecticut, 94, 95.
Redemptioners. See Indentured serv-
ants.
Redwood, Abraham, a leading Rhode
Island merchant, 60.
Refineries, sugar, at Newport, Rhode
Island, 67; at New York, 123.
Reformed, the, the strength of, in
Pennsylvania, 162.
Rehearsal, the, Boston news sheet,
27.
Religion, in Massachusetts Bay, 21-
26; in New Hampshire, 52-53; in
Rhode Island, 55-57; in Connecti-
cut, 79-82, 93-100; in New York,
121, 124; in New Jersey, 147; in
Pennsylvania, 162-163, 172-176, 178-
182, 203; in Newfoundland, 251,
269; within the Empire, 285-286.
Religious freedom, the guarantee of,
in Massachusetts Bay, 30; in Rhode
Island, 56; in Pennsylvania, 162;
within the Empire, 285.
Rensselaer Manor, New York, 108.
Rensselaerwyck, New York, 108.
"Report from the Committee appointed to enquire into the state
and conditions of the countries adjoining the Hudson Bay and the
Trade carried on there, etc."
(1749), 235.
"Report on the Lands in the Province of New York" (1732), by
Cadwallader Colden, 110.
"Report on the State of the Province of New York" (1774), 119.
Representation in Parliament, and
the London agencies, 107.
"Representations," the, of the Board
of Trade, 297.
Revenues, the, of New York, and
land grants, 116; of New Jersey,
and land mortgages, 136; of Pennsylvania, 190-192.
Revolution of 1689, the, 29.

Rhode Island and Providence Plantations, the value of the imports
and exports of, 9-10; the Boston
merchants petition the Crown
against the bills of credit of, 13;
the separate existence of, threatened by Massachusetts Bay, 18-19; a
commission to settle the boundary
between Massachusetts Bay and,
33; the sectaries of, 55; the founding of, 55; toleration in, 56; dis-
crimination against Roman Catholics in, 56; contrasted and compared with Connecticut, 57, 75;
the attitude toward the Jews in,
57; the natural resources of, 57;
the inhabitants of, 57; occupations
in, 57; aristocratic elements within, 58; the foreign trade of, 59,
67-68; the shipping of, 59; the
merchant princes of, engaged in
illicit trading, 60; the West India
planters protest against, 61; the
rum industry of, 64; the slave
trade and, 65; culture within, 68;
the government of, 69; public finance and private industry within,
70-73; the regulation of paper
money of, by Parliament, 74; the
decline of the commerce of, 74;
the public finances of, contrasted
with those of New Jersey, 136;
the making of anchors within, 217;
lack of a religious establishment
within, 285.
Rice, and South Carolina, 299.
Riots, land, on Livingston Manor,
113-114; in Dutchess County, New
York, and the use of British regulars, 115; in New Jersey, 149-154,
156.
Roads, in Connecticut, the repair of,
and compulsory work, 89.
Robbery, the punishment of, in Connecticut, 94; a capital crime in
Pennsylvania, 181.
Robson, Joseph, Hudson's Bay Company factor, the examination of,
by the parliamentary committee,
236; author of *An Account of Six
Years' Residence in Hudson's Bay*
(1752), 244.
Rochester, New Hampshire, a fortified post, 49.
Rodney, George Brydges, Governor
of Newfoundland, instructed to
protect the quality of the dried
cod, 259; the appointment of, as
governor of Newfoundland, 263;
the general instructions of, 263-
265; protests against the carrying
of Irish Catholics to Newfoundland, 266-267; the difficulties facing, in attempting to maintain
order, 268.
Roman Catholics, in Boston, 24; the
denial of religious freedom to, permitted under the Massachusetts
Bay charter, 30; the disabilities
of, in Rhode Island, 56-57; in New
York City, 121; in Pennsylvania,
162; a church for, in Philadelphia,
187; the predominance of, at St.
John's, Newfoundland, 251; the

INDEX

343

INDEX

Sussex, the County of, England, additional ironworks forbidden within, 208.

Swanley, Robert, appointed governor of Newfoundland by Baltimore, 274.

Sweden, the dependence of English industry upon the iron of, 210, 212, 213; restrictions on the importation of English goods into, by royal edict, 219-220; English exportations to, 220; the demand for a duty on iron imported from, 231; the loss of the markets in, by English hatters in favor of the French, 40.

Swimming, in Connecticut, the penalty for, on the Sabbath, 97.

Swords, to be possessed by all Connecticut householders, 91.

T

Tables, the playing at, forbidden in Connecticut, 98.

Talbot, Charles, Solicitor-General, gives an opinion on grievances against the Massachusetts Bay Church Establishment, 23.

Tar, of New England, 8; the premiums on American made, 218.

Taverns, in Philadelphia, the number of, 191; in Newfoundland, 253.

Taxation, the high rate of, in England, 107, 225; the low rate of, in Connecticut, 107; the absence of, in New Jersey, 136; the absence of, in Pennsylvania, before 1755, 191; in Ireland, 287; in Barbados and Jamaica, 294.

Tax Collectors, the town, in Connecticut, the election of, 90.

Taylor, Isaac, furnishes New England white-pine masts, 44.

Teignmouth, England, the interest of, in the cod fisheries, 252.

Tenantry, the system of, in New York, 119; the riotous conduct of the, in Hunterdon County, New Jersey, 151.

Thomas, George, Deputy Governor of Pennsylvania, circumvents the Assembly, 193.

Thomlinson, John, London agent of New Hampshire, on the appointment of Wentworth to office, 45.

"Thomlinson Papers," 49.

"Thoughts on the Iron Trade" (1750), 211.

Thurston, Mark, Accountant-General of the Court of Chancery, a member of the Hudson's Bay Company, 239.

Tidewaiter, the struggle over the appointment of a New York, 128.

Timber, the ship, of New England, 8; the preservation of, and the Massachusetts Bay charter, 32; the value of, 40-42; Parliament and the preservation of, 42-43; the exploitation of, promoted, 43.

Tippling, the punishment for, in Connecticut, 95.

Tithingmen, the town, of Connecticut, the election of, and duties of, 89.

Tobacco, the use of, and the Connecticut code of 1650, 95, 100; the sale of, forbidden in Newfoundland, 263; the regulation of the sale of, and the mercantile system, 287; discriminatory tariffs in favor of British colonial, 298; and the American colonies, 299.

Topsham, England, the interest of, in the cod fisheries, 252.

Tour Through Ireland by Two English Gentlemen, A (1745), 205.

Town meetings, in Connecticut, 86-91; qualifications for participation in, 87-88; the election of officials at, 88; ordinances passed in, 90; and the training of politicians, 90-91.

Towns, in Massachusetts Bay, the number of, 18-19; regulations regarding the creation of new, 20-21; in New Hampshire, and frontier defense, 48-49; in Rhode Island, the distribution of the "banks" among the, 70-74; in Connecticut, the comparative size of, and the rating of, for taxation, 75-76; the government of, 79-91; in New York, 120, 124; in New Jersey, and the provincial government, 147-148; in Pennsylvania, 185.

Townships, the granting of, about the Upper Connecticut River, 53-54.

Train bands, the radical tendencies of the, in Connecticut, 85; requirements for service in, 91; the organization of, 91; the election of the officers of, 92.

Train oil, the value of, exported from Newfoundland, 257, 258.

Tramount, Boston, 5.

Traveller's Magazine, The, 257.

Travels into North America (1772), by Peter Kalm, 121.

Travels through the Middle Settlements of North America, 1759-1760 (1775), by Andrew Burnaby, 41.

Treason, the punishment of, in Connecticut, 96; the crime of, and the Pennsylvania charter, 179.

Treasurer, the colonial, the election of, in Rhode Island, 69; in Connecticut, 84; the Assembly and the control of the office of, in New York, 127-128; in Pennsylvania, 194.

Treasurer, the town, in Connecticut, the election of, and duties of, 89.

Treat, Colonel Robert, Governor of Connecticut, addresses King William, 101-102.

Trepassey, Newfoundland, and the colonizing activities of Sir William Vaughan, 249.

Triangular trade, the, of Massachusetts Bay, 15-16; of Rhode Island, 60; and of Newfoundland, 256.

Trinity, Newfoundland, a garrison stationed at, 252.

Trumbull, Jonathan (later Governor of Connecticut), refuses the Connecticut London agency, 105-106.

344

INDEX

Winthrop, Major-General Fitz-John, Governor of Connecticut, goes to England to protect the charter, 102; opposes the commission of Governor Fletcher, 102.

Witchcraft, in Massachusetts Bay, 23; the capital law of 1650 against in Connecticut, 94, 95.

Wolf skins, brought out, of Hudson Bay in 1748, 235.

Wolverhampton, England, unemployment at the ironworks of, 214; the iron manufacturers of, desire a bounty on American iron, 231.

Wolverine skins, brought out of Hudson Bay in 1748, 235.

Women, of Pennsylvania, Mittelberger's description of the, 188-189.

Wood, an essential in the production of iron in 1750, 207; the wastage of, in the southeast of England, in iron production prohibited, 208; the lack of, about Dudley Castle and in the West Midlands, 208-209; resources in the valley of the Severn and the forests of Wales, 209; the shortage of, in England, leads to a shortage of bar iron and pig iron, 209; the price of, fixed by various factors, 212.

Woodbridge, New Jersey, the New England background of, 147.

Woodbury, Connecticut, the rating of, for taxation, 76.

Woodenware, of Pennsylvania, 183, 187.

Woods, of Newfoundland, the preservation of the, 264. See White pine.

Woolens, the export of Irish, restrained, 287.

Wool, the production of, in New York, 123; the importance of, to England, 298.

Worcester County, Massachusetts, the number of towns within, 19.

Worcestershire, England, the rise of the iron industry within, 209; and the making of nails, 214; petitions for relief by the ironmasters and ironmongers of, 219, 220-221.

Wrought iron, earlier and later methods of producing, 206; the amount of, shipped to the New World, 222.

Württemberg, the unhappy lot in Pennsylvania of immigrants from, 166-167.

Y

Yale College, a New England cultural center, 28.

Yards, premiums on American-produced, by Parliament, 43, 218.

York County, Maine, the number of towns within, 19.

York County, Pennsylvania, the creation of, 173-174; the representation of, in the Assembly, 177; the amount raised by excise in, 191.

Yorke, Philip, Attorney-General, gives an opinion on the grievances against the Massachusetts Bay Church Establishment, 23.

York Fort, the most important of the Hudson's Bay Company posts, 234; a description of, in 1750, 234; aid extended by, to the members of the Dobbs expedition, 245.

York, James Stuart, Duke of (later James II), grants land to Berkeley and Carteret, 152.

Z

Zinzendorf, Nicholas Lewis, Count, of Herrnhut, Saxony, Bishop of the *Unitas Fratrum*, the sermons of, banned from Hanover, 165.

347